FANNY CROSBY (1820-1915)

Blind since she was an infant, Fanny Crosby studied at The New York City Institution for the Blind, then taught there until her marriage to another gifted blind teacher.

Known for her courage and loving Christian spirit, Fanny Crosby became America's most prolific hymn writer. Her works include poems, cantatas, and many well-known songs such as "Blessed Assurance," "To God Be the Glory," "Close to Thee," and others.

Fanny Crosby's life and works continue to effect the lives of people today, providing inspiration and encouragement. You will be moved and amazed by her story and rejoice in Jesus Christ, who indeed was, and is, "Savior More Than Life to Me."

HEROES OF THE FAITH has been designed and produced for the discerning book lover. These classics of the Christian faith have been printed and bound with beauty, readability and longevity in mind.

Greatest care has gone into the selection of these volumes, with the hope that you will not only find books that are a joy to read, but books that will stir your faith and enlighten your daily walk with the Lord.

Titles available include:

Fanny Crosby, Bernard Ruffin

Dwight L. Moody, W.R. Moody

George Müller, William Henry Harding

John Wesley, C.E. Vulliamy

Fanny Crosby

Bernard Ruffin

Happy Birthday
Love Y.S.P '86

Barbour and Company, Inc.
164 Mill Street
Westwood, New Jersey

ISBN 0-916441-16-4
(Canadian ISBN 0-920413-90-0)

Published by: **Barbour and Company, Inc.**
164 Mill Street
Westwood, New Jersey 07675

(In Canada, HEROES OF THE FAITH,
960 The Gateway, Burlington, Ontario L7L 5K7)

EVANGELICAL CHRISTIAN PUBLISHERS ASSOCIATION ECPA MEMBER

Printed in the United States of America

CONTENTS

INTRODUCTION

The year is 1910. The place is Perth Amboy, New Jersey. A hackman stops to pick up two passengers. One is a middle-aged clergyman; the other is a withered old crone, apparently blind, ravaged and wasted almost beyond belief, bent nearly double with age. But as the coach jolts along en route to the railroad depot, the hackman becomes aware that there is something unusual about this ancient woman, seemingly straight out of one of Grimms' *Fairy Tales*. She is speaking to the clergyman. Her voice is not dry and quavering, as one might be led from her appearance to expect, but it is clear and high and mellow and young. Far from the senility that one might expect in one so venerable (she must be more than a hundred!), the lady's mind is as fresh and young as her voice. She evidently is a woman of great intellect and refinement. She and the clergyman are discussing some point of theology. The coachman listens intently to the wit and wisdom the old lady displays. When it becomes obvious that the driver is paying more attention to what she is saying than to the road, the minister speaks up.

"This is Fanny Crosby, the hymn writer," he says. The hackman is stunned. He stops his horse, takes off his hat, and weeps openly. Getting himself together, he proceeds to the depot, where he searches for a policeman and finds one. He introduces the old woman to him. "This is Miss Fanny Crosby that wrote 'Safe in the Arms of Jesus.' I want you to help this young man get her safely to the train."

The cop is stunned. "I sure will," he says. Then he says, falteringly, to the little old lady, "We sang your hymn, 'Safe in the Arms of Jesus' last week—at my little girl's funeral."

As he looks at the ground with reddened and shining eyes, "Aunt Fanny" takes his enormous arm in her skinny hands and says, with great feeling and tenderness, "My boy—I call all policemen and railroad men 'my boys,' they take such good care of me wherever I go—God bless your dear heart! You shall have my prayers! And tell your dear wife that your dear little girl is 'Safe in the Arms of Jesus.'" With these words, the constable broke down and wept openly.[1]

Who was this ancient crone, Fanny Crosby, this strange little woman dressed in the style of seventy years previous, with her green glasses and the crucifix on her breast? Who was this blind woman whose name was so revered by the man on the street?

Today, if Fanny Crosby is remembered at all, it is usually with a smirk or a sneer, as the author of gushy and mawkishly sentimental Victorian hymns which are the embodiment of all that is trite and hackneyed, all that is maudlin and cloyingly saccharine. Her name is a byword among many liberal-minded churchmen for bad church music and bad theology. She is often thought of as the personification of the neurotic woman whose syrupy literary efforts are the result of misdirected sex drives—that is, if she is remembered at all. For most people, the name Fanny Crosby conjures up an absolute blank.

Is it just as well that this strange dwarfish little woman is now forgotten? Was she indeed simply a third-rate hack poet whose fame ought justly to be confined to the pages of the Sunday school hymnals of several generations ago? Or was she more than most people today realize, a person whose life story is worth retelling? Is it best that she remain forgotten? Did she make any significant contribution to American civilization? Or is she simply a person who was tremendously overrated in her own day and is now rightly neglected?

How different was the place of Fanny Crosby in the estimation of our forefathers! Ann Cobham, a noted social worker at the turn of the century, wrote of her, "She is the most wonderful person living, and in my mind, has ever lived."[2] On the flyleaf of a collection of her reminiscences which was published shortly after her death in 1915, it is written:

> Everybody knows the name of Fanny Crosby. It is a question whether any name in the religious annals of America is better known. Who is there that has not heard and sung "Rescue the Perishing," "Draw Me Nearer," "Safe in the Arms of Jesus," and "Saved by Grace"? In far-off mission stations, down in the dark, unlovely underworld of cities, out on the trackless deep, in home and hall and church and camp, these hymns have brought solace and enheartment to millions. They are songs that will never die.[3]

Far from being the epitome of the bad hymn writer, Fanny Crosby, in her day, was considered by most people to be the greatest in America. As Johann Strauss reigned in Vienna as the "Waltz King" and John Philip Sousa in Washington as the "March King," so Fanny Crosby reigned in New York in the later nineteenth and early twentieth century as the "Hymn Queen." Charles H. Gabriel (1856-1932), himself a noted hymn writer and the author of several immensely popular songs, shortly after her death lamented the loss of the "queen of American hymn writers," whose "name, suspended as a halo above modern hymnology . . . will live on as long as people sing the Gospel."[4] William Alfred Quayle (1860-1925), a noted Methodist bishop as well as a poet and theologian, called Fanny Crosby the "modern Saint Cecelia."[5] George Coles Stebbins (1846–1945), a famous hymn writer and evangelical singer, attributed all his success as a hymn-tune composer to the poetry of the men and women who supplied him with verse, especially to his beloved "Aunt Fanny." "The most distinguishing thing about my life," he wrote in 1905, "has been my friends—Fanny Crosby—and Moody and Sankey. And but for them, 'nobody would never heard tell of me.' But they have made me what I am."[6] In his autobiography of 1924, Stebbins wrote, "There was probably no writer in her day who appealed more to the valid experience of the Christian life or who expressed more sympathetically the deep longings of the human heart than Fanny Crosby."[7] In 1904, the famous singing evangelist Ira D. Sankey, partner and colleague of the renowned D. L. Moody, said that the success of their evangelical campaigns was due, more than any other human factor, to Fanny Crosby's hymns.[8] And a modern Baptist hymnologist, William Jensen Reynolds, writing in 1963, commented that Fanny Crosby "to a greater extent than any other person . . . captured the spirit of literary expression of the Gospel-song era."[9]

During the era of the gospel song, a light, informal hymn written in the style of the popular ballad, Fanny Crosby reigned supreme. This would have encompassed, approximately, the years 1870 to 1920. Her hymns were sung all over the world. During an evangelical campaign in the British Isles, Ira Sankey took a short vacation in the Swiss Alps. There he was astounded to hear peasants singing, beneath the window of his inn, Fanny Crosby's "Pass Me Not, O Gentle Saviour," in German. That same hymn was said to have been a favorite of Queen Victoria and of the Prince and Princess of Wales. "Safe in the Arms of Jesus" was played by a brass band at the funeral of President Grant in 1885 and, the same year, was sung at the funeral of Lord Shaftesbury, a founder of the YMCA. During the early 1900s, an American clergyman, traveling through the Arabian desert, was astonished to hear Bedouins in their tents singing Fanny Crosby's "Saved by Grace," presumably in Arabic.[10] Any female hymn writer of any importance was termed another "Fanny Crosby." Caroline Sandell Berg (1832–1905), a Swede who wrote many excellent hymns, including "Children of the Heavenly Father," was known as the Swedish Fanny Crosby. A little blind Korean girl, famous around the turn of the century for her singing of Christian hymns, inevitably became known as "little blind Fanny Crosby."

But Fanny Crosby was known for more than her hymns. She was one of the three most prominent figures (D. L. Moody and Ira Sankey were the others) in American evangelical religious life in the last quarter of the nineteenth century. She did more than write hymns. She was a famous preacher and lecturer and was a devoted home mission worker. In many instances when she spoke at a church, people would be lined up for at least a block before the service began. She was venerated as practically a living saint in her later years; in fact she was often called "the Protestant saint" or "the Methodist saint." When she was at home she was a virtual "prisoner of the confessional" for the scores of people who came on pilgrimage from all over the world to see her and ask for her advice and prayers.

Fanny Crosby, in her ninety-five years, not only wrote around nine thousand hymns—more than anybody else in recorded Christian history—but also more than a thousand secular poems. In addition she was an eminent lecturer and a well-known musician, noted for her concerts on the harp and organ. She deserves some attention from readers in the second half of the twentieth century, if only for her great renown in the past and for the adulation in which she was held by our grandparents and great-grandparents.

As the mother of modern congregational singing in America, she should also be remembered for her great contribution to American Christian civilization. It was with her generation of hymn writers, a generation of which she was the chief example, that the popular congregational and Sunday school hymn originated. Before that time, most hymns were usually staid, formal, and rather cold. But Fanny Crosby and her colleagues worked to evolve and develop, if not to create, a kind of hymn which, written in the popular idiom, appealed to the emotions and feelings of the worshiper. In this sense she can be considered the grandmother of many of the modern hymns which are today so popular among younger worshipers, such as "Put Your Hand in the Hand of the Man" and "He's Everything to Me" and "We Are One in the Spirit." In fact, she can be regarded as the grandmother of all hymns that address the personal feelings and emotions of the singers, all hymns that are written in a popular idiom, all hymns that great groups of people love to sing.

The story of this woman of humble origins, blind almost from birth, who achieved fame as a poet, educator, and musician before becoming known throughout the English-speaking world as a hymn writer and finally almost as a saint, is one that ought to interest even those who in these pages meet the name of Fanny Crosby for the first time.

CHAPTER 1
THE BLIND GIRL

Southeast, New York, in Putnam County, was more of a geographical district than a town in 1820. It was a rural area, composed largely of forest and farmland, with a few tiny hamlets here and there, the largest being Doanesburg, then a thriving center with a Presbyterian church, a parsonage, a post office, a school, and even a library.

The countryside round about was dotted with trees and demarcated with those stone walls that are so typical of New England. The soil was not good, producing more rocks than crops, and it was virtually impossible for a small farmer to survive. Therefore, many men either hired themselves out as hands on the estates of one of the several great landowners or else combined with fathers, brothers, or cousins to farm jointly a substantial tract of land. Most of the more than 1,900 inhabitants of Southeast in 1820 were "peasants." In those days, the term did not have the pejorative meaning that it has today; it simply denoted rural working folk. Fanny Crosby often spoke in late years of the "humble peasants" from which she sprang.

Almost everyone in Southeast was of solid Yankee stock (except for about sixty Negro slaves), descendents of the original settlers of the Massachusetts Bay Colony and of largely English extraction. Familially, the area was comprised of clans, and in 1820 virtually everybody seemed to have been related to one another. There were only a few dozen family names in that area, and certain families were very large. The largest of the Southeast clans was the Crosby family, which numbered eleven households. But Southeast was full also of families by the name of Crane, Mead, Baley, Kelley, Foster, Barnum, Paddock, Weid, Howes, Comes, Reed, Hopkins, Dykeman, Gage, and Gay. Sometimes the various families that comprised a clan would be clustered in a settlement which bore their name. For instance, the community where Fanny Crosby was born was named for the Gays, who lived there in large numbers.

The men wore black clothing, and most of them sported full beards which were frequently allowed to extend almost to the waist. They tended to be heavy smokers, constantly puffing on big black cigars or clay pipes. They bore picturesque names of biblical or classical stamp, such as Enos, Abiel, Tartarus, Epaphras, Freeman, Ichabod, Anza, Peleg, Aruna, Myhajah, and

Ardola. The women, too, wore black, and their full-skirted "Basque dresses" with their stiff white collars and cuffs had buttons all the way down the front from neck to hip. Many of them had names as picturesque as those of their husbands: Mehitabel, Hepsibah, Jerusha, Patience, Temperance, Thankful, Ruhannah, Bethia.

They were pious folk, these peasants of Southeast. The Presbyterian church still taught almost unadulterated Puritan-Calvinist doctrine, with its tenets of "irresistible grace," "double predestination," and the need for a distinct personal conversion experience. Of a Sunday morning, people could be seen converging on Doanesburg from all directions, walking barefoot and carrying their only shoes, so as not to spoil them for "meeting," to the steps of the church, where they put them on.[1]

They might have been poor, but they were literate, managing somehow to sandwich between long hours of hard labor a few years at the little red district schoolhouse. There the children of Southeast would learn from a man or woman who had gone scarcely farther than the highest level of training that was being offered. But they learned! In this age, in which many high school and college graduates can or will do little more than sign a check or application, it may astound the reader that these "humble peasants," few of whom went beyond the fifth or sixth grade at most, would read and write poetry as they sat by the fire on winter nights, when their work was done. They were familiar not merely with jingles but could recite from Milton and Shakespeare and Chapman's Homer. All of them knew Bunyan's prose classic, *The Pilgrim's Progress*, and, of course, the King James translation of the Holy Bible.

If one had followed a winding road from the steps of the church at Doanesburg, on a day in 1820, after a walk of about a half hour he would come to a settlement known as Gayville. One of the half-dozen dwellings in that sylvan paradise was a small, rough, one-story frame cottage by the side of the road. Situated near the crest of a hill, it looked out onto a landscape of rolling hills, dotted with trees. Behind it was an open field, surrounded by a virgin forest, full of towering oaks and maples, with a thick underbrush. This was the home of Sylvanus Crosby, a veteran of the War of 1812 probably in his middle forties. Though he was a poor man, eking out a marginal existence through his farm labor, he knew his ancestry well, as did most of his neighbors. He claimed direct descent from William Brewster, one of the Pilgrim fathers. Arriving on the *Mayflower* in 1620, this Brewster had helped to establish Plymouth Plantation. Toward the end of the seventeenth century, one of his descendents, Patience Freeman, married a man named Eleazer Crosby.

Eleazer was the grandson of Simon and Ann Crosby, who had come from England in 1635 and settled near Boston. Simon Crosby came from an old Yorkshire family that dated back to the fifteenth century. Born in 1608, he married Ann Brigham (1606–1675), and came to the New World. He helped to found Harvard College, soon after his arrival, and died a few years later, in his early thirties. One of his sons, Eleazer's father, Thomas (1634-1702), was graduated from the college his father helped to found. Although never ordained, he conducted services as a "religious teacher" on Cape Cod and was also connected with the shipping business.

Eleazer begat a son named Isaac, who was born in Harwich, near Cape Cod, in 1719. Shortly after that the family moved to New Milford, Connecticut, and then to Southeast, New York. It is not recorded how long Eleazer lived, but Patience, his wife, lived to be 103 years old and until her early eighties made horseback trips alone, to Cape Cod and back, to visit relatives.

Isaac Crosby married a woman named Mercy Foster, who bore him nineteen children. The youngest of these was Sylvanus, born during the Revolution. Despite the fact that he was in his late fifties at its outbreak, Isaac volunteered his services during that war. When Sylvanus was born, he convinced his company commander to give him a leave of absence by claiming that he had "nineteen children at home and had never seen one of them."[2] Isaac won no laurels, but he did manage to return home alive and stay that way until he was more than a hundred years old. He and his descendents were proud of his service, and of the exploits of various other, distantly related, Crosbys during the Revolution. Fanny liked to recall some of the tales she was told as a child. "When General Warren was killed at Bunker Hill," she wrote years later, "it was a Crosby who caught up the flag as it fell from his hands."[3] There was another Crosby, living in nearby Carmel, whose name was Enoch. He gained such renown that James Fenimore Cooper wrote a novel based on his life, entitling it *The Spy.*

Around 1798, Sylvanus, about twenty-one years of age, married a girl named Eunice Paddock. Born October 3, 1778, Eunice was the third of twelve children (and eleven girls) of Nathaniel Paddock and the former Mary Crane. Eunice's grandfather, Colonel Thaddeus Crane, was a war hero. Wounded by a rifle ball during the Revolution, he was still living when Eunice and Sylvanus were married; he kept the metal that had passed through his body in a glass case on the mantelpiece as a grisly souvenir of his military service.

In time, Sylvanus and Eunice had four children, each six years older than the next. The eldest, born May 31, 1799, was named Mercy, after Sylvanus' mother. She was followed by Theda, born late in 1805, then Joseph, born early in 1811, and finally Mary, whom everyone called Polly, born late in 1817.

The entire Crosby family, parents and children, lived together in the little cottage. Sylvanus tried to farm the little plot of ground as best he could, scratching out an existence for his family. By 1820 he was not the sole breadwinner, however, for Mercy, the eldest daughter, had married and with her husband lived at home.

Mercy's husband, John Crosby, was an older man, perhaps not much younger than her father. Although he was probably some sort of cousin, this was nothing unusual for Southeast. Eunice Paddock's parents had probably been first cousins, and Eunice and Sylvanus were also related. But by the time Fanny Crosby came to write her memoirs, the fact that her mother and father were related (and were *perhaps* first cousins) had become a source of embarrassment, and she maintained that she did not know anything about his lineage. Most likely she knew but did not want to say.

Nothing is known of John Crosby, and since he died when Fanny was a baby, she had no personal recollections of him. She had always been told that he was an extremely ambitious, hardworking man who, like Sylvanus, seems to have been a veteran of the War of 1812.[4] He had been married before and had one daughter, Laura, who was about the same age as Mercy's sister Theda.[5] John Crosby hoped to acquire a farm of his own some day to provide a better existence for his young wife and the child they were expecting.

On March 24, 1820, two months before her twenty-first birthday, Mercy gave birth to her firstborn, a daughter, who was christened Frances Jane Crosby at the Doanesburg church, after one of her mother's numerous aunts, Fannie Paddock Curtis.

By late April, the Crosbys were alarmed. There was something wrong with the baby's eyes. In later years, Fanny spoke of a sickness which made her eyes "very weak." But, more disconcerting, the family was unable to obtain competent medical assistance. There was a doctor in the community, but he was away at the time.

Finally, however, they found a man who claimed to be a physician. Just who this man was, no one knows. Fanny, eighty-six years later, wrote of "a stranger."[6] She often spoke of him as a doctor, but insisted that he was totally untrained in medicine. Whoever he was, the Crosbys were horrified when he put a hot poultice on the baby's red and inflamed eyes. They were concerned about the extreme heat of the compress, but the "doctor" insisted that it would not hurt the child's eyes and would draw out the infection. When he had finished his treatments, it was apparent that the Crosbys knew more about medicine than the quack they had consulted. For, although the infection gradually cleared up, ugly white scars formed on the eyes, and as the months went by little Fanny Jane showed no response when objects were held before her face.

The "doctor" did not remain in Southeast very long after that. The Crosbys accused the man outright of blinding the baby and stirred up such indignation in Gayville and Doanesburg and neighboring hamlets that the unfortunate man, no doubt fearing lynching, fled the vicinity and was never heard from again.

Further disaster was to strike the hapless household of Sylvanus Crosby by the end of the year. November 1820 was cold and rainy. John Crosby,

20

however, a persistent and persevering man, continued to labor in the fields, even in the downpours. One night he came in badly chilled. The next day it was apparent that he was seriously ill. Within a few more, he was a corpse.

The Crosbys were devout Puritans, as they called themselves—or at least, as Fanny later said they did—and Mercy, a widow at twenty-one, was comforted in the hope that she and her husband would meet again one day in heaven. But, on earth, Mercy realized that her father could not support a household of six persons alone. So, shortly after her husband's body was lowered into an unmarked grave in the cemetery at Doanesburg, she hired herself out as a maidservant in a wealthy family nearby. Fanny Jane would be taken good care of by Mercy's mother.

Though they were desperately poor, the Crosbys, buoyed up by their devout faith, were a happy family. During the day, Grandmother Eunice and her middle daughter, Theda, kept house and cared for Fanny and Polly, who were more like sisters than niece and aunt. Joseph by now was no doubt assisting his father in farm work. In the evenings, when Sylvanus and Joseph and Mercy returned home, the family would sit reading and reciting poetry. As a little girl, Fanny Jane listened with rapt attention to the ballad of "Rinaldo Rhinaldine," the robber chieftain; she listened to the tales of Robin Hood; she heard her grandfather read from the *Iliad* and the *Odyssey*; she listened to her mother read from Milton; and she heard with eager ear her grandmother reading from the Bible.

Eunice took a special interest in Fanny and during the child's first four or five years was closer to her than was her mother. "My grandmother was more to me than I can ever express by word or pen." When it had become obvious to her that Fanny Jane was deprived of eyesight, she decided that she would be her granddaughter's eyes. She firmly resolved that Fanny Jane would not be a helpless invalid, dependent on others as so many people blind from birth or infancy were in those days. So she undertook to describe the physical world to the child in terms she hoped she would understand. Eighty years later, Fanny remembered "Grandma," as she called Eunice, "taking me on her knee and rocking me while she told me of the beautiful sun with its sunrise and sunset." How Eunice could describe colors to a child blind almost from birth is not so great a mystery, for Fanny Jane could perceive very intense light and could sometimes distinguish various hues. Eunice also taught the blind child about the birds:

> I knew the red-headed woodpecker, the red-winged blackbird, the mocking-bird with its white chin, and the bird with its garment of blue. One day I heard a strange sound coming from the meadow, saying, "Whippoor-will." Grandma told me about the bird which gave out that curious note and described its mottled wings and reddish brown breast, and its bristled mouth, with its white bristled tail.

21

How did Fanny understand what "bristled" meant? Eunice would place in her hands a surface similar to the one she was trying to describe. Afterward, whenever Fanny heard the sound of the whippoorwill, she knew the color and shape of the bird that produced that sound. Likewise, Eunice also taught her about the meadowlark, the cuckoo, the songsparrow, the goldfinch, the yellow warbler, the wren, and the robin.[7]

This remarkable woman, Eunice Crosby, a peasant from the remote backwoods of rural New York, was as skillful and successful in instructing a blind child as many with degrees were then and are today. She also taught her granddaughter about botany. By the time she was three or four, the violet was Fanny's favorite flower and would remain so for the rest of her life. In autumn, Eunice took Fanny on walks over the hills, telling her about the trees and their leaves. Fanny Jane came to know the trees as she did the flowers, by means of touch and smell, and the leaves by "handling and remembering." Eunice realized that Fanny's memory would have to play a more important role in her life than it would in a sighted child. So she began by having her exercise it. She was not harsh or dictatorial. Teaching Fanny by playing with her, Eunice would gather up piles of autumn leaves and have Fanny play with them. "Now what tree is *this* one from?" she would ask. In this way Eunice played an important part in Fanny's development. It was from the early training at Grandma's hands that she acquired a capacity for detailed description, and it was from this training that she acquired a wonderful memory.

Eunice also had a great influence on Fanny's religious development. All the Crosbys, John and Mercy included, were devout Christians, but Eunice seems to have been practically angelic. Grandma saw all the world as God's book and each natural phenomenon as a manifestation of God. Like many people of her day and of earlier generations, she saw nature as a mirror of the spiritual world. So, for Fanny, the walks she took with Grandma over the hills and through the fields were walks with God, as Eunice pointed out that every tree, every flower, every bird was put there by God and served his plan and purpose. Eunice taught Fanny and Polly that every natural phenomenon was not only a creation of God and served some purpose of his, but also was a symbol of some spiritual truth. She also taught the girls that whatever happens, good or bad, is a manifestation of God's delight or wrath. She taught them that not a sparrow falls to the ground without God seeing it, that every hair on the head is numbered. She instilled in them the conviction that God is an ever-present help in time of trouble.

Eunice was a tower of strength to her daughter Mercy in the first years of her widowhood. Often Mercy would become distraught by her difficulties. She had to work all day to support her child, whom she could see only at night. And then she fretted about Fanny Jane, wondering what would become of this little girl who was seemingly so hopelessly handicapped. When Mercy collapsed upon her rough cot, weeping, Eunice would go in to her, place her hard, horny hand upon her thin shoulder, and recite from a favorite hymn or quote the old Puritan adage which had been a favorite of Cotton Mather: "What can't be cured can be endured." In her nineties, Fanny Crosby would still be repeating that saying to all those who came to her in trouble.

From as early as Fanny could remember, Eunice would assemble her children and read the Bible to them. "The stories of the Holy Book came from her lips and entered my heart, and took deep root there."[8] Eunice did not simply read from the Bible without comment but took time to explain everything in terms children could understand. Sitting in her rocking chair, she would tell them of "a kind heavenly Father Who sent His only Son, Jesus Christ, down into this world to be a Saviour and a Friend to all mankind."[9]

Not only was Grandma a woman of the Book, she was also "a firm believer in prayer."[10] Prayer was essential to the Christian life, not merely as a form of mental exercise, or simply in meditating on God, but as a direct communication with her loving Savior. She taught Fanny that they should call upon God in every need and give thanks to him for everything good that happened. She taught that there was nothing too difficult for God to do and that, whatever their need might be, he could meet it. No matter how extravagant or unlikely their request, he would grant it—*if it was good for them.* If God did not grant the request, then they should not be downcast, for he had something in store for them better than their wildest hopes and expectations. They should rejoice, therefore, for the sufferings and frustrations of life could be borne patiently and cheerfully, because by means of these things they were being led to something better.

Every Sunday the Crosbys walked, like the other villagers, barefoot, shoes in hand, to the church. They went into the outlying horse sheds, tidied up, put on their shoes, and then climbed the two or three stone steps and went in to meeting. In winter, the wooden structure was heated by a potbellied stove set in the center of the sanctuary. It often grew very hot inside, with two hundred persons crowding the room, and the tobacco smoke issuing from the lips of most of the men made frequently for an insufferable atmosphere. The sermons seemed to last forever and were so often full of tedious vagaries of boring Calvinistic theology that people dozed throughout. At noon the congregation went home for dinner, then promptly returned to hear more preaching. "As long as they got home in time to milk the cows, they didn't mind,"[11] recalled a resident. There was no organ, and there were no hymns as such in the "Southeast Church." The cast of mind of the people of that area was still that of the first- and second-generation Puritans, and the theologians of the early days of Calvinism did not believe in "human hymns" (that is, hymns of human composition) and would use only the psalms, which were "dictated" to David directly from God. So most of the music consisted of psalms chanted in plainsong and, now and then, their metrical paraphrase by Isaac Watts, who lived and wrote a century earlier. The people of Southeast were only then getting to the point where they could accept even a paraphrase of the King James version of the psalter. A deacon at "the desk" would be the only person in the room with a text. "Lining out" the psalm, he would recite one line and the congregation would then repeat it, proceeding in this fashion until the entire psalm was chanted. This rather awkward brand of church music did not impress the child Fanny.

As a little girl Fanny Jane was quiet and pensive, but nevertheless cheerful. She was staunch friends with the postman, and one of the grand events of her week was to get the mail from him each Thursday. From the age of three, on pleasant days she would make her way with the ease of a sighted person to a large rock. There, under the watchful gaze of Grandma, she sat listening to the "voices of nature," all of which, she said, spoke a language familiar to her soul. Were it not for the persistent though well-meaning commiserations and "I wish you could see this or that," Fanny would not have known that she was different from other children. She was quite satisfied with her lot, not realizing that there was anything unusual or limiting about it.

Sitting on "her rock," Fanny daydreamed a great deal. Sometimes she imagined herself as a sailor, "standing at the masthead and looking into the storm." Sometimes she was a soldier. At other times she pictured herself as a clergyman, "addressing large audiences." And at other times the "leader of a gigantic choir . . . singing praises to God."[12] She loved to sing. By the age of five she knew such diverse songs as the stately "Hail, Columbia, Happy Land" and such rather crude ballads as the story of "Fourscore and Ten Old Bachelors." Eunice and Mercy let Fanny and Polly have quite a bit of freedom. Far from keeping the little girls constantly at her side, Grandma let them roam in the vicinity of the cottage. She and Mercy even permitted them to play outside at night, with the other children of Gayville, for Fanny, at least, could play in the night just as well as she could in the daytime.

CHAPTER 2
"OH, WHAT A HAPPY CHILD AM I"

One evening Fanny was playing with Polly and the other children outside the cottage when Mercy called her in. She wanted to speak to her alone. By the light of the dim and flickering homemade candles, she told her, "Fanny, I am going to take you on a little journey. We shall travel, first in a wagon, till we come to the bank of a beautiful river, with mountains on each side of it. Then we shall get into a sail boat and sail south for many miles. Then we shall come to a great city, larger than anything of which you have ever heard or thought. We will stay there for several days, and then go home again."[1]

From the time that it was apparent that Fanny was blind, Mercy had not given up hope for a cure. After five years, aided by generous contributions of neighbors from miles around, she felt that she had finally scraped up enough money to make a trip to New York City to procure an appointment for Fanny to be examined by Dr. Valentine Mott of Columbia University School of Medicine, one of America's finest surgeons.

For Fanny, the rather tedious trip by market wagon to Sing Sing and by sloop to New York was a wonderful and exciting adventure. She delighted in the "sea yarns" the captain told her, and she, in turn, regaled the crew and passengers of the ship with the little songs she had learned. The skipper enjoyed them immensely and periodically would send for her, tell her that he was "blue," and ask her to sing for him.

At the harbor of the "Great City" Fanny and her mother were met by a man named Jacob Smith, a friend of the family, who took them to his home on Roosevelt Street. Later that day. Mercy and Fanny were taken to Dr. Mott's offices, where Dr. Delafield, an eye specialist, had been called in. Fanny in later years remembered being given toys to play with by Dr. Mott, a man who seemed to radiate kindness and pleasantness of disposition. She remembered being examined by two doctors, the surgeon and the ophthalmologist, for what seemed to be ages. She remembered Dr. Mott laying his hand on her head and asking if she wanted him to do something that would make her see. She remembered shrinking back to her mother, murmuring, "No, sir," fearing the pain of a surgical operation (no anesthetics were available until the 1850s). She also remembered him saying, "Poor little girl." And she remembered that on the way back to Southeast, her mother was very silent and very sad.

Mott and Delafield confirmed the suspicion of Mercy and her parents that the "doctor" who had treated Fanny Jane's eyes had utterly ruined them. The poultice that had been applied to her eyes had burned her corneas, causing scar tissue to form. This made for a kind of vision, or lack of vision, which can best be compared to looking out of a glazed or iced window. The child could experience some light and color but little else. There was absolutely nothing they could do; the damage to the eye tissue was irreversible. Moreover, they said that the initial infection may have damaged the optic nerves, further complicating the cause of her blindness. Mott inveighed against the charlatan who, by his malpractice, had completely spoiled the child's already damaged eyes.

The words sank into Mercy's heart like daggers. Normally stern and staid, she burst into tears. Five years of saving and scraping, five years of hoping and expecting, had come to naught.

Mercy was so prostrated on the return voyage that Fanny was left almost entirely to herself—or, rather, to the care of the skipper and her fellow passengers. Fanny could not understand why her mother was so upset. She had a good time on the way back. She sat on the deck and watched the brilliant colors that were reflected by the setting sun on the waves of the Hudson. For she was not totally blind. Even in her eighties, she could still distinguish day from night. At that point in life a friend who assumed that she was completely blind remarked that she wished Fanny could see the sunlight of a particularly beautiful day. Fanny remarked, "I know it. I feel it. And I *see* it too!"[2] At any rate, little Fanny Jane had what almost amounted to a religious experience aboard the sloop that afternoon in the spring of 1825.

As I sat there on the deck, amid the glories of the departing day, the low murmur of the waves soothed my soul into a delightful peace. Their music was translated into tones that were like a human voice, and for many years their melody suggested to my imagination the call of Genius as she was struggling to be heard from her prison house in some tiny shell lying perchance on the bottom of the river.[3]

Back home, Grandma Crosby was there to comfort them and tell Mercy, as she was wont to do, something to the effect that "If the Lord does not want you to have what you have prayed for, then it is best for you not to have it." She assured her distraught daughter that God would provide for little Fanny Jane and that he had a useful future in store for her, even if she was always to be without sight.

While Mercy struggled to come to terms with the fact that her "poor little girl" would never see, Fanny was growing rapidly. About this time Mercy was forced to move to North Salem, six miles south of Gayville, where she was employed as a housekeeper. There was room in her employer's house for Fanny, so she decided to take her daughter with her.

North Salem was largely inhabited by Quakers, and Fanny Jane quickly learned the "plain language."

One good man and I became constant companions, and often when he was going to mill he found me a very willing passenger, and sometimes an uninvited guest. But whenever I persisted in going, he generally gave way after the first feeble resistence.

"No, thee ain't going with me," he would say; and I as surely replied, "David, I tell thee I *am* going to mill with thee."

"Well, get thy bonnet and come along."[4]

Unlike gentle Grandma, Mercy was very strict. Eunice was not of the school that taught "Spare the rod and spoil the child." Whenever Fanny Jane was mischievous, Grandma talked to her very gently, until she convinced the child of her fault and brought her to tears of penitence. On only one occasion did Fanny remember Grandma ever slapping her, and then Fanny was so upset that she took to her bed, wailing in a piteous manner. Eunice had then decided that she had learned the lesson and allowed one of her little playmates to ask her to come back out and play. When the little fellow asked her, "Will you come out and play with me?" Fanny threw a tantrum and screamed petulantly, "I'm going to hurt you, just like my grandma hurt me!" She picked up a rock and hurled it at him, but missed. Many grandmas would have then seen to it that Fanny was unable to sit for several days, but Eunice, seeing that no harm was done, exacted no further penalties. Mercy was much freer with the rod than her mother had been with Fanny, and this took some adjustment on the part of the child. Of her mother, she later said, "She was of the generation you *had* to mind!"[5]

From her pictures, Mercy seems the stereotype of the stern-visaged pioneer woman: spare and erect, with a long, bony face and a hawklike nose, hard, intense eyes, and pursed lips. She was not all discipline, however; she was a witty woman who liked a good time—whenever she had the opportunity. She was frantically devoted to her handicapped daughter and drove herself nearly to distraction in worrying about Fanny's welfare. To the extent that her meager means would permit, Mercy was always getting toys with which the little girl could occupy and amuse herself.

Fanny also played "early and late" with the other children of the village. As there was no crime problem, the parents did not have any worries about the children's safety and often let them play unsupervised. Soon the peasants of North Salem learned to their amazement that this little blind girl was certain to be a party in any childish mischief that was perpetrated in the community. In

27

fact, she became something of a tomboy. She learned to climb a tree "with the agility of a squirrel" and ride a horse bareback, clinging to the mane for dear life as the steed proceeded at a full gallop. She could also climb the ubiquitous New England stone walls and, when she tore her dress, she "managed to keep [the torn section] out of Mother's sight until I fancied she would not notice it, which was a rare occurrence indeed."

Grandma made it a point to visit Fanny several times a week in North Salem. While Mercy was busy with the domestic chores of the household where she lived and worked, Eunice continued to educate her grandchild, giving her portions of the Bible to memorize when she was about eight. Gradually, Fanny came to realize that she was unlike other children; the strange, unknown phenomenon of eyesight, which she lacked, seemed to be necessary for her to attain most, if not all, of her ambitions. In order to be a sailor, a preacher, or a musician, she had to go to school. Yet the path of knowledge appeared hopelessly barred to her. It irked her to hear people forever saying, "Oh, you cannot do this—because you are blind, you know," and "You can never go there, because it would not be worthwhile; you could not see anything if you did, you know."[6]

With these remarks in mind, Fanny Crosby, in later years, always insisted that blind people can accomplish almost everything sighted persons can. But for the blind little girl in the Puritan hinterlands of New York State, there seemed to be little hope of ever realizing any of her ambitions, and she became pensive and at times grew "very blue and depressed." It was then that she would creep off alone, kneel as Grandma had taught her, and ask God whether her blindness was to exclude her from being one of his children. She would ask him "whether, in all His great world, He had not some little place for me." Always of a mystical inclination, she felt that she heard his voice, saying, "Do not be discouraged, little girl. You shall some day be happy and useful, even in your blindness."[7] As a result of these prayers, her period of despondency passed, for a season, and at the age of eight she was able to compose her first attempt at verse:

Oh, what a happy child I am,
  Although I cannot see!
I am resolved that in this world
  Contented I will be!

How many blessings I enjoy
  That other people don't!
So weep or sigh because I'm blind,
  I cannot—nor I won't.

Although she as yet had not the "conversion experience" so essential in the Calvinism of her mother and grandmother, God was from the first a part of Fanny's life, and church in North Salem came to mean much to her. The only church was the Society of Friends. But the Quaker meeting, in which the speaker gave his sermons in a singsong manner of delivery, gasping for breath between phrases, was quite different from the deadly Puritan services at Southeast and so struck her fancy. Especially the singing caught her imagination. Throughout her life she would remember the "doleful" hymns. These grave, somber hymns were very much in New England at that time. They were frequently macabre poems set to eerie fuguing tunes.

In North Salem, as in Southeast, a great emphasis was placed on an emotional "conversion experience," without which one should dread to die. Because of this there was a great emphasis on mortality and the certainty of hell for the unrepentant. Numerous hymns told of careless sinners who, overtaken by a sudden death, died in despair. Even as a little girl, Fanny was revolted by scare tactics, which often hardened "sinners" in their unbelief rather than accomplishing their intended effect. This would have an effect on her lifelong attitude toward religious work.

However, with all justice to Fanny's neighbors, these hymns were not quite as horrifying to the ears of the people of that time as they would be for us today. Death was not a taboo subject of conversation by any means. Death and sickness and pain were taken for granted; they were not seen as an absurd intrusion upon one's existence. It was considered unnatural and downright foolish to assume that earthly joys last forever, and preparing for death was deemed of prime importance. The big question for the average person of the 1820s was not "Will I die?" or "When will I die?" or "How will I die?" The big question was, "When I die, where will I go?"

When Fanny was eight or nine, Mercy moved for a second time, this time over the state line to nearby Ridgefield, Connecticut, where she found domestic work. This time she was unable to live in the same house where she worked, and Fanny was left during the day in the care of the landlady, a Mrs. Hawley. Fanny Jane carried permanent memories with her of the Quakers in North Salem. Although she soon lost the habit of calling people "thee" and "thou," she loved, at times throughout her life, to don Quaker dress.

In Ridgefield, Mercy and Fanny lived right on the village green. Here they were once more in Presbyterian country. Mrs. Hawley was an arch-Calvinist, "an old Puritan Presbyterian who took everything in the Sacred Writ as literally as the most orthodox Scotchman could do."[8] She was not gloomy or severe, as many Puritans were, but was "kind" and "loved beautiful things."[9] Mrs. Hawley took over Fanny's education where Grandma Crosby left off. Fanny was now too far away from Southeast for Grandma to come regularly, but Mrs. Hawley resolved to take up Eunice's work. She set Fanny to the task of memorizing the entire Bible, giving the child a number of chapters to learn each week, often as many as five. These were repeated line by line, drilled into the little girl's head "precept upon precept." Being young and gifted with a phenomenal memory, Fanny had no trouble in mastering the books of Genesis, Exodus, Leviticus, and Numbers, as well as the four Gospels, by the end of the year. One wonders whether Mrs. Hawley actually burdened the child with the genealogies and the million and one cultic regulations and other minutiae in the Pentateuch. If she held every word in the Bible to be of utmost importance, as Fanny says she did, it seems likely that she did insist that her pupil memorize everything—genealogies, legal stipulations, and all!

At the end of two years Fanny could repeat by rote not only the entire Pentateuch and all four Gospels but also many psalms, all of Proverbs, all of Ruth, and "that greatest of all prose poems, the Song of Solomon."[10] This training sufficed Fanny for a lifetime, and from then on she needed no one to read the Bible to her. Whenever she wanted to "read" a certain portion of scripture, she turned a little button in her mind, and the appropriate passage would flow through her brain like a recorded tape. Whenever she visited Grandma in Southeast, which was fairly frequently, Eunice noted with great pleasure her progress in the learning of Holy Writ. Fanny was always a champion in the Bible-reciting contests that were held among the children and teen-agers of Ridgefield. Whoever could repeat the most verses would win a Bible, and the Bible came to be a part of her. "This Holy Book," she said when she was eighty-five, "has nurtured my entire life."[11]

Mrs. Hawley was not so strict a Calvinist as to believe that there was nothing worth reading outside of Holy Writ. She had Fanny memorize portions of edifying secular works, as well as many popular poems. When she had the time, Mercy also read to Fanny, and Fanny had vivid memories of her mother reciting "with great feeling" Milton's famous sonnet "On His Blindness." Mrs. Hawley also taught Fanny many "practical lessons." She told her the story of George Washington and his hatchet. "It was new in those days," Fanny wrote afterward, "and was emphasized more than at present." But even at eight or nine, Fanny had her doubts about the story. "It was one of the mysteries of my young life how he could have been so very good while the rest of us tried so hard and often failed to attain the standard of truthfulness that the Father of Our Country had set for us."[12]

The institution of the "singing school" was very popular in New England in those days, and in winter the young people of the village were visited by a singing teacher, who taught Fanny and her companions at Ridgefield from the famous *Handel and Haydn Collection* of Lowell Mason (1792–1872). This collection, which received its name from the Handel and Haydn Society of which its author was director, consisted mostly of songs and anthems in the musical style of classical European music. The *Handel and Haydn Collection* was also used by the church choir, of which Fanny Jane was a member. Years later she said, "I can still hear some of the sweet voices of my friends reverberating through the old Presbyterian meeting-house; the tuning-fork of the choirmaster as he 'set' the pitch; and the deep, mellow tenor of the minister as he answered the choir from the pulpit."[13]

The Ridgefield Presbyterian church was too poor to afford individual hymnals, and the deacons often lined out selections from Mason's collection in the same way that those at Southeast lined out psalms. But often they invented hymns of their own, to be sung to the tunes in the *Handel and Haydn Collection*. This usually turned out horrendously, and sometimes two or three deacons were required to finish a hymn of a few stanzas. Fanny at this time became acquainted with a tailor who was a Methodist and occasionally went to his church with him. She came to love the stately and beautiful hymns of Charles Wesley and Isaac Watts which were sung there.

Although Fanny was "the gayest of the gay" at times, at others she had recurring spells of moodiness and depression as she approached adolescence. She spent many evenings thinking and "reading" the scriptures. Her handicap came to depress her more than it had when she was younger. She seemed to acquire a chip on her shoulder. She put herself more and more in competition with her comrades, just "to show the world what a little blind girl can do."[14] She entered and won many Bible verse contests and took part in as many games with the neighbor children as she could, just to show everybody that she could do anything they could. She was never to outgrow this entirely. Even as an old woman, she was always terribly anxious to demonstrate to everyone that she could do anything a sighted person could. Even in her nineties, she insisted that the niece with whom she stayed allow her to do the dishes. When the good lady urged her to rest, saying that it was not necessary for her to do such chores, Fanny would accuse her of thinking that she could not do the job because of her blindness. "I'll wash those dishes, and they'll be clean when I get through!"[15]

In her eleventh and twelfth years, Fanny felt increasingly shut out of the world. She was beginning to realize that a great store of knowledge lay waiting out there, but, since she was blind and had no chance for an education, there seemed to be no way for her to tap it. It was a "great barrier" that rose before her, shutting away some of the "best things which I dreamed in my waking and sleeping hours." She attended the district school occasionally, but the local schoolmaster did not know how to instruct the blind and she would quit in complete frustration after a few days. As time went on, "what seemed frequently to me an oasis sooner or later faded like a mirage farther and farther into the dim and distant future."[16]

In the depth of her depression, she made one of her frequent trips to

31

Gayville, to visit Grandma and Grandpa, who still lived in the house where she was born. Eunice realized that the child was deeply troubled, and toward twilight one day they had a long talk together. Grandma sat in her rocking chair and Fanny poured out her heart. Then the two of them knelt down by the side of the doughty old chair and "repeated a petition to the Kind Father." After that, Eunice went quietly downstairs, leaving Fanny alone with her thoughts.

> The night was beautiful. I crept towards the window, and through the branches of a giant oak, that stood just outside, the soft moonlight fell upon my head like the benediction of an angel, while I knelt there and repeated over and over these simple words: "Dear Lord, please show me how I can learn like other children."

At once, she felt "the weight of anxiety" that had burdened her heart in recent months "changed to the sweet consciousness that my prayer would be answered in due time."[17] From then on, although Fanny often fell into depression because of the limited opportunities available to her, she treasured in her heart the confidence that ultimately the barrier that stood between her and "knowledge" would be demolished.

This was perhaps Eunice Crosby's last great gift to her granddaughter, this prayer for knowledge that moonlit night. Soon thereafter she fell ill. Knowing the end was at hand, she did not hide the fact from anyone. When Fanny next called, Eunice quietly told her that God would soon call Grandma away.

Fanny always remembered their last meeting. On that "rosy summer evening" in 1831, Grandma sat in her favorite rocking chair, but her voice was now a painful whisper. "Grandma's going home," she said, and told the frightened child that she would soon be in heaven. Fanny sobbed disconsolately before the dark silence was once more broken by the dying woman's faltering voice. She had one question to ask her beloved grandchild—her only grandchild. Would she meet her in heaven? "Tell me, my darling, will you meet Grandma in our Father's house on high?"

Fanny could feel Eunice "looking down upon me." There was another moment of silence. Then the child overcame the lump in her throat and "answered with emotion: By the grace of God, I will." Eunice, joyful, clasped Fanny to her bosom. Then they bowed their heads for one last prayer.[18] Not long afterward, Eunice Crosby, only fifty-three, died.

This last meeting was to haunt Fanny for many years thereafter. As we have seen, Eunice, like her neighbors, was a devout Calvinist who believed that one could have assurance of salvation only through a definite, dated, emotional "conversion." She hoped Fanny would have this experience, and her deathbed words were ultimately to induce it. In truth, however, Fanny really did not feel any different after leaving Grandma that last time than she did before she talked with her—at least concerning her salvation. The fact that she had not had a datable conversion experience was to weigh upon her mind at times. But now this anxiety was merged with her grief for "gentle Grandma," who had been the most influential person in Fanny's childhood and who had instilled in her much of her philosophy of life and much of her religious attitudes.

As Fanny entered her teens, she began to show clearly that she had musical talent. With a high, sweet soprano voice, she acquired a reputation locally as a singer. She mastered the guitar to the extent that she was constantly in demand at gatherings. She became an excellent horsewoman. She also attained fame as a storyteller. She liked to invent stories of charitable bandits, the type of robbers, she commented in later years, that "I have not been fortunate enough to meet . . . in real life." [19] These good bandits used to rescue poor wayfarers and send them on their journey with gold in their pockets. Now and then, "for the sake of variety," she threw into her narrative some bad robbers, "but, sooner or later, their chief would always emerge when they least expected it, and compelled them to return their dishonest gains." In the end, they would repent and reform, although "in some cases, a term in prison was necessary to settle them in their new purpose."

It was as a poet that Fanny Crosby attained her greatest fame in Ridgefield. She continued her poetic endeavors, commencing to write lyrics about events in the community. And she attracted attention by a youthful protest poem. Apparently there was a miller living near Ridgefield who had the habit of dishonestly mixing corn meal with his flour. Fanny wrote a poem on this subject, the first stanza of which read:

There is a miller in our town,
  How dreadful is his case;
I fear unless he does repent
  He'll meet with sad disgrace.

Neighbors thought the poem so good or the situation so in need of immediate attention that it was submitted to the editor of the nearest newspaper, the weekly *Herald of Freedom* at Danbury, whose editor was none other than Phineas Taylor Barnum, then in his early twenties and on the threshold of his lucrative career as a showman. Barnum liked the poem and wanted to print it in full. He took an interest in Fanny and would have probably blown her up in his paper as a "blind prodigy" had not Mercy intervened. She was astute enough to recognize the youthful Barnum's inclination for exhibiting things and people. Had she not put her foot down, permitting him to print just one stanza of her daughter's poem and forbidding him to print any more of her poetry, Fanny Crosby would possibly have been the first exhibit of P.T.'s fabulous career. Fanny, who did not like Barnum and was wont to make surreptitious cuts at him, wrote years later that she might, if Barnum had had his way, "have held an uncomfortable position in his hall of fame."[20]

Following the practice of the day, in which the chief theme of literary endeavors was death, Fanny tried her hand at writing obituary verse. For a while, whenever anybody in the neighborhood died, Fanny Jane Crosby would "cause my muse to shed a few sympathetic tears." Later, she felt ashamed of these youthful elegies. "How glad I am that none of these is preserved!"

When Fanny wrote a poem called "The Moaning of the Wind for the Flowers," Mrs. Hawley liked it so well that she sent a copy to Sylvanus in Gayville. Grandpa Crosby was enthusiastic about the poem and wrote Mrs. Hawley for copies of more of his granddaughter's works. He praised what in later years Fanny called "my poor little pieces" and hailed her to his friends and neighbors as a "comer." But he did not want to "spoil her and make her proud," so he instructed Mercy to communicate to Fanny none of his enthusiasm. It was not until years later that Fanny learned how proud her grandfather had been of her earliest poetic efforts. Unknown to Fanny at this time, Sylvanus told his friends, as he sat smoking his clay pipe, "That girl will bring great honor to this house, if she lives."[21]

In 1834, Mercy decided to move back to North Salem. In Ridgefield Fanny had spent some very fruitful years. It was there that she had come to know the Bible by heart, received her first rudimentary musical training, and met someone who would be most influential to her future. One of the children with whom she played on the green was Sylvester Main, three years her senior. A few years later he would marry Susan Lobdell, another of Fanny's childhood companions. It was "Vet" Main and his son Hugh's publishing house that would publish nearly 6,000 of Fanny's hymns and be one of the principal means by which her works gained access to America's hearts and homes.

CHAPTER 3
"MY HAPPY HOME"

At fourteen Fanny, always diminutive in stature, did not look her age. She was a lively little girl with jet black curls but not especially attractive; it was clear, however, that she was endowed with a personality of rare intensity and vitality which tended to express itself in passionate emotions, in violent sorrow as well as violent joy. Whatever she did—whether it was riding horseback, playing the guitar, singing, telling stories, or writing poetry—she did it with a fierce passion that was almost more than her meager frame could bear. It was to be so throughout her life.

But, as indicated earlier, she could not throw herself into education. Although she still attended the district school in spurts, the harried schoolmaster, given charge of more students than he could adequately handle, had absolutely no time to give the special attention and training she needed, so after attending classes for a few days Fanny, in despair, would drop out.

This on-and-off again pattern continued until November 1834, when Mercy read Fanny a circular about the newly founded New York Institution for the Blind. Certain that her prayers to God for a meaningful education had been answered, Fanny clapped her hands and cried out, "Oh, thank God! He has answered my prayer, just as I knew he could!" Seventy years of joys and sorrows later, Fanny could still describe that day as the "happiest ... of my life."[1]

For nearly four months, mother and daughter made preparations. Both of them knew that separation would be a difficult but necessary cross to be borne. "What will you do without me?" Mercy asked Fanny, undoubtedly asking herself mentally, What will *I* do without *you*? Fanny assured her mother that, as much as she loved her, she was willing to undergo any sacrifice to obtain an education. "You are right, my child," Mercy said, her voice faint and trembling, "I am very glad you have the chance to go."[2]

D-Day came March 3, 1835. That morning, Fanny was awakened by Mercy, who told her that the stagecoach was at the door. She had permitted Fanny to sleep until the last possible moment, no doubt in order to spare both of them the agony of a prolonged parting. Fanny was "thoroughly unnerved" and trembled so badly that she could scarcely dress. Her throat contained such a lump that she could only swallow a few morsels of the breakfast Mercy had prepared. Trying to force back her sobs, Fanny hurried from the house into the presence of the woman who was to be her traveling companion. She was fearful that she would break down completely if she should turn and say so much as good-bye to her beloved mother.[3] The traveling companion led her to a place in the coach; the stage lurched forward and rumbled onto the newly prepared road to Norwalk, Connecticut, where Fanny and her companion were to take a steamer to Manhattan.

The woman, whose name we do not know, tried to get Fanny to talk, but for an hour the girl was silent, too anguished even for tears. Her suffering was apparent. At length, the woman said severely, "Fanny, if you don't want to go to New York, we will get out at the next station and take the returning stage home. Your mother will be lonesome without you, anyway."[4] At this point, Fanny probably realized that a return to the frustrating and unrewarding life as the village bard in a rustic Yankee community was not a viable option for her. So she decided to "cross the Rubicon" by passing up the next station without disembarking.

"Had I returned to my mother that morning," she later wrote, "I would have cast away my pearl of great price, for it is not probable that I should ever have been brave enough to start again for the Institution." She set her teeth, and told her companion, "I will go on to New York."[5]

In the 1840s, Fanny was to write a poem about "The Rise and Progress of the New York Institution for the Blind." Funded by the state and also by the philanthropic contributions of concerned citizens, the Institution had been established only four years before Fanny arrived. It had started in 1831 with "three sightless orphans." Although similar institutions had been founded in Europe in the previous century, the New York Institution was only the second such establishment in the States, founded only two years after the Institution for the Blind in Boston. The instructors sought to draw the eye of the public by staging at schools and churches exhibitions of the work of the pupils. In those days, not very many people believed that the blind could be successfully educated. By means of these demonstrations the Institution acquired many benefactors. The authorities also sent flyers to all parts of the state; it was one of these that had reached one of Mercy's friends, who had forwarded it to her. The number of pupils increased so rapidly that the instructors were able to lease a private mansion on a pleasant country estate shaded by old willow trees. John Denison Russ, a thirty-four-year-old physician and Yale graduate, was then superintendent. By 1835, the Institution had thirty pupils. Occupying on Manhattan's West Side what is now the entire block bounded by Eighth and Ninth avenues and 32nd and 33rd streets, the estate was then in the country. It was not until 1840 that the built-up area of Manhattan extended as far as 14th Street. Kipp and Brown's Stage, which was the only means of "rapid transportation," extended only as far as 26th Street. George Frederick Root, who gave music lessons there in the 1840s and 1850s, recalled tramping from the end of the stage line to the Institution. "I crossed corn and potato fields, and remember occasionally being much disgusted at soiling my clean shoes in a muddy ditch where Madison Square is now."[6] The old mansion that housed the Institution faced Ninth Avenue, and was, for sighted persons, "in plain view of the Hudson," from the farther bank of which rose the lordly palisades of New Jersey. No skyscrapers barred one's view of it in those days. Only gently sloping lawns and fields lay between the Institution grounds and the beautiful river.

Dr. Russ (1801-1881), the superintendent, was much beloved of his pupils. Called a great benefactor of the blind, he invented a phonetic alphabet and worked diligently to perfect the system of raised characters and maps that Louis Braille had developed several years earlier in France. Russ came to the Institution when it was founded and served without pay for the first two years. Despite a busy schedule and heavy responsibilities, he was never too busy to take a personal interest in his pupils, even teaching Bible classes and reading to them from his favorite poet, Lord Byron.

It was to this school that Fanny Crosby arrived on March 7, 1835, and it was here that she would have some of her most important experiences. During the first days of her stay, Fanny was simply homesick. When evening came the first night, she was led to the little room that was to be hers. There "everything was strange" and nothing was in the place where she was accustomed to find it at home. This thoroughly disconcerted the poor girl, and she "could not keep the curl from coming to my upper lip." She sat on her trunk and tried to be brave and force back the tears. She was approached by the matron of the Institution, whom she described as a motherly Quakeress, who threw her arms about the girl's thin body.

"Fanny," she said, "I guess thee has never been away from home before."

"No, ma'am," said Fanny weakly, then added falteringly, "Please excuse me. I must cry." And she did, loud and long, until one of her fellow pupils succeeded in comforting her.[7]

Fanny soon overcame her homesickness—or, rather, it went away—and she got into the swing of things. Soon, the once-forbidding Institution became "my happy home," and in the next two decades she experienced "the brightest joys I e'er have known."[8] An outgoing girl, she rapidly made friends, and with her keen mind she quickly mastered her lessons. Among the subjects she was taught in the next few years were English, Grammar, Science, Music, History, Philosophy, Astronomy, and Political Economy. The lessons were given to the pupils in the form of lectures and readings. The instructors would read the lesson or lecture two or three times. This done, the pupils were expected to answer minute and detailed questions on the text that they had

37

heard. The next day they were to paraphrase the entire lesson. Fanny learned unusually quickly and well, and to the day of her death she was able to recite the entire text of *Brown's Grammar* word for word.

Fanny was "in love with" Grammar, Philosophy, Astronomy, and Political Economy, but she had trouble with Braille and Mathematics. She was taught to read the Bible, *Pilgrim's Progress*, and Coleridge's "Rime of the Ancient Mariner" in braille but apparently did so very slowly and laboriously. Although she said she could recognize a person instantaneously by the touch of the hand, she claimed that she had too poor a sense of touch in her fingers to master the raised alphabet. This she blamed on her guitar-playing, which calloused her fingertips. However genuine the causes of her difficulty, after she left the Institution Fanny rarely used braille. She kept a braille Bible, but even here relied more upon her memory and training. Whenever she wanted to read a book she would have someone read it to her; they had only to do so once and the contents were indelibly stamped upon her remarkable memory.

Mathematics was a "great monster" to her. This subject was taught by means of metal slates with holes in them with which the pupils could count and realize the numbers as they worked, and by means of three types which could be placed in different positions in a wooden frame to represent certain figures. Fanny was less than enthusiastic about this subject. "I have never been a very good hater," she said later in life, "even when the best material was provided for the purpose; but I found myself an adept at the art of loathing, when it came to the Science of Numbers." She managed to learn addition and subtraction. Multiplication was harder, and when it came to division Fanny balked entirely. In the Institution, the more advanced pupils were sometimes assigned to teach the newer ones. Anna Smith, who later became one of Fanny's most intimate friends, was teaching her—or trying to teach her— arithmetic. After two days of multiplication, she had to admit that her pupil had learned absolutely nothing. Dr. Russ was consulted and called Fanny into his office, threatening to "put me on the mantel."[9] As a result, Fanny got down to work and managed to learn the multiplication tables. Then Anna got to division. There Fanny's "patience failed." She was one of those persons who just cannot learn mathematics, no matter how hard they try. Although the Institution had the reputation of being more advanced in mathematics than schools for the sighted, Anna realized that Fanny had no aptitude for figures and told Russ so. The superintendent then wisely decided that Fanny could better spend her time in other studies, so he excused her from taking more arithmetic. "From that hour I was a new creature," Fanny recalled more than seventy years later. "What a nightmare I was escaping!"[10]

Fanny's favorite avocation continued to be writing poetry. The instructors read the pupils the poems of Thomas Moore, James Montgomery, Henry Wadsworth Longfellow, Alfred Lord Tennyson, William Cullen Bryant, and

Charles Wesley, as well as those of many long-forgotten authors who were well known in that day, poets such as Eliza Cook, Lydia Sigourney, Felicia Hemans, Martin Farquhar Tupper, Nathaniel Parker Willis, and George Pope Morris. Fanny tried to write poetry in imitation of all those authors whose works she studied. Her schoolmates, in turn, tried to write poetry in imitation of Fanny's. There are a few samples of her poetry from this period, but Fanny later passed them off as "crude efforts." Although her schoolmates thought at the time that her poems were good verse, she conceded that, in fact, "They were not." However, she would send these verses to her mother and grandfather, who doted over them.

Crude as these verses may have been, Fanny was considered adept enough at writing poetry to compose the words to a march by Anthony Reiff, a sighted music teacher. The march was sung by the very fine Institution choir at the laying of the cornerstone for the new institutional building in 1837. The verses do not seem particularly bad for a seventeen-year-old girl, especially one with only two years of formal education. And significantly, this first major poetic effort of which we have a record was a hymn:

This day may every bosom feel
A thrill of pleasure and delight;
Its scenes will in our memories dwell
When time shall wing his rapid flight.

Soon, however, Fanny's instructors noticed that she was developing a "swelled head." This was brought to the attention of Dr. Silas Jones, who had replaced Russ as superintendent in 1836, and he called Fanny into his office one morning. She entered expecting that "a new ode or other kind of lyric was to be ordered, to the honor of some distinguished person or event"; she was flabbergasted when Jones gave her a grave lecture about depending on "the favor and laudation of the world."

"Do not think too much about rhymes, and the praises that come from them. Store your mind with useful knowledge and think more of what you can *be* than of how you can *appear*." His words, Fanny recalled, "were bombshells in the camp of my self-congratulatory thoughts." Hot tears came to her eyes, but soon she recovered sufficiently to throw her arms around his neck and kiss him on the forehead. "You talked to me as my father would have talked if he were living, and I thank you for it."[11]

Whether or not Fanny's pride was checked immediately is not clear, but in the weeks and months and years that followed, the quality of her poetry rapidly improved. Before she was twenty she was the Institution's most promising pupil, a young lady who not only wrote poetry but, in addition to the guitar, which she had learned to play as a child, was proficient at the piano,

39

organ, and harp. She had the reputation of being one of the finest harpists in America.

Life progressed smoothly for Fanny during the late 1830s. These years at the Institution were pleasant ones, filled with hard work as well as pleasant diversion. A high-spirited girl, she later said she was sure to be part of any mischief that went on at the school. She would tease the postman mercilessly, hiding his pen and ink and letter book until he became frantic but always managing to stay out of his sight. When boys and girls who were "tenderly attached," as she said, held "spooning sessions," she and other pupils who could play the organ devised "preconcerted chords" which they struck to let each other know they were there. When she heard that the Institution's crop of watermelons was to be sold to raise money, she and a friend managed to steal a large melon, tricking the gardener by volunteering to listen for thieves while the old man caught a few minutes of sleep.

By then she had decided that in order to help support her "Mother Dear" she would become a teacher. Although she was not one of the regular instructors, she was being assigned to teach some of the subjects and skills to newcomers, just as Anna Smith had tried to teach arithmetic to her. Many years later Imogene Hart, whom she taught in this capacity, reminisced in a letter to Fanny that when she arrived at the Institution in 1839, "you were appointed to prepare me to join several classes that were well-advanced in their studies. You taught me grammar, geography, and knitting. You also labored very hard to teach me to sing 'second' in the hymn, 'Come, Ye Disconsolate.'"[12]

Dr. Jones became concerned that Fanny was devoting too much of her time to poetry, to the exclusion of her other studies. He decided to determine if she had real talent or if she was one of those people who write rhymes because they are poetry lovers. His way of determining this was to forbid writing any poetry for three months. He was convinced that if she was a real poet she could not withstand this "trial by fire," but if she were merely a dilettante the enforced layoff would not faze her. Fanny became so despondent that she could not do anything. After six weeks of failure in her lessons Jones called her to his office and began to reprimand her, demanding the reason for the poor work. Fanny's only excuse was that poetry occupied her thoughts to such an extent that it was impossible to keep her mind on other things when she was forbidden to write it. Jones became convinced that she was a real poet and relented, agreeing to allow her to write poetry if she would pay more attention to the lectures.

Shortly after this incident the confidence of the Institution's instructors in Fanny's poetic talent was strengthened by the visit of George Combe (1778–1858), the Scottish phrenologist. As a practitioner of character determination based on the shape and texture of the skull, Combe studied Fanny's head and remarked, "Why, here is a poetess! Give her every advantage. Read the best books to her, and teach her to appreciate the best poetry."[13] It has not been recorded whether or not Combe had been prompted as to Fanny's interests. In any event, Jones took Combe's advice conscientiously and found Fanny a teacher in poetic composition. The teacher was Hamilton Murray, a member of the Board of Managers, who claimed that while he could not write poetry he could teach others to do so. Murray read long passages of poetry to Fanny and required her to commit them to memory. He taught the proper use of rhyme, rhythm, and meter, pointed out the defects of her poetry, and had her imitate the works of well-known poets. He was very strict, one day assigning her the task of paraphrasing part of a poem by Nathaniel Parker Willis. Lunch was at noon, and at eleven forty-five Fanny had not written a word. Murray entered.

"Have you written those verses, Fanny?"

"I have not, Mr. Murray."

"Well, Fanny," he said, calmly but deliberately, "you understand—no verses, no dinner. It is now fifteen minutes to twelve."

By noon, she had the paraphrase, a half-dozen lines of blank verse. "I think I must have liked my dinner better than verse-making at that time," she remarked years later. From Murray, Fanny learned not only poetic technique but also rapidity of composition. It was owing to his instruction—or, rather, discipline—that in later years she was able to whip off as many as a dozen hymns a day. For all that Murray did, Fanny was eternally grateful. Of him she said, late in life:

With rare faithfulness and with much kindness, considering that his pupil was not a rich man's daughter, but a poor blind girl just starting in life, he toiled for my benefit. And though I could not pay him in money, he had my heartfelt gratitude. He has long walked the streets of the great Tuneful City: and I hope some day to meet him there, grasp him by the hand, and thank him once more.[14]

CHAPTER 4
"THE BLIND POETESS"

While Fanny was becoming the New York Institution's most promising student, her mother was beginning a new life. In Bridgeport, Mercy's brother, Joseph, had entered the saddlery business and become president of Crosby, May and Co. Saddle Goods. In 1836 Mercy left North Salem to live with Joseph, his wife, Maria, and their two-year-old son, Frank, at "Golden Hill" on the outskirts of Bridgeport. April of that same year saw another arrival in Bridgeport, this time from across the seas. Thomas Morris, born in Swansea, South Wales, in October 1799, had previously visited America and liked it so much that in early 1836 he informed his wife of his intention "of going to America forthwith." Two weeks later, Morris, his wife, Fanny, and his two young children, William and Jemima, set sail for America. Buying a plot of land one acre square very near to Joseph Crosby, he spent the "last picayune in [his] possession." By winter, however, his crops had yielded $500, rendering him "quite comfortable." Within a year, Morris had acquired a cow and $400 to $500 in capital. That fall, Fanny Morris, whose health had suffered ever since her arrival in the New World, was pregnant again. Morris wrote in his diary, "On the 18th of October she gave birth to our little Daniel, and on the 21st, I lost in her an undeviating and confiding friend whose virtues I knew not how to appreciate until I found they could not be recalled."[1]

Three months later, Morris was introduced to his widowed neighbor, Mercy Crosby. Only a month afterward, Mercy's seventeen-year widowhood came to an end with marriage to Morris on February 4, 1838. Mercy conceived, and in May 1839, at the age of forty, she bore Thomas a daughter they named Wilhelmina. Fanny was delighted. When she went to Bridgeport for her annual vacation it was with great joy that she took the new little sister into her arms, but shortly after Fanny returned to New York she received the heavy news that the baby was dead. At once she composed a letter and a poem which were copied out by James Chamberlain, a teacher at the Institution who would later be appointed superintendent. It was not only for Thomas and Mercy but also for Joseph and Maria, who had been shaken by the death of their little niece. To her family Fanny wrote:

The impression that her death has made upon my mind is a deep one, but this event teaches me a lesson, which, I trust, I shall never forget. Once I looked forward to future years, when she would not only be a comfort to you, but also to myself; but these fond hopes are blighted. Let us not repine, but cheerfully submit to the will of heaven.

Then, in a poem that foreshadowed a dominant motif of her later poetry, she wrote:

She's gone, ah yes, her lovely form
Too soon has ceased to bloom,
An emblem of the fragile flower
That blossoms for the tomb.

Yet, mother, check that starting tear
That trembles in thine eye;
And thou, kind father, cease to mourn,
Suppress that heaving sigh.

She's gone, and thou, dear aunt, no more
Wilt watch her cradle bed;
She slumbers in the peaceful tomb,
But weep not for the dead.

Kind uncle, thou art grieving too,
Thy tears in thought I see;
Ah, never will her infant hand
Be stretched again to thee.

She's gone, yet why should we repine?
Our darling is at rest;
Her cherub spirit now reclines
On her Redeemer's breast.[2]

The following year Mercy was again with child. On Sunday, August 9, 1840, while the church bells were ringing, Mercy bore Thomas yet another daughter. They named her Julia but called her Jule.

Fanny returned to New York in the heat of the 1840 presidential race. She was at that time an ardent Democrat and spent much of her time that fall, not writing verse in behalf of her candidate, but against the Whig candidate, the much-loved General William Henry Harrison. Either political campaigns were a lot more civilized then than now or Harrison must have been a man of angelic virtue, for his opponents, Fanny conceded years later, could not dig up a single item of smut with which to blacken his name. The mischievous poet managed to show her dislike for Tippecanoe in verse by altering his most popular campaign song, but despite her efforts Harrison was elected, and when he died, after only a month in office, Fanny was content to bury the hatchet with verse. Her quite conventional early American romantic elegy, perhaps because it was composed by a blind woman, received considerable attention through being published in the *New York Herald,* which at that time regularly carried a poetry column. A proud Grandfather Sylvanus, still living in Gayville, walked four miles each way to a nearby town where he was able to purchase a copy of the *Herald.*

After this, Fanny's reputation as "The Blind Poetess" grew. The students at the Institution were frequently invited to give demonstrations at schools, churches, and other places in order to demonstrate what the blind were capable of accomplishing. The pupils gave exhibitions of braille readings in geography, history, arithmetic, and other subjects, as well as singing and giving recitations. Fanny sang and played the piano, organ, and harp. The exhibition was always closed, however, by one of her "original poetical addresses." These pieces, filled with stock poetic diction, were written not at some unbidden impulse to reflect the outpouring of her soul but at the request of the managers of the Institution to demonstrate the capabilities of the blind and to solicit money. There was usually no extraordinary merit in these poems, although the form and style were impeccable. This technical perfection was what impressed her hearers. They were interested not so much in her poetic gifts but in her educability. She was indeed at this time the poet in residence, so to speak, of the Institution, and as she gradually attained a reputation it was just as much for what she symbolized as for what she wrote.

Nevertheless, even those listeners who saw Fanny simply as a symbol of the educability of the blind were impressed by certain attributes of her poetry, notably her descriptive powers. Fanny was much more impressive when she recited at soirees than she was on more official occasions, for then she was able to recite poems which she had been actually inspired to write. In some of her blank verse poems of this category, her fantastic descriptive powers were in evidence. The following lines come from "The Trial of the Faith of Abraham":

The aged patriarch, leaning on his staff,
Stood in the doorway of his tent, and watched
The gaily painted clouds which here and there
Were floating in the quiet evening sky
In strange fantastic forms, till, brushed away
By the light breath of the cool zephyr's wing,
They melted into air, and left the moon
Sole monarch of a train of radiant stars,

The bright attendants of her mighty reign.
And forth in brilliant majesty she came,
Touched with her silvery wand the tiny flowers,
And bade them fold their leaves, and lay their heads
Upon the bosom of their mother earth.[3]

Fanny was called to recite before many of the distinguished visitors who appeared at the Institution in the early days and were curious about this new phenomenon of educating the blind. President John Tyler, along with the Mayor of New York City and the entire City Council, suddenly appeared one day in June. The new superintendent, Peter Vroom, rushed into Fanny's room and told her about the visitors now waiting in the reception room. With fifteen minutes' notice Fanny prepared a poetic greeting for the President of the United States. At the appointed time, the poem was ready, and Fanny recited it before the eminent visitors and then sang a song. During the same period, the Governor of New York, William Henry Seward, later Lincoln's Secretary of State, visited the Institution. When the Governor was passing through the room where Fanny sat knitting, the young lady managed to let her ball of yarn slip to the floor. The ruse was successful. Seward bent down, picked the ball up, and gave it back to her with a few kindly words. One of the teachers saw that Fanny's "accident" had been intentional and reported it to Vroom. He laughed and said, "Oh, don't say anything about it to Fanny, for we never know what she will do next."[4]

Prominent visitors came from overseas too. From France, late in 1843, came Henri Gratien, Count Bertrand (1773–1844), Napoleon's old field-marshal, who had shared his master's exile on St. Helena before being pardoned and allowed to return to France. Fanny recited a poem written in honor of the elderly soldier, in which she referred to his ministrations to the Emperor in his last sickness. Bertrand was deeply moved and gave the young poet a box with "a piece" of the willow that grew above Napoleon's grave on St. Helena. "God bless you," growled the old field-marshal. "How I wish you could have known the Emperor."[5]

Around the same time, the Institution was graced by a visit from William Cullen Bryant, then forty-nine years old and America's leading poet. The author of "Thanatopsis" and "To a Waterfowl" appeared at a soiree. Fanny had no idea that Bryant was acquainted with her poetry. "I never imagined that he would greet me otherwise than conventionally, and as a stranger of whom he had never heard before." But, to her astonishment, Bryant recognized her as "The Blind Poetess" and told her that he was familiar with her verse, warmly commending her "poor little rhythmical efforts." He said she had real talent and potential and encouraged her to continue writing. "He never knew," Fanny wrote in later years, "how much good he did by those few words."[6]

While at the Institution Fanny became acquainted with many public people, and she also formed several warm friendships with her colleagues. Among these was Imogene Hart, who became a musician. Until they were in their eighties, she and Fanny corresponded, sending each other music and poems of their own composition. Then there was her roommate, Alice Holmes, a year younger than she, who had contracted a case of smallpox that left her blind at the age of nine, while en route with her parents from England to America. Miss Holmes, as "The Blind Poet of Jersey City," published several volumes of verse herself. Lucy Kingsbury was another of Fanny's friends at the Institution. She came in 1842 at the age of twenty-two after an accident in which a gun had discharged in her face and blown her eyes from their sockets. Fanny befriended the lonely, confused, and disfigured young woman, although she would see little of her after Lucy left the Institution several years later. But perhaps Fanny's fondest attachment during her Institution days was to Anna Smith, who had tried to teach her mathematics, and to whom she wrote:

Come, throw thy arms around me,
And press thy cheek to mine;
The love that thou has warmed me
Shall ever still be thine.[7]

In the summer of 1842, the Board of Managers decided that twenty of the Institution's best students should make a tour of the central part of New York State in order to demonstrate publicly the educability of the blind to induce parents of blind children to send them to the New York school. Of course, "The Blind Poetess" was a member of the company. They traveled west by what Fanny called "the highway of waves," the Erie Canal. Little "packet-boats," drawn by mules, made their way up the "artificial river" laden with both freight and passengers. In one of these Fanny and her colleagues traveled first to Schenectady, then to Rome, Utica, Syracuse, Rochester, and, finally, Buffalo. At each of these cities, and also in some of the smaller towns along the way, a reception was held in which the mayor and prominent citizens would speak and hundreds of townsfolk would throng the place of exhibition in order to satisfy their curiosity about the strange tales of blind people being taught useful trades. The pupils sang, gave addresses, described their school, and made other recitations. Fanny played for them on the piano and harp and sang and recited poems.

At the end of the canal in Buffalo, the party disembarked and made its way to Niagara, where from Goat Island the pupils experienced the falls. Fanny was very enthusiastic. Not only did she spiritedly take in the various descriptions of sighted persons (she always said that one advantage to being blind is that one got to "see" things from many different points of view, as different people described them), but she also was able to hear "the trumpet-voice of the King of Cataracts proclaiming the power of the Almighty Hand." What Fanny could not see, however, she was able to compensate for by imagination. "I could imagine those great rocks that had stood for ages, while the river-billows went sweeping over them night and day, summer and winter, century after century."[8]

In May 1843 the Institution held its twelfth-anniversary celebration at the New York Tabernacle. Fanny, as on other such occasions, was asked to compose and recite a poem. On June 22, the New York State Senate visited the Institution as a body. Again "The Blind Poetess" was asked to perform.

That summer Fanny was designated to go with a company from the Institution on another tour of New York State. It was an arduous task being "exhibit number one." It was tedious to travel from little town to little town, to hear pompous mayors give vacuous speeches oozing with shopworn platitudes, to hear condescending officials make flowery pledges of future support that were never meant to be, to hear lachrymose old women bleat their unwanted commiserations. People would ask that infuriating question, "How long have you been—er, ah—that way?" Once a hotel room clerk asked that question of one of the managers, who had twenty-twenty vision but who was assumed to be blind because of the institution he represented. "Why, I've been this way all my life," he replied, and chuckled to himself as the clerk shook his head and put his hand on his shoulder and told him how sorry he was to hear that.[9] Frequently people would ask how blind people, when they ate, managed to get the food to their mouths. Fanny always liked to respond to this question by saying that they would take a string and tie one end to the table leg and the other to their tongues and work the food up to their mouths along the string. Several weeks of answering questions of this nature and of composing "original poetical addresses" to be read at each stop left Fanny completely exhausted.

The tour brought Fanny one tremendous benefit, however, albeit one which would not be fulfilled for fifteen years. While the company was giving an exhibition at Oswego, New York, a woman there was so impressed that she decided that the Institution in New York was the place to send her own blind son. She brought the boy and introduced him to Fanny. She told the twenty-three-year-old poet that her little boy was going to be coming to the Institution at the earliest possible opportunity and that she wanted him to be Fanny's personal charge. "Take good care of my boy," Mary Van Alstine said of her twelve-year-old, not realizing that Fanny would take such good care of little Alexander that he would later marry her!

That fall Fanny was a regular instructor at the Institution. She was teaching Rhetoric, Grammar, and Roman and American History. It took a great deal of work to prepare for her courses, and, although exhausted after a full day's work, she frequently stayed up until 2 A.M. composing poetry. The strain had a deleterious effect on a constitution insufficiently recovered from the summer's exertions. By winter, some of the managers were afraid that Fanny might be developing tuberculosis, but the Institution doctor, J. W. G. Clements, assured them that all she needed was rest. For this reason, he recommended that she forego meeting her classes for a while and skip the upcoming visit to Washington, D.C., in which she was scheduled to recite poetry before members of Congress. Fanny did not mind not meeting her classes, but she yearned to go to Washington. Finally, Clements decided that she would worry herself into a fever if she did not go and permitted her to do so, provided that she did not overly exert herself. Fanny's joy, however, turned into apprehension, when she learned the great importance that was being pinned on her poetic presentation. The managers were trying to get Congress to pass legislation to create institutions for the blind providing free education to children so handicapped in every state in the Union. They hoped that Fanny could pull on their heartstrings with her poetry to such an extent that they would be moved to enact such a bill.

On January 24, 1844, between demands by John Quincy Adams for the "Orders of the Day," Congressman Davis of Indiana moved that the use of the Assembly Hall "be granted on the evening of the Twenty-Fourth . . . to the managers of the New York State Institution for the Education of the Blind for the purpose of exhibiting the proficiency of their pupils in the academic and mechanical arts."[10] The use of the hall was granted. That evening at seven thirty, seventeen pupils from the Institution gave their "concert and exhibition" in the Capitol. In later years, Fanny would sometimes speak of being the first woman to address Congress. But it would appear, from the account given in the *Washington Daily Globe*, that the exhibition was not strictly an appearance before Congress, at least in the usual sense. Although the event was held in the Capitol and a number of Senators and Representatives, including John Quincy Adams, James Buchanan, Andrew Johnson, Hannibal Hamlin, Stephen A. Douglas, Thomas H. Benton, Jefferson Davis, and Alexander Stephens, were in attendance, Congress was not in session but was only granting the Institution the use of their Assembly Hall. Congressmen as well as private citizens were admitted to this public event by paying a twenty-five-cent admission fee.

The program opened with the band (and with a company of seventeen, one wonders what sort of a band it could have been!) playing "Grand March" by Küffner. This was followed by a "Christmas Anthem"—one month late—sung by the choir. Next was a piano solo, "Storm Rondo" by Steibelt, given by an anonymous pupil. Next, the company of students was examined in grammar. This was followed by the band's rendition of a popular waltz by Johann Strauss, Sr. Then a pupil sang an air entitled "Fortune's Thorns." (This may have been Fanny, but whether it was or not is not recorded.) This was followed by an examination in arithmetic, which, in turn, was followed by a march from Bellini's popular opera Norma, played by the band.[11] When this was finished, Fanny gave her "poetical address." When she had recited her long poem of thirteen stanzas, the Congressmen burst into applause so loud that it sounded like thunder to Fanny and frightened her. At the conclusion the Congressmen, impressed by Fanny and her presentations, insisted that she give an encore. Drawing on her remarkable memory, she cast around for a poem of a nature suitable for the occasion and came up with an elegy written that summer upon the sudden death of Tyler's "lamented Secretary of State," Hugh Legare, who had suffered a heart attack while laying the cornerstone at the new Bunker Hill Monument. Fanny recited the poem flawlessly. By the time she closed, the Congressmen were weeping audibly. Legare's sister, who had read the poem in the papers the previous summer, was there to see her, and met Fanny at the chamber door and gave her a beautiful ring. John Quincy Adams, the hard-boiled, crusty ex-President, came up to the young poet and wrung her hand. But Congress, for all its weeping, did not realize the Institution's proposal to establish more institutions for the blind.

On the way back to New York, the company stopped in Trenton and, on January 27, gave an exhibition there before the governor and legislature of New Jersey at which Fanny, as usual, was called upon to recite. She returned to New York almost in a state of collapse. She did not meet any of her classes that spring but spent it working on the first volume of poetry that she would publish.

By April her little volume of poetry, entitled The Blind Girl and Other Poems, was ready for publication. The book was 160 pages long, and among the poems it contained were "The Blind Girl," "The Rise and Progress of the New York Institution for the Blind," "To the Heroes of Bunker Hill," and the poetic addresses she had made on public occasions over the past several years, through which she had distinguished herself. The preface was written by Fanny's friend and mentor, Hamilton Murray. Since the book was being published partly to raise money for the Institution, Murray used the preface to make a pitch for the reader's purse. Exaggerating Fanny's strained state, he wrote ominously of the poet's "declining health" and appealed to the heart of the prospective reader to buy the volume and recommend it to his friends, if for no other reason than the charitable one of making comfortable her declining days. A final step was necessary. The publishers requested for the frontispiece a daguerrotype of the author.

Photography was then only about five years old in America, but the new art had taken hold very strongly, and everyone with any substance was taking advantage of this means of recording their features for all time. So it was not an unusual request that Fanny's publishers made, but sitting for a picture was

49

for her a new experience and something of an ordeal. The exposure required several minutes, and in that interval the subject was obliged to sit stock-still lest the image be blurred. This is probably why one so seldom sees smiling faces on old daguerrotypes. One of the New England literati observed that in photographs the hands usually appear clenched "as if for a fight, or as in despair" and the eyes are fixed "as if in a fit—or in madness—or in death." Years later, Fanny observed that "the restless Fanny Crosby . . . would be obliged to sit still for . . . five whole minutes." On the first attempt, she failed. Sometime during the prolonged exposure, something struck her funny bone, and she had a fit of giggles and ruined the plate. The photographer, perhaps accustomed to such occurrences, tried again. This time Fanny endured the "veritable inquisition . . . to the length of five whole minutes."[12]

Interestingly enough, this first photograph, taken in the early days of photography of a woman who lived into the era of snapshots and the box camera, which could more easily capture facial expression, is the only known picture of Fanny which shows her smiling! She does not appear to be in ill health. Fanny stood only 4 feet 9 inches tall and claimed never to have weighed as much as 100 pounds, but this, of all her photographic likenesses, without a doubt shows her at her heaviest. A beauty Fanny Crosby definitely was not, even in these early days. She had a rather long horse face and a small, blunt, nondescript nose, and the lips, parted in the smile, reveal somewhat prominent front teeth with a gap between them. Dark rectangular spectacles entirely obscure the sightless eyes. The ears are "jug-handled." The hair is thick and wavy, parted in the middle and pulled backward in curls that hang to the shoulders. The unevenness of the shoulders, so evident in later portraits, is scarcely detectable here. Although a lock of Fanny's hair which has been preserved in the Fanny Crosby Memorial Home at Bridgeport is light blond, the hair appears dark in this photograph. This accords with a statement she made in old age in which she spoke of the long black curls she had in youth.

The Blind Girl and Other Poems was published in the late spring of 1844. It enjoyed a moderately good sale, and the name of Frances J. Crosby, or Fanny Crosby, became more familiar. What was Fanny Crosby like as a poet? Was she an utterly untalented hack or did she have true genius?

Fanny Crosby was nationally acclaimed for her verse long before she gained fame as a hymn writer. But "The Blind Poetess" may have been noted more for being blind than for being a poet. She was seen by most people as a symbol of what the blind could do, and her poetry was viewed simply as a manifestation of that larger accomplishment. However, even had her poems been written by a sighted person, they would have claimed attention. It is not known how many secular poems she wrote, although they probably number in the thousands. She seemed to exude verse. She wrote verse for every occasion in her life and that of her friends: anniversaries, weddings, birthdays, funerals, church events, national events, tea parties, and anything else that could possibly be the subject for a poem. Whenever she left the house of a friend after a visit, she bestowed upon her host a few lines of verse. One is led to wonder whether or not it was more natural for her to *speak* in verse than in prose. In normal daily conversation not only was she likely to use poetic or quasi-poetic expressions like, "In the Institution I touched the poetic garment of Mrs. Sigourney, sat long at the feet of Bayard Taylor, slaked my thirsty soul at the living streams of Frances Ridley Havergal, and drank deeply from the chalices of Longfellow, Whittier, Holmes, and Lowell,"[13] she was also likely to burst into outright verse, such as her after-dinner remark:

Now just as sure as I'm a sinner,
I know I've had a very good dinner.

Fanny wrote many poems for publication. As we have seen, she was a regular contributor to the poetry columns of various New York newspapers, including the *Herald* and the *Tribune*. She had poetic battles with her friend William Wye Smith in the pages of the literary weekly, the *Saturday Emporium*. He would write a poem expressing one sentiment and she would rebut him in verse in the next issue. She published four books of poetry: *The Blind Girl* in 1844; *Monterey and Other Poems* in 1851, *A Wreath of Columbia's Flowers* in 1858, and *Bells at Evening* in 1897.

The quality of Fanny's verse varies wildly, even within her published collections. Looking through any one of her volumes, with the possible exception of the last one, the most untrained person can readily tell that many of the poems are weak and undistinguished—even blatantly bad—as these lines from "The Indian's Lament," published in *Monterey,* demonstrate. The Indian tells a gracious white lady:

Lady, I sigh for that far-off shore
Where they tell me the red man shall weep no more;
I hear the Great Spirit whispering now
As I turn to look on thy sunny brow.

However, the very same brain that produced some appallingly banal lines was also capable, at the same period, of writing the following excerpt from "Samson with the Philistines," which she was to publish in *Bells at Evening:*

His hair had grown. He knew it. But his eyes—
Would they return? Would he again behold
Or sun or moon or stars or human face?

O, heaven! In all our catalogue of woes
Can there be one that so afflicts the mind
And rends the very fibres of the heart
Like that which comes, when in our riper years,
We lose, and by a single stroke of Thine,
That sense, which of all others, most we prize,
That glorious avenue through which we range
The fields of science, poesy, and art,
And trace Thee in Thy excellence divine
Where Thou hast left Thy Name in living light
On Truth's immortal page, Thy Holy Book?
O, to be left at midday in the dark!
To wander on and on in moonless night!
To know the windows of the soul are closed,
And closed till opened in eternity!
They who have felt can tell how deep the gloom,
And only they who in their souls have learned
To walk by faith and lean on God for help,
To such a lot can e'er be reconciled.

So, although a great deal of Fanny's poetry bordered on doggerel versifications of common experiences or sentimental themes, she was capable of writing something better. Henry Adelbert White (1880–1951), her great friend, himself a poet and for many years a professor of English at various universities, admired Fanny's poetry and considered her a first-class writer. George Henry Sandison (1850–1900), a literary critic and editor, admitted in 1897 that in many of the gospel hymns the literary critic could not "discover at once the full-orbed genius of a poet," but maintained that Fanny was "naturally a classical poet," and that, when it came to secular verse, hers was frequently of excellent quality, of which the "imaginative power and beauty would astonish those who knew her only as the writer of the sweet and simple songs of the Gospel."[14]

Fanny Crosby wrote in the mode of the popular poets of her day. When one thinks of the poets of the first half of the nineteenth century, he usually thinks of such shining lights as Byron, Keats, Shelley, Wordsworth, Tennyson, or perhaps their American counterparts: Longfellow, Bryant, Whittier, Poe. But there was in that day an army of poets who were immensely popular but almost totally forgotten now. They wrote in the style of, or perhaps in imitation of, the masters but lacked their depth, content, and poetic finesse. Nevertheless they exercised an enormous appeal for the common reader. The names of Lydia Howard Sigourney (1791–1865), Nathaniel Parker Willis (1806–1867), George Pope Morris (1802–1864), Martin Farquhar Tupper (1810–1889), and

Eliza Cook (1818–1889) mean little or nothing to the modern reader, but they were household words a century or more ago. When we look at some of their poetry, it does not seem exceptional. But the average reader did not expect poets to say very much that was profound; rather, they were to stimulate the emotions by treating a familiar theme versically. The themes of home, motherhood, unrequited love, the flag, and patriotism may be sneered at today, and those of death and grief and old age, uneasily avoided, but the nineteenth-century reader of poetry liked to have sentiments connected with these themes put into verse. It might be said that, for many readers, the test of a poet's success was how readily and how much they had been made to cry.

Poetry was demanded frequently on public occasions. We do not usually have a poetic introduction to our favorite television programs, but in the nineteenth century the Chatauqua Assemblies, which in many ways fulfilled the role of television, frequently opened and closed and were otherwise graced with poetic addresses. Whenever a distinguished person visited a town or city or an institution, some local poet was usually enlisted to greet them in verse. Whenever a famous man or woman died, numerous elegies appeared in local papers or were read at the funeral or wake. The trivial, banal, and humdrum contents of some of these addresses and elegies would not, by the standards of today, be considered as fit for poetic expression, but the patrons of a century ago demanded the versification of their significant experiences. To them, the rhyming, the rhythm, and the flowery words were all important. They did not read a poem so much for the ideas that the poet was expressing as for the poet's facility in expressing in rhyme and verse an idea which was simple and previously assumed to the point of being trivial.

It was in such a literary milieu that Fanny Crosby wrote most of her secular poems, and in most of them, like the other poets of the day, she aimed at putting some common sentimental theme to rhyme. Many of her poems are exceptionally imaginative, and the few really serious poems she published are good, judged by the standards of the time, although they are usually imitations or paraphrases of the work of the top-flight poets of the day. Profound for the genre in which they were written, they embody several striking qualities. One of these qualities is a great power to arouse the emotions. Perhaps this power lay in part in the simplicity of her line and in the intensely personal treatment of her themes. She dealt in everyday actions, wringing the heartstrings, so to speak, not so much by high-flown language as by homey examples and allusions, such as a dying child trying to comfort his mother by reminding her that after he is gone she will be able to sleep late.

Fanny Crosby never achieved fame as a major poet. Her situation did not encourage being a serious poet in her own right. She had the opportunity to compose precious little serious verse. As we have seen, she was expected by the public and the managers of the Institution to be "The Blind Poetess," drawing attention to the Institution and the blind by skillful imitation of popular poets. Had she presented something entirely new and original, the public would not have been as well entertained as was the case when she rehashed a familiar theme made popular by another writer. Fanny's role as "The Blind Poetess," far from being that of a really major poet, was that of an entertainer, through whom the Institution could best raise money and attract attention. Although she must have been aware that her poetic talents were not being permitted to develop as they might, yet she was content with this role. She was grateful to the Institution for providing an excellent education without cost, and she was willing to do anything she could for its managers, even if this meant sacrificing a genuine poetic potential.

CHAPTER 5
PRESIDENTS, GENERALS, AND BRATS

Success as "The Blind Poetess" did not go to Fanny's head; she did not acquire the artistic arrogance common to so many men and women in the world of culture. This fact is illustrated by an incident which took place shortly after *The Blind Girl and Other Poems* was published.

One afternoon, Fanny was asked to show a visitor through the Institution. During the tour of the building, the man happened to catch sight of a stack of volumes of *The Blind Girl* which were being sold there. "Oh, here is the Fanny Crosby book," he said enthusiastically. "You must know her, I suppose."

Far from chiding the man for not recognizing such an eminent person of letters on sight (her picture was in the front of the book), the young woman merely nodded and let the visitor go on.

"Is she a likable girl?" he asked.

Keeping a straight face, Fanny shook her black curls gravely. "Oh, no! Far from it!" she replied.

Silence. Then the visitor, perhaps first expecting more and then realizing that no further tidbits of Crosbiana were forthcoming, said, "Well, I am sorry to hear that." Perhaps his guide was jealous of her, he thought. "But I will take one of her books. Will you please tell her?" Thereupon he gave Fanny his card.

When he was gone, Fanny learned that her visitor had been none other than Johann Ludwig Tellkampf, an eminent professor at Columbia College, and regretted her playfulness. "That incident," she later wrote, "brought to mind the Scriptural advice, 'Be not forgetful to entertain strangers, for thereby some have entertained angels unawares.'"[1]

And, so, through the sales of *The Blind Girl*, the name of Fanny Crosby became familiar in many households in New York and nearer New England. How proud her grandfather would have been of her! But, alas, Sylvanus now slept with his Eunice in the little cemetery at Doanesburg.

The success that the book had was not enough to bolster Fanny's overworked constitution, and by the end of the spring term Dr. Clements feared a collapse, so he ordered Fanny to spend the summer at home, in complete rest.

Events both joyful and tragic had transpired since she had last visited her mother's home two years previously, and her vacation must have been just as great a comfort to her mother as it was beneficial to her. There was a new addition to the Morris family. On Christmas Day, 1843, Mercy, now nearly forty-five, presented her husband with a living Yule gift: their third daughter, Carolyn.

In spring, however, disaster struck. Thomas had for some time been interested in the teachings of Joseph Smith, the Prophet of the Church of Jesus Christ of Latter-Day Saints, whose devotees were active in the Bridgeport area. In April, just as suddenly as he had decided a decade before to come to America, he announced to Mercy that they were going to join the Prophet and his "Saints" at Nauvoo, Illinois. But Mercy was made of somewhat different mettle than Thomas' more compliant first wife. A sixth-generation descendent of the founders of the Massachusetts Bay Colony, she was not about to leave New England and go off to parts unknown. Still less was she willing to renounce the faith of her fathers. She adamantly refused to go with Thomas; neither would she permit their daughters to go. Thomas was equally stubborn. He was going, with or without Mercy, and he was taking his children by his first wife with him. So, on April 10, Thomas Morris left Mercy and Bridgeport and, with Jemima and Daniel, set out for Illinois. William, his oldest child, now fifteen, had a mind of his own and wanted no part of his sire's adventures. When he heard of his father's plans, he ran away and did not return to his stepmother until he knew that his father had left without him.

Thomas Morris made his way to Nauvoo, Illinois, just in time to witness the assassination of the Prophet in June. One group of followers then began their journey toward Utah, and Morris went with them. He managed to reach his destination and ended his days as a gardener to Smith's successor, Brigham Young. He never returned to Bridgeport, and Mercy was never to see him again.

It was on the heels of this tragic desertion that Fanny returned to her mother's household. The rest and change of environment proved extremely salutary for her, and in September she returned to New York in perfect health, to the amazement of her colleagues, who, by their reactions, seemed to indicate that they had never expected to see her alive again.

Life resumed as before at the Institution. Fanny quickly got back into her routine of teaching and giving recitations of her poetry for the numerous dignitaries who visited the Institution. From this time on, many of these worthies were well acquainted with the name of Fanny Crosby, for during the summer months *The Blind Girl* had circulated still farther among the literary circles of the East.

One celebrity who had previously visited the Institution and who now took a new interest in Fanny was Horace Greeley (1811–1872), the famous newspaper editor. He and Fanny had met at a New Year's Eve party the year before where, much to her disappointment, the famous newspaperman had little time for her. But when the two met again in September 1844, Greeley seemed unable to run out of things to say to "The Blind Girl." They discoursed on such divers subjects as history, literature, social ethics, and political economy, until Greeley expressed a desire to hear Fanny recite some of her poems. Fanny complied. Greeley was impressed and invited her to contribute poems to his newspaper, the New York Tribune. The Tribune, then just three years old, already was an influential daily. It was a liberal paper, backing the Whig party and social reform. Although Fanny was "an ardent Democrat," she was progressive in her political and social outlook and admired Greeley and most of the ideas which were supported by the paper. She accepted his offer and left her meeting with him in transports of delight. "I hardly knew whether I walked or flew to my room that night; I was so proud at having been recognized as a poet by such a great genius as Horace Greeley."[2] By this time, Fanny was also contributing to several periodicals. Besides contributing poems to James Gordon Bennett's New York Herald and the Saturday Emporium, as she had for several years, she also was writing for the Saturday Evening Post and the Clinton Signal.

But the celebrities Fanny met were not all from the literary world. She came to make many friends from the world of politics. That fall, ex-President Martin Van Buren took her out to dinner. A man of fashion and elegance, Van Buren was charmed by his young guest, and Fanny became attached to the sixtyish former President, whom she came to call "My Little Magician," after one of his political soubriquets. "Down to his dying day," she later wrote, "he was one of my closest friends."[3] What she meant by "closest friends" is questionable. Despite her piety, Fanny Crosby was something of a name-dropper, even in old age, and often referred to various prominent persons as her "close friends" when she had only met them a few times. There is no evidence that her relationship with Van Buren went beyond an occasional dinner engagement.

The following year, Fanny had the honor of meeting her fourth President, the newly inaugurated James K. Polk. First Tyler, then John Quincy Adams, during the Washington trip, then Van Buren, and now Polk. Polk and his staff made an official visit to the Institution in 1845, and Fanny was drafted, as usual, by the current superintendent, William Boggs, to recite a poem of welcome which expatiated upon the glories of the republican form of government.

The next year Fanny was again in Washington and once more in presidential society. In April, delegations from the institutions for the blind in Boston, Philadelphia, and New York appeared before Congress. The benefactors of the blind who wanted to establish free institutions for the visually handicapped in every state thought that it was now time for another demonstration. A bill was in preparation which would be introduced within a month by Representative John W. Tibbats (D-Ky), which dealt with the matter, so they thought. It was decided that the existing institutions should demonstrate to the lawmakers that educating the blind was a useful and worthwhile undertaking. Once again, Fanny was chosen to recite her poetry, not only in a special gala being given by the Congressmen for the blind students, but also before a special House subcommittee which had been appointed to study the subject of the need for creating institutions for the education of the blind.

At any rate, while in Washington, Fanny and her colleagues were invited to dinner at the White House. The President remembered Fanny from the previous year. "Well, Miss Crosby," he asked, "have you made any poetry since I saw you last year?"

"Yes," she replied, "I have composed a song and dedicated it to you."

Polk was taken aback. He wanted to hear it, so, after dinner, he escorted her to the music room, where, seating herself at the piano, she gave an "important recital" for him, singing him her new song.[4]

Fanny once again met John Quincy Adams, who, having finished his term of office some fifteen years before, was now a respected member of the House. While in Washington, Fanny heard him deliver one of his last important addresses, in which he argued that the United States should accept the $500,000 which the British scientist, James Smithson, had left to the United States of America for "an establishment, under the name of the 'Smithsonian Institution,' for the increase and diffusion of knowledge among men." There had been opposition by certain Congressmen, notably John C. Calhoun of South Carolina, who maintained that Congress had no power under the Constitution to accept a gift of the type of Smithson's bequest. It was to oppose this point of view that "Old Man Eloquent" spoke out on April 23, 1846, with Fanny listening in one of the galleries of the old House chamber. She noted that the "audience was so still that the faintest noise in any part of the room seemed to be very loud." This, however, was a phenomenon due more to the acoustics of the room, now known as the "echo chamber," than to the silence which was then reigning. The harsh, dry voice "fell upon our ears with a strange cadence that echoed in my memory for many years after the voice itself had ceased to be a great and commanding force in the councils of our nation."[5]

Shortly thereafter, the Smithsonian bill passed both House and Senate roll calls. The bill for the institutions for the blind did not fare nearly so well. The climax of its backers' two-year fight occurred on May 8, when Tibbats introduced a much-altered bill. In its final form the bill called for the setting aside of a certain amount of public lands for establishing a library or printing house for the blind. It was a far cry from what the managers of the existing institutions hoped it would be. But even in its final form, the blind bill had vigorous opposition. One representative argued that if there was to be set up a library for the blind, then libraries for the deaf and mentally defective ought also be set up. It was soon proposed that the bill be referred to the Committee of the Whole on the State of the Union. Tibbats, alarmed, spoke out. "I hope those in favor of the bill will vote against such a motion. If it is sent to the Committee of the Whole on the State of the Union, it will never again be reached in the world!"[6] But Tibbats' pleas were to no avail. The bill was indeed sent to the Committee of the Whole and, as he had warned, it never surfaced. On May 13, the *Congressional Globe* reported that Tibbats made "an ineffecutal motion to take up the bill for the benefit of the blind."[7] But after that the bill was never heard from again, and the benefactors of the blind gave up any hope for obtaining any kind of congressional action in behalf of their goals.

As Fanny looked back over the years on the second trip to Washington, she remembered it not for the legislation that she and her colleagues failed to persuade the legislators to pass but for the many distinguished persons that she met. She had "seen" Adams once more, and had been introduced to many other Congressmen, including two future Presidents, James Buchanan and Andrew Johnson. She had again met President Polk and also, for the first and only time, his wife, Sarah. Fanny was deeply impressed by this pious and serious-minded woman and always remembered her with deepest affection.

Back at the Institution, Fanny sometimes grew weary of her position as poet laureate. It was an annoyance to the young woman to be "expected, whenever anything unusual happened, to embalm the event in rhyme and measure." Yet, as we have seen, this was what her public demanded. Fanny, or "Fan," as she was often called now, was obliged, for instance, to celebrate in verse the killing of a mouse by a girl there at the Institution. On another occasion (the Institution must have hosted a large army of mice in those days), she was asked to write about an incident in which a teacher at the Institution awoke to find a mouse in his long, disheveled hair. Although mildly annoyed to be asked to write such nonsense, Fanny always considered it more important to please others than herself. If this was what made her friends happy, she would write it, even if it meant sacrificing time she would have otherwise spent in writing genuine poetry.

Whenever she heard of the death of any prominent person, she automatically sat down and compiled an elegy, knowing that one would be expected of her. An embarrassing situation once occurred when she heard a newsboy crying, "Daniel Webster dead! Read all about it! Full accounts of the melancholy event here! Daniel Webster dead! Read all about it! Get the full story here!" Hurrying to her room, Fanny began to write an elegy and was repeating the verses aloud when a friend overheard and informed her that Webster was in fact quite alive and that the "news" of his death was all a "get-up to sell papers." Fanny, however, did not throw the poem away, and five years later when Webster died it saved her the labor of writing another.

In February 1848, a capital opportunity occurred for Fanny to ply her talent of writing mortuary verse. On the twenty-third of that month, former President John Quincy Adams succumbed to a brain hemorrhage. Since in those days, before television and radio brought a state funeral into the homes of all Americans at once, public funerals were usually held for revered statesmen in every major city. It was two weeks before the body arrived in New York on March 8, aboard the *S.S. Vanderbilt*. The funeral cortège proceeded from the Battery up Broadway to City Hall with bands playing Handel's "Dead March" from *Saul*, the dead march from Rossini's *Semiramide*, and a popular march of the day entitled "Napoleon's Funeral." Thousands watched the hearse pass by. Fanny composed an elegy entitled "Weep Not for the Dead," in which she employed the pagan device of representing the soul of the dead man in the form of a bird.

At the same time that New Yorkers were bidding farewell to John Quincy Adams, they were welcoming Henry Clay, the great statesman from Kentucky. He was already in the city at the time of Adams' funeral. The day before Adams' body had arrived, he had come on the very same boat. Crowds of people swarmed toward the *Vanderbilt*, at Pier One, North River, to see Clay.[8] The seventy-one-year-old Senator "appeared in excellent health and bore himself with the vigor of a young man."[9] From the pier, amid tumultuous cheers of welcome, Clay, who hoped to be nominated to run for President on the Whig ticket that year, was escorted to a public reception for which tickets cost thirty dollars. There he was received by the Mayor, City Council, and various prominent citizens of New York. Immense crowds followed his progress up Broadway from the Battery to the New York Hotel.

On the eighth, Clay was one of those who took part in the Adams funeral. On the ninth, he toured the city's various institutions. That afternoon, he paid a call at the Institution for the Blind. It was a warm, hazy day, and the Senator was driven in a carriage drawn by four gray horses. When he arrived at the Institution, at the Ninth Avenue entrance, he found a banner hanging over the gateway, reading "Welcome, Henry Clay."

James Chamberlain, who had succeeded William Boggs as Superintendent two years before, gave him a long-winded introduction. The *Herald* reporter recorded that Chamberlain next introduced "Miss Crosby" to the Senator. They shook hands; then Fanny began to recite. The reporter noted that during the recitation Clay seemed "much affected." When Fanny's greeting was concluded, she recalled later, "Mr. Clay stepped forward, and, drawing my arm in his own, led me slowly to the front of the platform." Facing the audience, he said, "This is not the only poem for which I am indebted to this lady. Six months ago, she sent me some lines on the death of my dear son." [10]

Thirteen months before, Henry Clay, Jr., had become a casualty of the Mexican War and Fanny had indeed written a poem, "On the Death of Colonel Clay." Friends had persuaded her to send a copy of the poem to the Senator, and this was his first acknowledgment of receiving it. His voice trembled as he told about the poem. Then "he did not speak for some minutes, while both of us stood there, weeping." [11]

Scarcely more than two weeks later, the pupils of the Institution were honored by the visit of yet another celebrity. This time, General Winfield Scott, the great hero of the generally popular Mexican War, called upon the students. It was he who had captured Mexico City less than a year before and had triumphed in the "halls of Montezuma." Now, like Clay, Scott was seeking the Whig nomination for the Presidency. When he arrived in New York on May 24 for a brief visit and a reception in City Hall, the reporters for the *Tribune*, who had several weeks before commented on the youthful appearance of the seventy-one-year-old Clay, described the corpulent, sixty-four-year-old soldier as looking "very bad." It was noted that when he responded to the introduction he was given at his reception, his voice was "feeble." [12] Despite his apparent ill-health, the general, like Clay, decided to undertake a tour of some of New York's institutions.

On May 25, "Old Fuss and Feathers" appeared unexpectedly at the Institution for the Blind. The short notice of his visit caused a flurry of activity on Ninth Avenue, but, as Fanny said more than a half century later, "there was still no emergency for which our superintendent, Mr. Chamberlain, was not equal." While he feverishly struggled to prepare a program of welcome for Scott, Chamberlain asked Fanny to prepare for entertaining the unexpected guest. She went to meet him in the parlor and talked with him for some time.

Fanny had a lifelong fascination with war, a fascination that seems quite incongruous with everything else that is known of her gentleness and sensitivity. Even when she was an old woman, she used to say how proud she was of the fact that she had had relatives in every single military conflict in which the United States had ever been involved, from the American Revolution down to the imperialistic Spanish-American War and Boxer Rebellion. She had enthusiastically supported President Polk's policies in the Mexican War and had written several poems celebrating that frightful conflict, poems containing lines like:

In the halls of Mont'zuma
now revel the grave,
'Tis thine arm that hath
conquered the Mexican slave,
Thou hast burned thy sword

in the enemy's breast,
They quailed at thy glance—
Thou hast laid them to rest.

She recited some of these lines to Scott, and they were too much even for this military man. He was repelled. When Fanny gushed, "How did it seem when you really found yourself in the halls of Montezuma, General? Did you feel like shouting?" The General growled, "No. I felt like falling on my knees and thanking God for the victory." He went on to tell Fanny that war was not a picnic; "war is a *terrible thing*—demoralizing, degrading, cruel, devastating in all its immediate effects." Then he paused and fished for some reason to justify it. "Would to God it were not sometimes necessary, in order to accomplish results!"[13]

Fanny never forgot the General's comments. It puzzled her to hear so highly esteemed a military hero speak with such distaste of his livelihood. She remembered his words to her a decade and a half later, when General Sherman uttered his pithy epigram, "War is hell."

Since Scott had come on such short notice, Fanny had no extended poetic address prepared with which to welcome him, but while the General was being shown exhibitions of the pupils' work she managed to get up a four-stanza "Chorus." Published later in *A Wreath of Columbia's Flowers*, the poem begins:

Hark! Hark! What merry shouts of joy
    Proclaim a conqueror near;
He comes; a noble hero comes,
    Oh! bid him welcome here.

The third stanza reflects the afternoon's conversation:

Yet, sheathe thy sword, for gentle peace
    Her silvery wing hath spread,
Where thou to meet thy country's foe
    A fearless band has led.

The "Chorus" concluded:

Hurrah! Hurrah for General Scott,
    His name we'll proudly sing;
The north, the south, the east, the west,
    Shall with his triumph ring!

After this welcome, Scott gave a short talk in which he commented on the afternoon's conversation with the poet. "No, we did not revel in the halls of Montezuma," he said, "we lived on one meal a day." [14]

The summer of 1848 the Institution was greeted by another august personage: the President himself. Polk, who was in ill health, was not running for office again. He had come to the Institution unexpected and unattended and told the startled administrators that he did not want a reception. He happened to be in the city and had come to the grounds of the Institution simply for a rest. He remembered their tranquil beauty, and he would be pleased if the administrators did not make a "big to-do" about his presence. Since Fanny and Polk had met, Superintendent Chamberlain asked her to accompany the President on a leisurely stroll around the grounds..

There is no record of Fanny Crosby ever walking with kings, but though she did walk with Presidents, she never lost the common touch. Throughout these years when she was the premier attraction of the New York Institution for the Blind and was spending many hours of the day that were left over from escorting dignitaries around in writing poetry for magazines and newspapers, as well as for herself, she was still loved by her pupils as a devoted teacher and as an affectionate friend.

CHAPTER 6
AT THE CROSS

The year 1848 had been a vintage year for eminent visitors. In 1849, the Institution and all of New York, as well as much of America, saw another visitor, a less comely and genial one. The guest whose visit made the greatest impact on the Institution was a visitor from the Orient, the ghastly pestilence.

The Pale Horse was first seen galloping through Russia, India, and Persia (now Iran) in the spring and summer of 1846. Shock waves of alarm were felt as far away as America as foreign dispatches brought bone-chilling reports that 20,000 had died of cholera in Persia in a few months' time. News that the pestilence was working its way westward caused great alarm and consternation on the European continent. In August 1848 the "Death Blow," as cholera was called in the Orient, struck Berlin, and the next month it infested London.

By the spring of 1849, New Yorkers were made uneasy and nervous by reports that the death toll in Britain alone was 70,000. Many people seemed to die of sheer panic. In America, strange portents presented themselves to unnerve the fearful. Terrifying apparitions were reported in the sky above Baltimore. Several witnesses claimed to have seen a sixty-three-foot "sea serpent," six feet in circumference, rise from the waters of Long Island Sound and invade nearby Westchester County to kill sheep and cattle.[1]

At the Institution, Fanny and others calmed the more terrified residents with the assurance that the future was in God's hands. Fanny impressed upon her pupils, as it had been years before impressed upon her by her grandmother, that "the good Friend above that had been so merciful to us thus far would not desert us now; that He would do all things best for us, both in this world and in the next." So "we rested secure in His promise that we should all be held in the hollow of His hand. And so we prayed—and waited."[2]

The epidemic had first broken out in New Orleans the previous December, when a ship from Le Havre docked there after having buried at sea seventeen victims of the scourge. Soon 3,500 died in New Orleans. The Pale Specter invisibly permeated the sailing ships, the flatboats, and the steamers that continually left in all directions from that southern port, and the pestilence was brought to Memphis, St. Louis, Cincinnati, and Chicago, as well as to smaller towns and villages. In May, cholera broke out in the East. At the Institution, Jim Chamberlain thought it best to dismiss the pupils for an early vacation because the scourge was much less severe in the country than in heavily populated areas. Some pupils, for one reason or another, were unable to return home and Fanny and certain other members of the faculty decided to remain, "being convinced that God would take care of us and that we could be of some help."[3] Then, on May 17, three people died of the disease in a lower Manhattan tenement; the disease had struck New York.

Fanny volunteered her services as a nurse to help the Institution's physician, Dr. Clements, attend to those stricken in the school and immediate vicinity. On June 19 it was learned in New York that former President Polk had died of the disease four days earlier in Nashville, Tennessee. Public buildings were ordered closed and flags flown at half staff in memory of the man who had three short months before been the nation's President. What reaction Fanny had to the news we do not know, but she was too busy to write a memorial poem. All her time was occupied making "cholera pills," which were two thirds calomel and one third opium.

By mid-July, 500 to 800 a week were dying in Manhattan; in two months' time, 2,262 New Yorkers had succumbed to cholera. On July 15, a new cholera hospital was set up at 30th Street, between Seventh and Eighth avenues. Less than two weeks later, a school just one block from the Institution was turned into a cholera hospital. Here Fanny and Dr. Clements labored to relieve the stricken. Apparently, the sick from the Institution were taken there. Ten of the pupils died. Fanny remembered one little girl who told her, "Miss Crosby, I am going home and I just wanted to bid you good-bye and tell you that I love you." Her death nearly broke Fanny's heart. As she toiled away in the hospital on 35th Street, she became increasingly overwhelmed; "The horrors of the situation grew upon us day by day." A half century later, she could still hear "the harsh cry of the truckman, 'Bring out your dead!' It sometimes rings in my ears to this day!"[4] When her patients died, they were usually removed as quickly and quietly as possible, but "I remember my fright at sometimes stumbling over coffins in the halls, on my way from room to room."[5]

In the midst of this epidemic, Fanny was called upon to welcome to the Institution, with a poem, of course, the white-haired Irish priest Father Theobald Mathew, who had chosen this dreadful time to observe the Institution for the Blind. Since he was a world-famous figure, Chamberlain thought that Fanny ought to leave the hospital for a while and give her customary welcome. Mathew, who was then fifty-nine years old, had a tremendous reputation on both sides of the Atlantic as an evangelist. A member of the Capuchin Order of the Roman Catholic Church, he was a great advocate of Temperance, and during his lifetime he led nearly 700,000 to sign pledges of total abstinence from alcohol.

In addition to being a famed preacher, Mathew was said to have worked many miracles of healing, and while staying at the Irving Hotel he expressed a desire to visit the Institution. Far from an imposition, his visit was "like the visit of an angel to a house of death." The Capuchin was much impressed with Fanny's great piety, and when he left he laid his hands upon her head to bless her. "His touch seemed to me like that of a saint who had been permitted to leave his abode in heaven for one single moment to cheer the desolate children of earth."[6] It was perhaps from knowing Father Mathew that Fanny acquired her great love and respect for the Roman Catholic Church.

However comforting the visit of Mathew, Fanny was not able to withstand the horrors of that summer much longer. Already, she had been sent to Brooklyn for a three-day rest, and shortly after the visit Fanny felt certain that she herself was coming down with cholera. She liberally dosed herself with the cholera pills that she had been making and went to bed. By the next morning all her symptoms were gone, but when Chamberlain learned that his most valued teacher had almost contracted the pestilence, he ordered her to take a vacation. So, in early August Fanny left for Bridgeport, to remain until fall when she was summoned back. Nevertheless, the "terrors of that summer" remained with Fanny, and, increasingly occupied by thoughts of death and desolation, she fell into a state of deep depression. She tried to occupy her mind by organizing a new collection, *Monterey and Other Poems,* which would be published a year later. Her mental state is evident in the preface, which sounds as if it were written by an old woman. She spoke of "health sadly impaired" and an "inability to discharge those duties from which I have hitherto derived a maintenance."

During the abbreviated semester of 1849-1850, she was able to meet few classes. She suffered from no specific disease, but only from a feeling of "sadness and depression."[7] This was in part due to her anxiety about her eternal destiny. Had she succumbed to the pestilence, where would she be now? Would she have been as ready to meet her Maker as her beloved President had been? The last meeting with her grandmother weighed deeply on her mind. She knew well that that Puritan lady believed in the distinct emotional "conversion experience," and yet Fanny had not experienced it. She began to doubt her own faith. She doubted whether her life was totally consecrated to the service of God, as she felt it should have been. It occurred to her that for the last several years she had tried to "hold God in one hand, and the world in the other."[8] Although she had never lost her profound faith in God and in his goodness, she grew increasingly convinced that she had not taken seriously enough the lecture that Superintendent Jones had given her long ago when he warned of allowing success to go to her head. She felt that perhaps she had allowed herself to live too much for fame and worldly recognition. She had enjoyed being acclaimed as "The Blind Poetess," but she came to question its worth; what did it mean in the face of death? In the past few years she had striven after worldly honors, worldly success, but to what end? Had she been pursuing a phantom? Had she been betraying her Lord and dishonoring the memory of her grandmother?

66

Fanny attended a series of revivals that fall at the Methodist Broadway Tabernacle on 30th Street. The Methodists were then growing rapidly in numbers and influence in America. Fanny, reared in a cold and colorless Calvinistic Presbyterian church, was drawn to their warm and lively services and their fervent and comparatively cheerful hymn singing. As early as 1839, Fanny had attended Methodist "class meetings" at the Eighteenth Street Church. Here the pious came together once a week to sing, pray, "testify," and read scripture in free-flowing and informal meetings that appealed to many young persons. Often the leader, without prior warning, would call upon someone: "Brother ———, will you testify tonight?" And "Brother ———" would talk about all that God had done for him. In her teens and twenties, Fanny had attended these class meetings twice a week, once at Eighteenth Street and once at the Institution, where that church sent a man every Thursday evening to lead a meeting. But, in her own words, in these years she had "grown somewhat indifferent to the means of grace,"9 whatever that meant, and she attended simply to provide the worshipers with music for their meetings. She played only "on the condition that they should not call on me to speak,"10 and a decade later Fanny was still afraid to "testify" in the meetings.

Fanny had a close friend named Theodore Camp, who was a teacher of Industrial Science at the Institution and who suggested that the troubled young woman go with him to the revivals at the Broadway Tabernacle in the fall of 1850. At first she apparently hesitated; then one night she had a vivid and disconcerting dream. In it, "it seemed that the sky had been cloudy for a number of days and finally, someone came to me and said that Mr. Camp desired to see me at once. Then I thought I entered the room and found him very ill." The dying Camp, who in real life was to live for another fifty years at least, said in the dream, "Fanny, can you give up our friendship?"

"No," replied Fanny. "I cannot. You have been my advisor and friend, and what could I do without your aid?"

"But," replied Camp, "why would you chain a spirit to earth when it longs to fly away and be at rest?"

"Well," Fanny replied, "I cannot give you up of myself, but I will seek Divine Assistance."

"But, will you meet me in heaven?"

"Yes, I will," Fanny said, "God helping me." This, it will be remembered, was the response she had given to her dying grandmother.

Then, in the dream, just before he died, Camp spoke his last words: "Remember, you promised a dying man!"

Then the clouds seemed to roll from my spirit, and I awoke from the dream with a start. I could not forget those words, "Will you meet me in heaven?", and, although my friend was perfectly well, I began to consider whether I could really meet him, or any other acquaintance, in the Better Land, if called to do so.11

Now Fanny was convinced that as things stood she could not. Although, from all indications, she had never ceased to be a deeply religious woman, she was certain that she had denied the faith in which she had been reared and had allowed it to take second place in her life to literary and social concerns. She felt "roused from a comparative state of indifference."[12] With her conviction that God was working for the best even in the terrible cholera epidemic and her conviction which she had, apparently, at all times, that he would do all things well in her life, it is hard to believe that she was really ever indifferent. The important thing is that she believed herself to be so. She felt that there was something terribly lacking in her spiritual life.

So she began to attend the revivals with Camp every evening in the autumn of 1850. In those days the service was highlighted by a long, emotional sermon, punctuated by cries of "Amen!" and "Hallelujah!" and other similar interjections. Not only were there articulate cries, but convulsive sobbings and ecstatic outbursts took place, and it was not uncommon for the frenzied worshipers to leap from their seats and run about or fall to the floor. When the preacher concluded the sermon, usually spiced with abundant references to hellfire and the fiery consequences of failure to heed the gospel message, those interested in joining the church were invited to come forward and be prayed over. People would go to the front of the Tabernacle and kneel on the floor—dirty, carpetless, and frequently cold—often for as long as two hours while deacons and elders placed their sweaty palms on the candidates' clammy foreheads, praying aloud for conversion. It was at this time that the seekers were expected to "get religion" in an emotional "conversion experience," usually leaping to their feet and shouting ecstatically that they were "saved," that they had entered upon a new relationship with God, and that everything was different in their life now.

Thrice during the fall meetings Fanny had gone to the altar in the Tabernacle. Twice she got down on her knees and the frenzied elders all but crushed her skull, laying hands upon her head and roaring prayers for her conversion, and twice the hours went by without her "getting happy." Finally, on November 20, Fanny, now torn with frustration and anxiety, was led for a third time to the altar. This time she was frantic. "It seemed to me that the light must come then or never." She was there alone that night, for no other candidates had presented themselves. For hours the deacons and elders prayed but nothing happened. The congregation began to sing Isaac Watts's "grand old consecration hymn," "Alas and Did My Saviour Bleed." Finally, at the fifth and last verse—"Here, Lord, I give myself away. Tis all that I can do"— it happened. Suddenly Fanny felt "my very soul was flooded with celestial light." She leaped to her feet, shouting, "Hallelujah! Hallelujah!" In her ecstasy, "For the first time I realized that I had been trying to hold the world in one hand and the Lord in the other."[13]

Although this experience is sometimes spoken of as a "conversion," it is difficult to review Fanny's life up to this time without getting a distinct impression of her Christian convictions from earliest childhood. However, something very significant happened at this time. Although the experience almost certainly was not the beginning of her Christian life, it certainly marked a pronounced deepening of it. It was perhaps what would be called by today's "charismatics" the "baptism of the Holy Spirit." Years later Fanny spoke of it, saying, "The Lord planted a star in my life and no cloud has ever obscured its light." [14]

There was, however, no sudden or dramatic change in her way of life. She admits, "My growth in grace was very slow, from the beginning." She still had a great reluctance to speak in public about her religious faith. Finally, about a week later, she forced herself to "testify" at a class meeting, but she could not shake the feeling that the devil was tempting her to pride through pleasure at this newfound ability for public Christian witness. Nevertheless, the November Experience, as she called it, was a watershed of sorts in Fanny Crosby's life. Although she soon realized that it did not solve all her spiritual problems, it marked the beginning of a deepening Christian experience and a beginning of the total dedication of her life to God. Like most other young people, Fanny had previously lived in hopes of making a name for herself in the world, of making money, of attaining other rather routine earthly goals. Now increasingly she came to feel, in the words of one of Watts's hymns:

All the vain things that charm me most,
  I sacrifice them to His blood.

One thing is very peculiar about this conversion experience. Usually, when this occurred, the convert became a member of the church in which he or she had been converted. But Fanny did not join the Broadway Tabernacle—or any other church, for that matter. Nobody knows why. In any event, the November Experience is frequently alluded to in many of her hymns and poems. It is in "At the Cross," written about 1900, and is described in more detail in the long, unpublished "Valley of Silence," written about two months before she died at age ninety-five.

I walk down the Valley of Silence,
Down the dim, voiceless valley alone,
And I hear not the fall of a footstep
Around me, save God's and my own;
And the hush of my heart is as holy
As hours when angels have flown.

Long ago I was weary of voices
Whose music my heart could not win,

Long ago I was weary of noises
That fretted my soul with their din;
Long ago I was weary with places,
When I met but the human and sin.

I walked through the world with the worldly,
I craved what the world never gave,
And I said, "In the world, each ideal
That shines like a star on life's wave
Is tossed on the shores of the Real,
And sleeps like a dream in its grave.

● ● ●

And still did I pine for the Perfect,
Yet still found the false with the true,
And sought, 'mid the human, for heaven,
But caught a mere glimpse of the blue,
And I wept where the clouds of the mortal
Veiled even that glimpse from my view.

And I toiled on, heart-tired of human,
And I moaned, 'mid the masses of men,
Until I knelt long at an altar
And heard a voice call me—since then
I have walked down the Valley of Silence
That is far beyond mortal ken.

Do you ask what I found in this Valley?
'Tis my trysting place with the Divine,
For I fell at the feet of the Holy,
And above me a voice said, "Be Mine."
And there rose from the depth of my spirit,
The echo, "My heart shall be Thine."

She concluded:

Do you ask how I live in this Valley?
I weep and I dream and I pray;
But my tears are so sweet as the dewdrops
That fall from the roses in May,
And my prayer, like a perfume from censers,
Ascendeth to God night and day.[15]

The "Valley of Silence," more than any of her writings, explains the mystical experience of November 20, 1850.

CHAPTER 7
THE VOICE OF LOVE

In April, following Fanny's conversion experience, the celebrated English poet Martin Farquhar Tupper arrived at the Institution, accompanied by the Governor, the Mayor, and members of the City Council. The self-assured Englishman with side-whiskers and balding head was one of the most popular poets alive. A decade before he had published his *Proverbial Philosophy*, a volume of poems of immense length and somewhat vacuous content. With such titles as "Of Compensation," "Of Humility," and "Of Anticipation," the poems were didactic versifications, often dry and pompous and abounding in quasi-religious platitudes. Although his verse was the despair of most serious critics, for thirteen years this volume sold thousands of copies.

Fanny was chosen to address Tupper in the assembly arranged to welcome him. She seems to have had little respect for him and, if we can believe Fanny, the visit did not turn out well for Tupper. The Englishman had come expecting only a quick tour, but Chamberlain surprised him by announcing that he had scheduled an assembly in which the poet would address the students. (That was Chamberlain's way: most eminent visitors, expecting only a tour of the buildings and grounds, to their horror frequently found themselves being escorted into a teeming auditorium to make an address for which they had made no preparations.) In his autobiography, Tupper speaks of "an address by a blind lady (the name was Crosby)." He then says that being asked "on the spur of the moment" to speak, he answered "in a speech and a stave that took the room by storm."[1]

Somehow he seems to protest too much; Fanny's account of his appearance is less flattering to the poet. She recalled that Tupper tried to recite one of his poems, "Never Give Up," but got only as far as the third line, "Throw off the yoke with its conquering fetter . . . "

He fumbled and sputtered embarrassingly until Fanny, seated directly behind the lectern, whispered, "Yield not a moment to sorrow and care." Tupper breezed through the remainder of the first stanza but did not get very far into the second when he again forgot the lines. Fanny again prompted him, but Tupper, in Fanny's words, "evidently not wanting to continue, in spite of his title, 'Never Give Up,'" sat down, remarking to the audience, "It is of no use. This lady knows my poem better than I do myself, and therefore I will sit down."[2] His words still sizzle with pique. Evidently Tupper found the blind lady's helpfulness more of a taunt than an aid, and perhaps this was why he gave so cursory an account of her in his autobiography.

Tupper was not the only visitor to the Institution from the cultural world during these years. Fanny was much more impressed by visits by Jenny Lind and Ole Bornemann Bull. The soprano, known as the "Swedish nightingale," was brought by P. T. Barnum to America in September 1850, shortly before Fanny's religious experience. The "fabulous showman," through adroit advertisement and public relations, had drummed enthusiasm in America for the opera star to fever pitch. When she disembarked in New York harbor, a crowd of 40,000 jammed the piers, streets, and tops of nearby buildings, and bands serenaded her with such American anthems as "Hail, Columbia, Happy Land" and "Yankee Doodle" as she passed through many triumphal arches of flowers to the coach that would take her to her hotel.

Fairly early in her lengthy American tour, Miss Lind arranged to visit the Institution. As she waited for the "nightingale" to arrive, Fanny was tense with expectation. "My heart was like an overflowing cup, my joy a living fountain, my body light as a feather."[3] She was so excited that she could not eat her breakfast. During her concert of operatic arias, Swedish folk songs, and American patriotic airs, Fanny "could imagine that I was in heaven and hearing an angel sing."[4] She later said that she never expected to hear such singing again until she heard "the choirs of the Eternal City." Fanny finally got a chance to meet the blond, blue-eyed soprano personally, at, of all unlikely places, a wake! She always held Miss Lind in highest esteem, both as an artist and as a person. Not so her mentor: Franny always used to crack, "Why were Jenny Lind and P. T. Barnum calculated always to agree and never have any difficulty? Because Jenny is always for giving and the other is always for getting!"[5]

When Ole Bull, the Norwegian violinist, visited the Institution a year later, Fanny was similarly impressed. "I can weep over it even now," she confided to a friend years later. As he played, "the birds sang, the brook rippled, the rain fell, the thunder roared, the sunbeams danced, the bells pealed, the angels sang. . . . Burning tears of joy coursed down my cheeks and a light celestial threw its halo over my brow."[6]

During these years, as always, Fanny maintained close ties with her family, going to Bridgeport every summer and often bringing friends with her. Mercy and the children, now living outside the city limits in the "Fairfield Woods," were enchanted by the visitors from the Great City. In manner, speech, and dress they seemed so very different from the rustic inhabitants of that rural community. Years later Fanny's older half-sister, Jule, would recall the fascination with which, as a tiny girl, she first sniffed the perfume that Fanny brought on her visits. Even though Mercy was a stern disciplinarian, she was also an inquisitive and open-minded woman who never condemned her daughter for her perfumes and jewelry. She also took an interest in the culture of the city and welcomed her daughter's guests, whether students or professors, eagerly following their conversation. Mercy usually got along very well with Fanny's city friends, delighting them with her Puritan customs, New England cooking, and picturesque Yankee twang.

Fanny had good times with her family at the cottage in Fairfield Woods. "How well do I remember that small family group," Fanny has recalled, "the two little sisters snuggling up to me and clinging to my hands, and Mother sitting close by, and listening to it all with an indulgent smile, which I could feel, though I could not see." Jule and Carrie insisted that "every poem that I composed since I saw them before" be "duly recited and subjected to their criticism." Fortunately, however, these junior literary critics were unabashed admirers of their sister's work. So great was their enthusiasm that "it would not have been exactly comfortable for any one rash enough to have intimated to them that their big sister was not the greatest poet of ancient or modern times!"[7]

Little Jule aspired to be a poet herself and imagined that she could achieve her goal by creeping unobserved into her big sister's room at night, when she was composing poetry, and copying exactly her physical gestures and position. When the Muse refused to come, Jule abandoned all hope of following in Fanny's footsteps. But she did attain her dream of traveling to the Great City to visit her celebrated sister when, in the autumn of 1852, Mercy put the "little maid from the Fairfield Woods" on the train for a stay of nearly a week with Sister Fan. Jule fancied that she had achieved the zenith of eminence when Fanny permitted her to lead a group of blind students to the platform of the Methodist Broadway Temple, where they were to give a presentation.

In the fall of 1853, a young man named William Cleveland was appointed head of the literary department of the Institution. Shortly thereafter he was able to arrange the hiring of his sixteen-year-old brother, who was to teach reading, writing, arithmetic, and geography to the younger children, as well as serve as a clerk in the office of the new superintendent, T. Colden Cooper. The boy's name was Grover. Shortly after the Clevelands arrived, William consulted Fanny "in regard to the boy." Fanny, now the "preceptress," or dean of students, was recognized as the best-loved teacher on the faculty, a woman to whom both teachers and students came in times of difficulty. The father of the Clevelands had died recently, quite suddenly, William told her. "Grover has taken our father's death very much to heart, and I wish you would go into the office . . . and talk to him once and a while."[8] Of course, Fanny agreed to do so.

The boy Fanny met was quite mature for his age and, although very thin, was almost six feet tall and wore "a very respectable goatee."[9] At this time young Cleveland was quiet, introverted, and "chary of giving his confidence to many people." This reticence, Fanny concluded, came not "from any vanity of feeling, but from his natural reserve." She was soon able to win his confidence, and he entered into a deep friendship with the older woman "fully and unreservedly."[10] Fanny, motherlike, immediately took the young teacher under her wing. For the still-unmarried poet, now in her mid-thirties, "Grove" was like a son. He began to confide in her and she watched over him with maternal solicitude, frequently warning him when he seemed to be overly absorbed in bookish pursuits. "Take care of yourself, that you do not study too much and injure yourself."[11] Grove would, in turn, read to Fanny from his favorite poets: Lord Byron and Thomas Moore. He also volunteered to serve as Fanny's amanuensis, copying down the poems she dictated. The fact that Grove and Fan worked in this way on the job irritated Superintendent Cooper, and he began to give them a difficult time. There was no love lost between Fanny Crosby and T. Colden Cooper. Cooper is one of the few people Fanny genuinely detested (P. T. Barnum was another), and in her various autobiographical accounts she never refers to him by name but simply as a "cruel incompetent."[12] Fanny felt that Cleveland's copying poems for her was not in violation of any of the school's rules. Moreover, Grove was directly responsible to her and not to Cooper, the ultimate authority being the Board of Managers. Therefore Cooper's complaints about Cleveland appear unjustified; as dean of students, Fanny was "entitled to the privilege of making my own requests, whenever and of whomsoever I wished, provided that I was not breaking any of the rules or customs of the school."[13] One day Cooper flew into Grove's office while the youth was copying a poem dictated by Fanny and snapped, "Miss Crosby! When you want Mr. Cleveland to copy a piece for you, I will thank you to ask *me*. *My* clerks have other work to do than copy poetry!" Cooper then stormed out in high dudgeon, slamming the door, leaving Fanny seething and brooding, but saying nothing to anyone. Nevertheless she did not give up the practice of having Grove copy, and several days later Cooper again stormed into the office. This time he exploded and forbade Fanny even to speak to Cleveland again without his permission. Fanny was now at a loss as to what she should do.

Cleveland stepped in to give a few words of advice. "Now, Fanny Crosby, how long do you intend to allow that man to harrow up your feelings like that?" he asked soothingly.

"But, what can I do to stop it?" she asked.

"By giving as good as he sent it!" said Cleveland. "Give him a few paragraphs of plain prose, that he will not very soon forget."[14]

Fanny was reluctant to speak harshly, even if she were within her rights to do so. "But, Grove, I've never been saucy in my life."

"But it is not impudent to take your own part, and you never will be taught independence and self-reliance any younger," said the youth, lecturing the middle-aged teacher and dean as if she were his own daughter. "Now," he said, "we will try an experiment. Come down to-morrow and ask me to copy another poem for you. I will do so, and then Cooper will come in, as usual, and you will see the consequences! But, in any event, make up your mind never to let anyone impose on you."[15]

So concluded Cleveland's protoinaugural address. It would seem that to be lectured like a child by a boy half her age would have been nearly as offensive to Fanny as Cooper's insolence, but she accepted Grover's counsel; she agreed to stand up to Cooper, as he had advised her. (It is interesting that Cleveland never volunteered to say anything to the blustery superintendent, but then his job was not as secure as Fanny's.)

The next day Fanny was dictating to Grove when Cooper again stormed into the office, and this time he exploded with curses, insults, and threats. Fanny turned and said icily, "I want you to understand that I am second to *no one* in this Institution except yourself, and I have borne with your insolence so long that I will do so no longer. If it is repeated, I will report you to the managers."[16] Without another word, Cooper, put down, slunk out of the office and never gave Fanny trouble again.

The Clevelands hated the Institution. Fanny may have liked it, but apparently the physical appearance of the "Sing-Sing marble" structure was such as to make those sighted persons on the staff envy their blind colleagues. Both Grover and his brother found the building hideously ugly and the life there depressing. The Institution had deteriorated under the new superintendent. Cooper was apparently a character straight out of a Dickens novel; during his regime the Institution became overcrowded (there had been about 60 students in 1850; three years later there were 116), and the children were treated more as inmates than pupils. Cooper believed that his students should never forget that they were wards of the state, and he instituted severe punishments for very minor offenses and whippings for major ones.[17] The Cleveland brothers resigned in late 1854.

About the same time that she met the young Cleveland, Fanny came to work with a man who, though less important to American history, was to be more important to her career and future. She had known George Frederick Root for ten years. An American born the same year as Fanny, Root had studied for some years in Europe, and upon his return he worked diligently, as Lowell Mason had done, to introduce European-style music to America. He even went so far (as many musicians and artists did at that time) to Europeanize his name to George Friedrich Wurzel. Like many cultured people of the day, he considered native American music rather crude and employed elements of the music of Handel, Haydn, Mozart, and Beethoven and others to write suave and sophisticated popular songs.

Root had given music lessons at the Institution as early as the 1840s, but it was not until the 1850s that Fanny really came to know him as a person, rather than as a teacher or colleague. One day in 1851, Root was playing the piano and Fanny was listening. The poet was deeply moved by the strains of an original composition, which sounded so much like the music of some European master. "Oh, why don't you publish that, Mr. Root?" she asked.

Root, a small, bearded man, looked at her with his piercing, birdlike eyes and said, "Why, I have no words for it."

"Oh, I can think of words," she said. "Your melody says:

'O come to the greenwood, where nature is smiling,
Come to the greenwood, so lovely and gay,
There will soft music, thy spirit beguiling,
Tenderly carol thy sadness away.'"

Root was enthusiastic. "I can use you!" he said. "I need someone to supply words to the songs that I write. Would you be willing to do that?"

Fanny was too busy to work with Root until the next summer, when she was offering some courses at the Normal Academy of Music at North Reading, Massachusetts. Root, along with Lowell Mason, was a director, and it was here that Fanny began to supply words for his tunes.

Fanny wrote several songs that first summer. Root supplied all the music, Fanny all the words. At least two pieces became fairly popular when published. The first was entitled "Fare Thee Well, Kitty Dear," which, according to Fanny, "describes the grief of a colored man on the death of his beloved." Its content was trite and superficial, but it contained the tearful sentimentality that many people in those days looked for in a song. It was her first hit.

I saw the smile of evening die
In beauty on the southern sky,
And, as I marked that fairy scene,
So mild, so lovely and serene,
A strange wild sound, yet sweet and clear,
In tones like these I chanced to hear:

Chorus:

Fare thee well, Kitty dear,
Thou art sleeping in the grave so low,
Never more, Kitty dear,
Wilt thou listen to my old banjo.

Fare thee well, Kitty,
Fare thee well, Kitty,
Fare thee well, Kitty,
Fare thee well, Kitty dear.[18]

The other hit song was "The Hazel Dell." It dealt with a similar theme, the death of a beautiful woman:

In the Hazel Dell my Nelly's sleeping,
Nelly loved so long!
And my lonely, lonely watch I'm keeping,
Nelly, lost and gone.
Here in moonlight often we have wandered,
Through the silent shade;
Now, where leafy trees are drooping downward,
Little Nelly's laid.[19]

Root was pleased, recognizing Fanny as "a lady . . . who had a great gift for rhyming, and better still . . . a delicate and poetic imagination." That fall he put her to work again, this time on an absurd composition called "The Flower Queen," which Fanny later called "the first American cantata."[20] Intended for female voices, the plot concerns a disgruntled old man who, weary of the world, decides to become a hermit but is led back to human society through the agency of a chorus of talking (or, rather, singing) flowers. It was billed as appropriate for "academies, female seminaries, and high schools," as well as for "concerts, anniversaries, and other festive occasions." Root already had the preposterous plot in mind but wanted Fanny to render the various themes into poetry suitable for singing. So Root "used to tell her one day in prose what [he] wanted the flowers or the recluse to say, and the next day the poem would be ready."

In fact, sometimes Fanny had two or three poems for Root. The musician generally "hummed enough of the melody to give her an idea of the metre and rhythmic swing wanted, and sometimes played to her the entire music of a number" before she undertook the work. After he received Fanny's poems, Root rarely saw fit to modify and had only to choose between the alternate versions which Fanny had written for him. With the poems chosen, Root "thought out the music" in its final form while going to and from classes on the bus.

"The Flower Queen" was soon in immediate demand and became popular all over the East Coast. Accordingly, the next summer Root and Crosby tried their hand at a similar composition, "The Pilgrim Fathers." This time Lowell Mason collaborated with Root in writing the melody to the poems Fanny provided. Still later Fanny collaborated with Root and William B. Bradbury in turning out the cantata *Daniel*. But neither of these two pieces attained the popularity of "The Flower Queen."

During the summer of 1855, Fanny and Root once again concentrated on writing songs. Several became hits, including another slave song, "They Have Sold Me Down the River," another death song, "Proud World, Goodbye," as well as "Birth of the North" and "O, How Glad to Get Home." Three songs they wrote that year became especially popular: "The Honeysuckle Glen," about the death of a beautiful maiden; "Rosalie, the Prairie Flower," which became more popular than anything Fanny had ever written before; and, on the same subject, "There's Music in the Air," which was sung in schools and colleges well into the twentieth century.

At this time nobody knew that Fanny Crosby was the lyricist for these songs, as they appeared solely under Root's name. Although the royalty on "Rosalie" alone amounted to $3,000, Fanny received but a dollar or two! Root bought the poems from Fanny, published them himself, and reaped the benefits of their popularity alone. He considered that he had no further obligation to Fanny after paying the standard fee that publishing companies normally paid their poets. Even in his autobiography, although he acknowledges Fanny as the author of "The Flower Queen," Root never cites her as having written the lyrics to "Rosalie," "The Hazel Dell," and "The Honeysuckle Glen."

At the same time that Fanny was writing hit songs for Root, she became reacquainted with another man who was to prove even more important in her life than the little musician who had so exploited her talent: her future husband. "Some people," Fanny commented years later, "seem to forget that blind girls have just as great a faculty for loving and *do* love just as much and just as truly as those who have their sight." At thirty-five, Fanny "had a heart that was hungry for love,"[21] but she was still a spinster. By the 1850s, an increasing output of poems on frustrated disappointed love perhaps betrayed her frustration. However, in 1855 the Institution acquired a new teacher, Alexander Van Alstine, whom Fanny had met as a boy years ago during a tour at Oswego, New York. Since then, "Van" had studied for a few years at the Institution and had become a brilliant pupil. Then in 1848 he was enrolled at Union College at Schenectady, becoming the first pupil from the Institution to attend a regular college. Although his chosen vocation was music, Van also studied and mastered Greek, Latin, Philosophy, and Theology, because he felt that being a well-rounded scholar would enable him to become a better musician. There is no record of his graduating, but by the early 1850s Van had a teaching certificate and was giving music lessons in the public schools of Albion, N.Y. (near Rochester). In 1855, he returned to the Institution as an instructor of music.

At first, Fan and Van had merely a platonic relationship, based on their mutual love of music and poetry. Van became deeply interested in Fanny's poetry, and Fan, herself an accomplished musician, became interested in Alexander's "sweet strains of music." And, in her words, "thus, we soon grew to be very much concerned for each other." In the fall of 1857, Van left the Institution and began to give private music lessons in Maspeth, Long Island, in what is now the borough of Queens. Fanny was prepared to follow him. The "cruel incompetence" of Colden Cooper had made the Institution, once her "happy home," into a dreary and unpleasant place. The children were mistreated, the teachers underpaid, the building was ice cold in winter, and the meals grew increasingly bad. Devoted teachers like Van and Fanny felt that they could no longer function to the best of their ability under Cooper's Spartan regime. Deciding that it was now time to terminate her long relationship with the Institution for the Blind, Fanny handed in her resignation on March 2, 1858, and headed toward Long Island, marriage, and an independent life.

Most likely traveling by bus, ferry, and stage, she reached the little town of Maspeth, where she was married to Van in a private ceremony on March 5. He was twenty-seven, she was thirty-eight. Her existence would be altogether changed now. She was no longer the center of attention that she had been in the Institution, visited and feted by visiting dignitaries. She was no longer living near the nation's greatest cultural center, recognized by everyone as the famed "Blind Poetess." She was now a housewife, married to a struggling teacher of music, living in rented rooms in a country town where few of the residents, mostly farmers and merchants and laborers, realized that their blind, dwarflike neighbor was a nationally known poet. Yet this life pleased her, for she never liked publicity and the attendant crowds. Now, for the first time in two decades, she was back where she loved to be, in the country, and she felt that she was living to benefit not so much the general public but her husband. In the spring of 1858, Fanny seemed to be on the threshold of her dream come true.

About Fanny's married life, we know almost nothing. In fact, precious little is known about her husband, who remains quite a shadowy figure. We do not even know how his name was properly spelled. According to the U.S. Census of Oswego County, New York, where he was born, his mother's name was spelled "Van Alstine." He also appears in the records of the New York Institute for the Blind as "Van Alstine." However, his death certificate and burial record read "Van Alsteine," as do the Brooklyn City Directories of 1901 and 1902. If he was of German extraction, as his death certificate indicates, it would seem that the original form of his surname would have been "von Alstein" or "von Allenstein"; if his forebears were from Holland, as one census report indicates, the prefix "Van" would probably be correct. In later life

Fanny always spelled her married name (which she used only on strictly legal documents) as "Van Alstyne," but her husband seems never to have used the alternate spelling.

Alexander Van Alsteine, Jr., was born in Oswego, N.Y., on February 18, 1831. We know little about his parents. His father, sometimes known as Wells but also christened Alexander, died before 1850. In one of her autobiographies, Fanny speaks of him as being "from the banks of the Rhine,"[22] and indicates that he emigrated to the States as a young man. "He was an engineer by profession, and bore a prominent part in the construction of the Welland Canal."[23] His wife, the former Mary Dowd, was born in England in 1798 and lived over eighty years. The couple also had a daughter, Elizabeth, born in 1834.

Of Van's childhood, nothing is known, although a magazine article written in the 1880s indicates that he lost his sight in early childhood as a result of sickness.[24] The two pictures we have of him indicate a handsome man, slender, with a finely chiseled Teutonic face. Unlike most men of his generation, he was clean-shaven. He did not always wear dark glasses.

Van specialized in the organ and was well known as one of the New York area's finest organ virtuosos, but was also proficient in other instruments, including the piano and cornet. When he was at the keyboard, his features were said to have been transformed and to have worn a look of unutterable delight.[25] He was a jovial and easygoing man, apparently well liked by everyone who knew him. His mission in life was to make his beloved European classical masters available to the common people, and he concentrated on providing music lessons to poor children at low cost. In order to support Fanny and himself, he served as paid organist in various churches in the area.

In the late spring and early summer of 1858, Fanny was busy compiling a third volume of poetry, A Wreath of Columbia's Flowers. In the preface, she expressed concern that many Americans preferred foreign to American literature. The verses that Fanny presented in this volume, published later that year, certainly did not demonstrate the worth of native American poetry. Even she admitted that of the four volumes she had published (as of 1903), this one "suffered more than the others from the need of careful pruning and revision."[26] While there are many excellent poems in the collection, many are trite. For the first time, Fanny included three short stories: "The Home of Medora," "Annie Herbert," and "Philip Synclare, or the Traitor's Reward." Besides the stories, there were poems on various subjects, ranging from the Metropolitan Police Force, to unrequited love, to the death of Daniel Webster. The quality of the work is not good, and A Wreath of Columbia's Flowers was the least successful volume of verse Fanny Crosby ever published.

Meanwhile, as Fanny's status in life underwent a drastic change in the year 1858, there were changes in her family circle. Fanny's Uncle Joseph, with his wife and two children, Frank and Ida, had gone to Savannah, Georgia, to open a regional branch of Crosby and May Saddle Goods, of which he was the president. There he contracted tuberculosis and died on May 2, after making a will in which, among other bequests, he left $500 (a huge sum in those days) to Fanny's mother and to Theda and Polly, his other sisters. The same year Fanny's sister Julia was married to Byron Athington of Bridgeport. Jule was no longer the mischievous little sprite who disturbed her sister's attempt to write verse. Now a plump, dark-haired young woman, short, but still a head taller than her older sister, Jule had been for two years apprenticed to a dressmaker. At the age of eighteen, she fell in love with and married Athington. Twenty-one years old, he had come to Bridgeport to be apprenticed to a coach-lamp maker. Now he was a full-fledged member of the firm of White, Bradley & Co. Byron and Jule lived in Bridgeport proper, while Mercy continued to live in the Fairfield Woods with fourteen-year-old Carrie.

About 1859 Fanny became a mother: "God gave us a tender babe."[27] However, this joy was not destined to last, for soon "the angels came down and took our infant up to God and His throne."[28] This was perhaps the greatest misfortune of Fanny's life. Even years later she did not like to talk about it. We do not know whether the child was a girl or boy, much less what happened to it. Fanny's step-grandniece, Florence Paine, who lived with the poet for six years, heard her go into great detail about many aspects of her life but never heard her mention the child. All that the younger relatives knew about this episode in Fanny's life "was that there was a child who died in infancy. There doesn't seem to have been much mention of whether it was a boy or girl."[29] When Fanny made the brief statement about the "tender babe" being taken by the angels in an oral biography to her friend, the Rev. Samuel Trevena Jackson, she spoke of the birth and death of the child as "something that only my closest friends know."[30] Even then, she fell silent after a few sentences.

After this tragedy, most of Fanny's dream of a quiet secluded life on rural Long Island seemed to have been exploded. At first prostrated with grief, she gradually recovered, but she longed to return to familiar surroundings. What was once a rustic paradise had now become an inferno, and she longed to escape from the scenes of her suffering. So she and Van returned to Manhattan, about 1860, and took a room a few blocks from the Institution. The New York City to which they returned was a city engulfed in the zeal of religious revival.

81

CHAPTER 8
A PURPOSE FOR LIVING

The revival began before Fanny left the Institution and grew to tremendous proportions during her stay in Maspeth. There had been two or three previous revivals in American history, starting with the First Great Awakening in the 1740s. Now, in the late 1850s, on the heels of an economic depression, there was again an intensified interest in religion, and a full-scale revival, sometimes called the Second Great Awakening, swept the nation. Apart from the workings of the Holy Spirit, there were certain human factors that tended to foster the revival.

One was the growth of the Sunday schools. "Sunday school" originally was the name for the nineteenth-century equivalent of today's night school, in which working people were given an opportunity to pursue a secular education by attending classes on their only day off from work. Soon, however, religious education, especially for the young, became popular on Sunday, too.

A second factor was the growth of mission societies. These were societies not only for the propagation of religion but also for the abolition of such evils as slavery, liquor, and tobacco and the amelioration of other social ills. During the 1840s and 1850s, there was a great growth in home mission societies, dedicated to spreading the holy gospel of Jesus Christ among the increasingly large numbers of unchurched in the nation's rapidly growing towns and cities.

The most significant of these groups was the Young Men's Christian Association. First introduced in England, the YMCA appeared in America in the early 1850s. Its goals were to promote "evangelical religion," to cultivate the living of the Christian life, and to improve "the mental and spiritual condition of young men."[1] The YMCA provided devotional meetings and classes for instruction in the Bible, as well as mission and Sunday schools. In addition, it engaged in social action, organizing community relief activities to help the needy and oppressed in a material way. Libraries and reading rooms were set up, and lectures were held "to amuse, interest, and instruct."[2] To spread the gospel, the YMCA sent young men to preach on city street corners, on wharves, in firehouses, and sometimes in tents.

It was in this capacity that the career of D. L. Moody, with whom Fanny Crosby's name would become inextricably linked, had its beginnings, on the

North Side of Chicago. Moody achieved great success in bringing young boys from the slums to participate in the Y's programs and, through the activities and fellowship provided by that organization, to become successful and respected Christian citizens. In New York, too, the YMCA was active. Here, the guiding light was Dr. Howard Crosby (1824–1891), a distant cousin of Fanny's. The young pastor of the Fourth Avenue Presbyterian Church was a charter member of the New York YMCA and its second president. He considered the YMCA an "extension of the church" and labored to spread its work among New York's 700,000 inhabitants.

Partly owing to the zeal of men like Moody and Howard Crosby, but mostly to the Providence of God, revivals began to occur in the Great City and in other parts of the country in late 1857. Prayer meetings sprang up all over the New York area, and conversions were professed daily. So great and so widespread were the revivals that various newspapers gave them extensive daily coverage. Between 1858 and 1860, it was claimed that 50,000 conversions occurred each week in the nation and that each week some 10,000 were united with a church for the first time.[3]

Whether or not these figures are exaggerated—and they may not be—the Second Great Awakening was deeply felt everywhere. The New York Tribune, for example, printed telegrams from various parts of the country in which people reported their conversions. "Dear Mother," wrote a young girl, "the revival continues. I too have been converted." "My dear parents," wrote a youth, "you will rejoice to hear that I have found peace with God." "Tell my sister," wired a man, "that I have come to the cross of Christ." Headlines were made when Orville (called "Awful") Gardner, a heretofore dissolute boxing champion, was suddenly and dramatically converted. The revival encompassed not only the old, who met in groups like the Norfolk Street Methodist Church's "Flying Artillery," which spent the whole day in noisy and ecstatic prayer, but also the young, who were converted in droves at the various colleges all over the country, making for a dramatic decrease in gambling and drunkenness on many campuses.

Many churches in New York undertook a "systematic visitation program," in which laymen visited homes both wealthy and destitute. Christian folk went from door to door, witnessing to faith in their gracious God and Savior, in dingy attics and squalid cellars as well as in elegant parlors and opulent drawing rooms. They asked their hosts whether they too had made their peace with God. If the meeting ended amicably, the visitors would invite their hosts to attend Sunday school and inquirers' classes. And many of the people who were visited, far from dismissing their callers with the curse or threat to call the police that the modern-day person would expect, actually promised to come to Sunday school. And they came in droves! As many as twelve hundred people a day packed into the John Street Methodist Church alone for its noonday prayer meetings. The city churches could scarcely accommodate the multitudes who crowded their sanctuaries and Sunday school rooms, athirst for the Living Waters of the gospel.

Fanny's life was much affected by the revivals. She began attending the John Street church, where she became active in the sewing societies, knitting garments for the poor. She also attended the prayer meetings there and at Henry Ward Beecher's Plymouth Congregational Church, getting to know the celebrated pulpit orator, whom she soon came to count as one of her friends.

In the midst of the revival, the Civil War broke out. Every man in the area of Bridgeport where Fanny's relatives lived was drafted or enlisted. Byron Athington, her brother-in-law, enlisted in the First Connecticut Artillery. He had, at twenty-four, just acquired the entire business of White, Bradley, which he gave up to answer the call of his country. Fanny's "brother," as she called her mother's stepson, William Morris, also enlisted.

Fanny was very proud of her relatives. Formerly a Democrat, then a Whig, she was now an ardent Republican and would remain so for the rest of her life. Quite a jingoist, she had always carried a miniature silk flag with her, but now she took to wearing it pinned to her blouse. Her fanatical ardor for the Union cause almost led her to blows. Fanny was eating at a Manhattan restaurant one evening when a southern lady was irritated to the point of hysteria by Fanny's flaunting of the emblem of the Union.

"Take that dirty rag away from here!" she snapped, when she saw the flag.

Fanny, to the astonishment of her companions, flew into a towering rage and sprang from the chair, rushing in the direction of the insulting voice. "Repeat that remark at your risk!" she threatened. The manager, attracted by the shrill cries, came onto the scene just in time to prevent the two women from coming to blows.[4]

On another occasion during the war she was invited to the hotel suite of an admirer who, unknown to her, was from the South. Fanny did not realize that the lady was a Southerner until she was offered some cake and asked if she would object to eating something that came from the South. Fanny ate it, but confessed that she nearly vomited afterward.[5]

The war progressed, and back in Bridgeport there were further changes in the family circle. Fanny's first cousin Frank had died the previous November of tuberculosis at the age of twenty-six, to be followed in April 1861 by his mother, Maria. Fanny's sister Carrie had recently married a man named Lee Barnum, and Mercy had gone to live with the newlyweds in an apartment on Grand Street in Bridgeport. The war was not kind to the Morris clan. William contracted tuberculosis. It did not kill him for nearly two decades, but upon his return he passed it on to his little son, Walter. Athington was severely wounded in Virginia in 1863 and would never fully recover.

All these events only intensified Fanny's patriotic devotion. During the war she began to write patriotic songs that were set to music by Dan Emmett and other musicians. Among the songs she composed at this time were a series written to be sung to such popular airs already existing such as "Bruce's Address" and "Wait for the Wagon." They are of blood-curdling bellicosity. In the "Union Song," she wrote:

> Rebel hosts your flag profane,
> Traitor blood your swords shall stain,
> Onward! to the battle plain—
> Strike! for liberty!

and

> Death to those whose impious hands
> Burst our Union's sacred bands,
> Vengeance thunders, right demands—
> Justice for the brave.

In "Song to Jeff Davis," she urged menacingly:

> Come, thou vaunting boaster,
> Jeff Davis and thy clan,
> Our northern troops are waiting,
> Now, show thyself a man.
> Advance with all thy forces,
> We dare thy traitor band,
> We'll blow thy ranks to atoms!
> We'll fight them hand to hand!

> • • •

> Now, Jeff, when thou art ready,
> Lead on thy rebel crew,
> We'll give them all a welcome—
> With balls and powder too!
> We spurn thy constitution!
> We spurn thy southern laws!
> Our stars and stripes are waving,
> And Heav'n will speed our cause.

The song ends with a threat to decapitate the southern leader.[6]

It is truly remarkable that, from the pen of a woman whose work is distinguished for its sentiment and sensitivity, even saccharine sweetness, these cruel, raucous lines should pour forth. There is nothing charming or appealing about these songs. They are too cruel to be loved. One would imagine that Fanny Crosby might well have written hit Civil War songs, since most of the popular songs of that period were distinguished for their emotional intensity, their sentimental nature, and their relating the war to personal situation, and Fanny was very good at writing verse of this sort. But Fanny's Civil War songs were savage rallying cries, devoid of even a touch of warmth or human interest. Because of fanatical patriotism, Fanny found herself unable to write in a medium in which she normally excelled, and so she failed to capitalize on an opportunity for success.

As long as her mind was not on the war, however, she still retained her touch. And in the midst of the war she was given the opportunity to use her gift of writing verse in a way that would bring far more recognition than her secular poetry, her musicianship, or her work as a teacher had ever accomplished.

Fanny was still depressed and at loose ends since the death of her child. The bitterness, hatred, and vindictiveness of her war songs undoubtedly reflects a lingering unhappiness which even a move back to familiar surroundings had failed to alleviate. Even more than a decade after her conversion, Fanny still continued to experience a "dark night of the soul." Her spirits began to improve only gradually, as she involved herself in church work and sewing societies. But soon she was to find a new hold on life. She had always been eclectic in her churchgoing and at forty-three was not a member of any church. Partial for years to Methodism, she frequently attended the John Street church. In addition, she often went to the Plymouth Congregational Church in Brooklyn to hear her friend Beecher, who was her favorite preacher; the Fifth Avenue Presbyterian Church, whose pastor was Dr. John Hall; and the Fourth Avenue Presbyterian Church of her cousin, Howard Crosby. She was no stranger to Trinity Episcopal Church and especially liked to go there when the young, dynamic Phillips Brooks from Boston was guest preacher.

Fanny also attended the Dutch Reformed Church at 23rd Street. The pastor of that church, the Rev. Peter Stryker, was delighted to make the acquaintance of the "Blind Poetess" and thrilled when she responded to his request to write a New Year's Eve hymn. He knew that Fanny was at loose ends, and early the next year he came to her and told her about a friend, William B. Bradbury, a musician who, since the revival had begun, had been engaged in writing hymns. Bradbury very much needed someone to provide lyrics for his melodies, and Peter Stryker recommended that she see Bradbury at once. Fanny agreed to go.

The Second Great Awakening brought about great changes in American hymnody, as the need was felt for a type of hymn that would match the new approach in presenting Christian doctrine. Lowell Mason, considered the father of American church music, had long before set forth his "canons," and these instructions concerning the aim and nature of hymnody, published in his widely circulated *Church Psalmody* in 1831, were still definitive for American hymnwriting two and a half decades later. "The sentiments and imagery," he wrote, "should be grave, dignified." Also, "Whatever is unscriptural, groveling ... light, [or] fanciful ... should be avoided," because it tended to "check the flow of the soul." Moreover, "All familiar and fondling epithets or forms of expression, applied to either person of the Godhead, should be avoided, as bringing with them associations highly unfavorable to pure devotional feeling."[7] Mason called for a heavy emphasis on sin and hell. He disparaged any hymn that tended to make the worshiper "feel good," as all emphasis should be on the "sinner's" unworthiness and his need for repentance.

These stern hymns were now falling out of favor. Their theology may have been impeccable, their music may have been considered excellent by all experts, but they just did not touch the heart. The "revived" of the 1850s and 1860s wanted hymns that were personal and also light and informal. A few of those written in the past fit this description and were well used, such as "My Faith Looks Up to Thee" by Ray Palmer, "Nearer, My God, to Thee" by Sarah Flower Adams, "Just As I Am, Without One Plea" by the Englishwoman Charlotte Elliott, and "Abide with Me" by the Rev. Francis Lyte. People wanted more hymns of this type, and of the type of Charles Wesley's "Jesus, Lover of My Soul" and A. M. Toplady's "Rock of Ages."

Already some musicians were answering that call. Our old friend George Root had turned to Sunday school music from the beginning of the revival. During the late fifties and early sixties he wrote (to whose lyrics we do not know, but not to Fanny's), such songs as "When He Cometh," "Come to the Saviour," "Ring the Bells of Heaven," and "In the Midnight Watches." With their simple words and catchy tunes, similar to those he wrote for "Just Before the Battle, Mother" and "The Battle-Cry of Freedom," Root's hymns gained immediate popularity. Another composer of Sunday school hymns was a Baptist minister, Robert Lowry, of whom we shall learn more later. In 1864 he wrote an all-time hit, "Shall We Gather at the River?" which became an immediate sensation. Within a year's time, "there was not a child from the gutter or a mission waif who did not know it."[8]

The most important and prolific hymn writer of the period was William Batchelder Bradbury. We have mentioned him as a collaborator with Root and Crosby in the cantata *Daniel,* published in 1853. Born in York, Maine, on October 6, 1816, Bradbury first studied music under Lowell Mason. Early in his career, he helped introduce the organ to American churchgoers. Bradbury was appointed organist at New York's Baptist Tabernacle while still a young man, and there he started singing classes. For many years at the Tabernacle he held an annual Juvénile Musical Festival that was one of the biggest musical events in the city. More than a thousand children gave a concert of classical and semiclassical choral pieces that Bradbury had arranged and conducted. At thirty, Bradbury went to Europe, where he studied composition for two years in England and Germany. After returning to New York, he began to manufacture Bradbury pianos and compose songs and other musical works, even trying an opera: *Esther: The Beautiful Queen.* His melodies, like Root's, applied much of the style of the European masters to American music and were often adaptations of actual melodies by Beethoven, Handel, and other major composers. Bradbury's songs were distinguished by their "easy, natural flow" and his harmonies by their simplicity and naturalness.[9]

Bradbury was not appreciated by everyone. Some complained that he was neither singer, performer, nor composer. Others claimed that he was ruining American music with his melodies, often written in outright imitation of European composers. But he endeared himself to many of the faithful by his musical settings of "Just As I Am," "He Leadeth Me," "Saviour, Like a Shepherd, Lead Us," and "On Christ, the Solid Rock, I Stand." The tunes may have been sneered at by highbrow musical experts, but they were loved by masses of people. Here, at last, were hymns everyone could sing.

But not only did Bradbury desire to provide a light, melodic musical setting for already existing hymns, he also wanted to set newly written poems to music. He was not satisfied, however, with the quality of much of the verse that was submitted to him, most of which was either too heavy or just doggerel. He was overjoyed, therefore, when Stryker informed him in January of 1864 that he would shortly be meeting a lady who would probably be the answer to his problems.

Fanny, too, was enthusiastic about her forthcoming visit, and at this time she had one of her periodic dreams or visions, which were remarkable in that she, who had never been able to see anything but the faintest rays of light, saw everything vividly and in detail. She described the vision, which she said was "more than a vision—it was a kind of reality—with all my senses at their fullest"—in this way:

I was in an immense observatory, and before me was the largest telescope I had ever imagined. I could see everything plainly. ... Looking in the direction pointed out by my friend, I saw a very bright and captivating star, and was gradually carried toward it—past the other stars, and any amount of celestial scenery that I have not the strength even to describe.

At last we came to a river and paused there. "May I not go on?" I asked of my guide. "Not now, Fanny," was the reply. "You must return to the earth and do your work there, before you enter those sacred bounds; but ere you go, I will have the gates opened a little way, so you can hear one burst of the celestial music."

Soon there came chords of melody such as I never had supposed could exist anywhere: the very recollection of it thrills me.[10]

Fanny now felt God had given her a new reason for existing; she was convinced that he wanted to use her talents in the field of writing hymns. In later years, whenever she was discouraged and tempted to stop working, she had only to recall the vision of January 1864, and the very remembrance of that experience was enough to sustain her.

Fanny had an appointment with Bradbury on February 2. She arrived at his office at the Ponton Hotel on Broome Street and was greeted by the composer. He was a very thin man with a pinched face, framed by a lionlike mane of thick, bushy dark hair and a gigantic beard. His deep-set eyes gazed with great intensity beneath beetling brows. Fanny could not see his face, but she could perceive his character. Not only was she subject to visions and trances but also she had that strange faculty of reading a person's character from the "overtones" that emanated from him. She liked Bradbury even as he liked Fanny, for he immediately put their relationship on a first-name basis. "Fanny," said he, "I thank God that we have at last met, for I think you can write hymns; and I have wished for a long time to have a talk with you."[11] Bradbury then introduced Fanny to his assistant, her old friend from Ridgefield, Sylvester Main. Vet had come to New York many years before to open a music school. He was now a prominent churchman, a pillar of the Norfolk Street Methodist Church and a well-known soloist in the churches of New York.

Fanny and Bradbury had their talk. As she started back to her rooms on Ninth Avenue, she left with an agreement that she would return within a week with a hymn by which Bradbury could sample her abilities. "It now seemed to me that the great work of my life had really begun."[12]

Three days later, she was back with a three-stanza poem which began:

We are going, we are going
To a home beyond the skies,
Where the fields are robed in beauty
And the sunlight never dies.
Where the fount of joy is flowing
In the valley green and fair,
We shall dwell in love together,
There shall be no parting there.[13]

Bradbury was enthusiastic. The hymn was everything he had been looking for. Light and informal in verse, it was nevertheless reasonably good poetry and also contained great warmth and emotional power. He decided to use "We Are Going" in the hymnal he was then preparing.

89

The next week, Bradbury sent for Fanny in haste, saying that he needed a war song (he also published secular music). He suggested, as the first line, "There's a sound among the mulberry trees," but Fanny flatly rejected that line for the more euphonious "There's a sound among the forest trees." Bradbury then played the melody for which she was to write the words. It was difficult, but after hearing it two or three times Fanny was able to count the measure and find suitable words. Within a day, she had written several stanzas, the first of which is:

There's a sound among the forest trees,
Away, boys! Away to the battlefield, hurrah!
Hear its thunders on the mountain! No delay, boys!
We'll gird on the sword and shield,
Shall we falter on the threshold of our fame, boys?
The light of morn appears, Hurrah! Quick to duty!
"Up and at them," once again, boys! Hurrah for our volunteers.
They are coming from the North,
They are coming from the West,
Where the mighty river flows,
From New England's hallowed soil,
Where our Pilgrim Fathers rest
And the star of freedom rolls.[14]

It does not look like much, but when Fanny presented the song to Bradbury's secretary, he was incredulous. Playing it over on the piano, he said, "How in the world did you manage to write that hymn? Nobody ever supposed that you, or any mortal, could adapt words to *that* melody!"[15] Bradbury had in fact given her the cruelly difficult melody to test her, and she had passed the test with flying colors!

When Bradbury appeared that morning and heard the hymn, he said, "Fanny, I'm surprised!" Then he added, "And now, let me say, that while I have a publishing house you will always have work!"[16] And so Fanny went to work for the firm of William B. Bradbury and Company.

CHAPTER 9
W. B. BRADBURY & CO.

Fanny became part of a group of poets and musicians who compiled the Sunday school hymnbooks published by Bradbury, joining Mary Ann Kidder and Josephine Pollard in a "trio" who produced the bulk of the poems Bradbury and his colleagues set to music. The first hymnal Bradbury issued to which Fanny contributed was *The Golden Censer* (1864). "We Are Going," which was given the title "Our Bright Home Above," and "There's a Cry from Macedonia" were credited to Fanny. She may have contributed other hymns but Bradbury, following the practice of Root and other publishers, did not always designate the authors. Other hymnals followed.

Most of Fanny's hymns would appear under the name of "Miss Fanny J. Crosby." This was more than a pen name, for, following the custom of many professional women of the day, Fanny had never taken her husband's surname. When they were married, Van realized that his middle-aged bride had a career and a reputation of her own, and he felt that to have her change her name was tantamount to subordinating her career to his. So Van encouraged Fanny to maintain her own career and name. Fanny variously called herself "Miss Crosby," "Mrs. Crosby," or "Madam Crosby," and whenever, for legal reasons, she had to write her married name, she used, as we have seen, the spelling, "Van Alstyne."

Fanny was deeply affected by Lincoln's assassination in April 1865. She had met the man whom she called "a lofty cedar," towering above all other figures in American history, on at least one occasion, and called him "Captain Lincoln" after his old rank in the militia. Years afterward she could recall in verse the "night of deepest gloom" when the news was telegraphed to New York that "a noble chieftain" had been laid low.

The Civil War was now over but Fanny's work as a hymn writer was just beginning. Bradbury was preparing still another hymnal, and Fanny was asked to supply hymns. Usually the music came first. Bradbury would give Fanny a tune for which she was to provide the words; often he would give her the title and subject too. This was not always the case, however, and frequently she was allowed to choose the topic, often providing the poem before Bradbury or one of his colleagues provided the music.

There were almost infinite variations of the ways in which the Crosby-Bradbury hymns came about. Sometimes Fanny's poems were inspired by trivial bits of conversation, as, for instance, the one afternoon when she, Bradbury, Vet Main, and an eminent musician and singer named Philip Phillips were "discussing various things" and Phillips looked at his watch and realized that he had to go. "Good night," he said, "until we meet in the morning."

When he had left, Fanny turned to Bradbury and remarked, "If I write a hymn for that subject, will you compose the music?" The composer agreed, and Fanny wrote a funeral hymn:

Goodnight! Goodnight! Till we meet in the morning,
Far above this fleeting shore;
To endless joy in a moment awaking,
There we'll sleep no more.

●　　●　　●

Goodnight! Goodnight! Till we meet in the morning,
There from pain and sorrow free,
With Him who died from the grave to redeem us,
We shall ever be.[1]

As it turned out, however, it was Robert Lowry, author of "Shall We Gather at the River?" who set the poem to music.

One of Fanny's more distasteful duties as Bradbury's colleague was to revise other people's hymns. She was quite wary of doing this, for several years before, the *New York Ledger* had asked her to revise a poem called "Charlie and I." When the woman who had written the poem saw the alterations and learned who had made changes, she went to see Fanny and took her to task for ruining her "masterpiece." It was only through the intervention of Mary Ann Kidder, the Ledger's poetry editor and a personal friend of Fanny's, that the blind author was reconciled with the irate poet. While working with Bradbury, therefore, she always made it a point to ask permission of the author before revising a poem. Many of the poems submitted to Bradbury had good themes but were terrible as poetry, and thus there was a genuine need for revisions.

Bradbury was a sick man when he and Fanny first met, and he told her from the start that he knew he had but a short time to live. In April 1866 he was so ill that he had to go south in hopes of regaining his health; there he remained all summer.

In the meantime Fanny was not idle. She reported regularly to the office to prepare poems and receive melodies for the new volume. In the past two years her talents had also come to the attention of other writers and publishers of church music. One of them was Phoebe Palmer Knapp, who became one of Fanny's most devoted friends. Born about 1835, the daughter of a prominent New York doctor, Walter Palmer, and his wife, Phoebe, a mystic theologian who taught a doctrine of "spiritual perfection," young Phoebe was married to Joseph Fairchild Knapp, who later founded the Metropolitan Life Insurance Company. Mrs. Knapp was what would now be called a social activist, and she claimed to "care more for the active movements of the world of society than for spiritual abstraction."[2] Her understanding of Christianity was to aid the poor and foster social reform. By the time she was thirty and Fanny met her, she was actively involved in many political and social activities and had already given away large sums of money to the poor.

Phoebe Knapp was an attractive woman, tall, slim, with fine, regular features, intense eyes, and dark, curling hair. Although she was deeply concerned about the plight of the poor, she did not by any means disdain the life of the rich. She was a lavish dresser, given to wearing elaborate gowns and diamond tiaras. The "Knapp Mansion," a palatial residence on the corner of Bedford Avenue and Ross Street in Brooklyn, was a New York institution. There she held a European-style salon in which she entertained most of the prominent people of the day. Almost every Republican president, Union general, and Methodist bishop was entertained there at one time or another, and her evening musicales were the talk of the town. In her music room was one of the finest collections of musical instruments in the country, and many well-known artists and performers were from time to time her guests. Phoebe Knapp was not liked by many people. Very talkative, she had the reputation of being a smothering, possessive, strong-willed woman, and a bizarre eccentric. She considered herself a better musician than she actually was and gave vocal recitals, despite the fact that her soprano voice was thin and weak.

Nevertheless, Fanny came to love Phoebe, and Phoebe saw to it that Fanny was a frequent habituée of the Knapp Mansion, allowed free access to the music room and to its piano and organ. Here too, over the years, Fanny was introduced to many national dignitaries including Presidents Grant, Hayes, Garfield, McKinley, and Teddy Roosevelt. Here she frequently conversed with her friend Henry Ward Beecher as well as his sister, Harriet Beecher Stowe. At the Knapp home she also came to know the bloody General Sherman, the temperance crusader Frances Willard, and the poet Alice Cary. Phoebe would have willingly done more for Fanny, who was living in poverty, but the poet refused her beneficence. One thing that Phoebe wanted Fanny to do was write poetry for the hymns she composed, and Fanny readily obliged. She provided Phoebe with many poems which the wealthy lady set to music and published through a brother who owned a publishing company.

Another musician who became seriously interested in Fanny's talents was Philip Phillips. Known as "The Singing Pilgrim," he was fourteen years younger than Fanny but had for several years been gaining nationwide renown through his services of song. His rendition of hymns in a beautiful baritone voice had considerable influence on those who heard him. One day Phillips and Bradbury were going shopping and Phillips laughingly said to Fanny, who was in the office, "Fanny, I wish you would write a hymn and have it ready when I return." To his great amazement, when he returned Phillips found that Fanny had indeed written a hymn—one of three or four stanzas![3]

And so Phillips had occasionally called upon Fanny to provide him with a hymn or two for his various evangelistic services. Now in 1866, he was busy preparing a hymnal to be entitled *The Singing Pilgrim, or Pilgrim's Progress, Illustrated in Song for the Sabbath School and Family*. It was centered around John Bunyan's seventeenth-century classic of the pilgrimage, or progress, of a man named Christian to the promised land. The book was still universally read and known.

Phillips asked Fanny to write hymns based on the thought contained in various selections from the book. He himself would provide the tunes. He gave her a selection of seventy-five quotations of a few lines, each which Fanny memorized and from these selected forty which she thought appropriate for the composition of a hymn. Then she composed forty poems in her head and, when the last one had been completed, dictated all of them, one after the other, to her secretary at Bradbury's office.

Phillips and everyone else was amazed at Fanny's phenomenal memory, but she made light of it, saying that every person without sight has to develop his or her memory and that others could do it too if they were placed in a situation in which they could not refer to the written word. In any event, Fanny's forty hymns comprised the bulk of Phillips' hymnbook, *The Singing Pilgrim*, which became very popular and was widely circulated. Nevertheless, few people knew who wrote these popular hymns, for Phillips, like Root, paid Fanny a dollar or two for her efforts and then published them under his name.

Fanny's life was not spent entirely in the Bradbury office. As we have seen, she often visited Phoebe Knapp. She also spent a great deal of time with her neighbors in the various tenements in which she and Van boarded in Manhattan. Staging her own soirees in the dingy houses in which she lived, she gathered together many of the residents for an evening of song, accompanied by her guitar. How much time she spent with her husband is questionable; they seem to have gone their separate ways. Van had his circle of friends and round of activities and Fanny had hers, and the couple seemed content to have it that way. Both retained a lively interest in the other's career without really becoming a part of it. Although he preferred classical organ compositions, nevertheless Van took an interest in Sunday school hymnody and occasionally provided a melody for his wife's lyrics.

Bradbury returned from the South in the fall of 1866, apparently improved in health. The following year *Fresh Laurels* was published. In addition to that title hymn it contained eleven hymns attributed to Fanny Crosby or one of her numerous pen names. These included "Beautiful Mansions," "I Love the Name of Jesus," and "Away! Away!" Although of varying quality, they showed simplicity, directness, emotional power, and a relationship to daily life—characteristics which were to be the earmarks of her art.

Fanny and Van had moved several times during this time, in 1867 they were living at 88 Varick Street, on the Lower West Side, near what is now the entrance to the Holland Tunnel, between Watts and Canal streets, in one half of the third-floor garret. Fanny's immediate neighbors were a fifty-year-old Negro washerwoman from Georgia named Mary Laverpool and her children, James, John, and Eliza, and a twenty-year-old colored porter named George Johnson. This tenement, where thirty-three people were crowded into an unbelievably small space, was far from the worst of New York's slums. All Fanny's neighbors seem to have been respectable working-class people. The neighborhood included dressmakers, goldbeaters, hackmen, carriage painters, truckmen, and grocery clerks. Ethnically it included large numbers of Irish, Germans, and Negroes. Fanny and Van were part of the minority of white Anglo-Saxons. Nevertheless tenement living was no luxury, with no outside ventilation or running water in the rooms. Fanny and Van could have lived in better circumstances if they had so chosen, but she insisted on giving away all that she received that was not required for their basic needs. Fanny wanted to live with the poor and as one of them, for she believed part of her mission in life was to them. It is for this reason that she tried to organize evening diversions for her neighbors, and it was mainly for the poor that most of her hymns were written.

In these hymns she addressed people like Mary Laverpool, who was most likely a former slave; Charles Jacko, an immigrant carpenter; Jacob Seamon, a shoemaker; and Isaac Broton, a colored porter. It was for these people who saw the good things in life going to others but passing them by that she wrote hymns like:

Pass me not, O gentle Saviour,
Hear my humble cry;
While on others Thou art smiling,
Do not pass me by.

and it was for those who had taken refuge from the buffetings of life in alcohol and dissipation that she wrote:

Rescue the perishing,
Care for the dying,

Snatch them in pity from sin and the grave;
Weep o'er the erring one,
Lift up the fallen,
Tell them of Jesus the mighty to save.

Fanny Crosby's hymns arose from this milieu, and it was for people even more wretched than those among whom she lived that she wrote, those wretched souls who "seemed drunk half the time" and had to sleep on the rooftops in summer because of the stifling heat, those at the bottom rung of the social ladder, those who lived, destitute, in dwellings unspeakably filthy and falling apart, with no windows and doors, who had to collect rags, bones, and driblets of coal that fell from the wagons that passed by.

For these unfortunates she wrote "When I'm Resting by the River in the Beautiful Forever," "O the Morning, Happy Morning, That Will Break on Yonder Shore," and "I Know There's a Rest That Remaineth for Me." Many people, noting the great volumes of her hymns on the hereafter, have accused Fanny of lulling those who sang her hymns with hope of "pie in the sky," but she knew that for many people it was either pie in the sky or no pie at all!

She also wrote verses for the wealthy, urging social activism, such as:

When, cheerful, we meet in our pleasant home,
And the song of joy is swelling,
Do we pause to think of the tears that flow
In sorrow's lonely dwelling?

Let us lend a hand
To those who are faint and weary,
Let us lend a hand
To those on the pilgrim way.

● ● ●

"Remember the poor" was the great command
Of the Gentle, Pure, and Holy,
For the choicest fruit and richest gain
Are found among the lowly.[4]

But mostly Fanny's hymns were geared to the humble. Many have supposed that the extreme simplicity of most of her hymns was because she could do no better. This was not true; she wrote the hymns as she did because she wanted them to be understood by the common people. Her goal was not to compose poetry that would be admired by college professors and literary critics but rather would be easily understood by washerwomen, carpenters, porters, and grocery clerks. Fanny felt the same way about music. She apparently knew and loved Italian opera, was an excellent soprano, a fine organist, and the best harpist of her day. She was skilled at the piano and knew well the compositions of Beethoven and Chopin and Mendelssohn. But she also knew that most people did not comprehend this music. The congregational hymn was for the untrained singer, and music for the congregation should be something in which every worshiper could participate. So for Fanny Crosby the best poetry for the congregational hymn was pop verse and the best music was the pop tune.

It was in November 1867, after completing the libretto for an oratorio by Philip Phillips called *The Triumph of the Cross,* that Fanny first met a man who was to be her most frequent collaborator and the composer of the tunes to her most successful hymns. William Howard Doane was a wealthy manufacturer, the president and general manager of J. A. Fay and Company, a firm which manufactured woodworking machinery. Born in Preston, Connecticut, on February 3, 1832, the son of a cotton goods manufacturer, Doane began his successful career at the age of sixteen in his father's firm. At nineteen he joined J. A. Fay and Company as the head of their financial department. At twenty-four he was given responsibility for the company's Chicago branch, and at twenty-eight he moved to Cincinnati, where he became vice-president of the firm. A year later, in 1861, he became its president.

Howard Doane also had a second career. From earliest childhood, he was precocious in the field of music. At sixteen he wrote a song titled "The Grave Beneath the Willows." Throughout his early years in business Doane directed choirs in churches and led various musical societies. He had a good voice and became rather well known in Cincinnati as a church soloist.

Music was simply a hobby for Doane until he was thirty, when he suffered a heart attack and nearly died. A devout Baptist, Doane interpreted his illness not as the result of the tension and overwork to which he had been subjected for over a decade but as chastening from the hand of a God who was displeased with something in his life. He decided that God wanted him to devote more time to writing sacred melodies and had sent the attack to give him time to think over the priorities in his life. Almost immediately after his recovery, he compiled a book of hymns called *Sabbath School Gems,* which was followed by *The Sunbeam* in 1864 and *The Silver Spray* (co-edited with Theodore Perkins) in 1867. Doane was dissatisfied with his hymns and felt that they lacked suitable words. Like Bradbury, he tried for a while to write the words himself, but he was no poet, and the people he engaged to write lyrics were no better.

In November 1867 Doane was in New York attending the American Institute Fair. During his stay he visited a friend, the Rev. Dr. W. C. Van

Meter, who directed what was known as the Five Points Mission. Van Meter knew that Doane wrote hymn tunes and asked him for a melody to use on the anniversary of the founding of his mission, which would occur in a matter of days. Doane replied that the melody would be no problem but did he have words? Van Meter gave him a poem which he thought might be suitable.

Doane did not like it and searched through his briefcase in vain for something better. Then, kneeling on the floor of his hotel room in prayer, he asked God to send him a poem suitable for use at the anniversary celebration. He also asked God, as he had asked him many times before, to send him a poet who could supply religious verse suitable for music. At once, he heard a knock on the door. Opening it he saw a little boy with an envelope addressed to Mr. William Howard Doane. The letter in it read: *Mr. Doane: I have never met you, but I feel impelled to send you this hymn. May God bless it.* It was signed, *Fanny Crosby.*[5] Accompanying the note was a poem that began:

> More like Jesus would I be,
> Let my Saviour dwell with me,
> Fill my soul with peace and love,
> Make me gentle as the dove;
> More like Jesus as I go,
> Pilgrim, in this world below;
> Poor in spirit would I be—
> Let my Saviour dwell in me.[6]

The words seemed veritably to sing themselves to him. What song could be more appropriate for the anniversary of a home mission than one that appealed to God for the grace to be "more like Jesus"? Doane had no trouble writing a gentle, easy tune for these words. He once again prayed, giving thanks to the Almighty for sending him not only the poem but his long-sought poet.

Doane went to Van Meter the next day and offered to play the hymn for him. They went to a neighboring church, where Van Meter agreed to pump the organ while Doane played and sang. Before they had completed the first verse, Van Meter, bursting into tears, had become so emotionally affected that he could no longer pump the organ. He managed to pull himself together within a few minutes and Doane started once more. But after another verse Van Meter could no longer restrain himself. His eyes shining, he came from behind the organ and threw both arms around Doane's neck, crying, "Oh, Doane, where did you get that poem?"[7]

Doane told Van Meter about receiving it in an envelope and inquired about the author. Van Meter either gave him an address or referred him to someone who did so. However, Doane found it inconvenient to call on Fanny that day, and the next he had business commitments in Cincinnati, so he resolved to find her the next time he was in New York.

Since summer it had been apparent to most of his friends and associates that Bradbury was slowly and painfully dying of consumption. It was owing to his illness and his inability to set her poems to music anymore that Fanny had been urged by Bradbury's friend, Robert Lowry, to send her latest poem to Howard Doane. Before that, on his last day at the office, Bradbury had called Fanny in for a final talk. "These interviews have been very pleasant to me," he said. "But they will soon be over. My life's work is done."

Fanny, who had not imagined that her friend and mentor was so near death, almost broke down, distraught at the thought of losing "a friendship I have enjoyed so much."

Bradbury tried to reassure her, saying, "You will not lose a friendship though I am going away from you, but rather strengthen it by striving to carry out my ideals. . . . You must take up my life-work where I lay it down." He made it clear that he expected her to assume leadership in the Sunday School Hymn Movement when he was dead. He bade her an affectionate farewell, saying, "I am going to be forever with the Lord, and I will await you on the bank of the River."[8] Racked with excruciating pains, he took to his bed in Montclair, New Jersey, where he died on January 7, 1868, at the age of fifty-one.

Fanny was heartbroken at Bradbury's death. She attended his funeral, where, according to a request the composer had made shortly before he died, the choir sang the first hymn that he and Fanny had written together: "We Are Going, We Are Going to a Home Beyond the Skies." After the services, as Fanny filed by the casket, she broke down in tears. It was then that she heard a mysterious voice, "clear and beautiful," which said to her, "Fanny, pick up the work where Bradbury has left it. Take your harp from the willow, and dry your tears." Several others heard the voice but could not determine its source. Fanny, however, took it as a mandate from heaven to carry on Bradbury's work.

CHAPTER 10
"MUSIC FOR THE MASSES"

After Bradbury's death, the publishing company was reorganized by his colleague, Sylvester Main, and a local merchant named Lucius Horatio Biglow (1833-c.1910). Although Vet Main occasionally wrote music, he and Biglow were primarily businessmen, and they generally left the work of producing hymns to the various poets and musicians who were associated with the firm. Of these Fanny Crosby rapidly became the most prominent, and in many ways was responsible more than any other person for setting the style of the hymns that the new company produced for the next half century. Although she seldom wrote the music, the fact that she pronounced on the suitability of the numerous tunes that were submitted to her for lyrics made her influential even in that area.

Soon after Bradbury was buried, Howard Doane returned to New York and went to the address he had been given. Alas, it was an old address, and he was told that Fanny Crosby was no longer living there. After a few days of searching and being given incorrect addresses, he arrived at 88 Varick Street about eight thirty one evening. He was horrified at the dilapidated condition of the old tenement house and was unnerved by the stares of the seemingly numberless tenants of all colors, who gawked at the impeccably dressed gentleman with the fashionable Vandyke beard. When he got to the attic floor, he knocked on the door to which he had been directed and a strange, ugly, almost hunchbacked little woman wearing green glasses appeared.

"Could you please direct me to Miss Fanny Crosby?"

"*I* am Fanny Crosby," replied the dwarfish woman, who immediately welcomed him into her room and showed him a chair.

Gradually Doane became aware of another fact that shocked him even more than the squalor of the habitation: Fanny Crosby was blind! He had never known that, and since Fanny could navigate in her own home without any need of assistance, this fact was not immediately apparent.

Fanny soon put him at ease. "God bless your dear heart!" she said. "Oh, how glad I am to find you! I have been trying to find you for such a long while, and now, at last, I have succeeded." Doane forced Fanny to accept reluctantly what she understood to be two dollars, the standard fee for a hymn. When he left, she discovered that Doane had given her twenty!

Thus began a collaboration that would last for forty-seven years. Howard Doane and Fanny Crosby came to be close personal friends, and Fanny often spent her summers with Howard and his wife, who was also named Fanny, and with their daughters, Ida and Marguerite. Despite their close friendship, as was the case with many Victorian friends, they were never on a first-name basis. Doane always called Fanny "Mrs. Crosby" and she called him "Doane" or "Mr. Doane."

Doane, who was to set over a thousand of Fanny's hymns to music, was not a great musician. He was best at writing simple, straightforward, marchlike tunes. His melodies are distinguished for their catchiness and seemed to rely heavily on the tradition of such songs as "Hail to the Chief" and "Columbia, the Gem of the Ocean." His tunes were rather regimented and mechanical, and he often resorted to tenor-bass counters in the choruses, simply to get through a long note. At his best his work was melodic, but even so usually lacked sweetness and mellifluity. At worst, it could be insipid and boring. Fanny, however, liked to collaborate with Doane; as we have seen, she believed that simple, catchy tunes were best remembered and understood by most people. One must remember that in those days there was little opportunity for people to hear a melody repeated a number of times. There were no records or radios, most people were too poor to buy a piano, and many were too poor even to afford hymnals. So when one first heard the tune of a hymn, it was a matter of memorizing it then or not at all. Fanny felt that the best tunes for congregational singing were those which could be memorized in one or at the most two hearings. And Doane's tunes, while not particularly pretty, were of the type that no one would have trouble singing, even the first time. Doane often butchered some of Fanny's more complicated and reflective poems, but he was able to make hits of some of her more simple ones.

Howard Doane was truly as remarkable in his accomplishments as was Fanny. He was a rare breed, a Christian business tycoon. Although fabulously rich, he apparently came by his fortune entirely honestly and was never accused of greed, injustice, corruption, or any of the other faults common to men of his wealth. He gave a large percentage of his income to charitable institutions in a time before income tax laws made it expedient for rich men to do this. For instance, he donated a pipe organ to the Cincinnati YMCA and built a library, chapel, and gymnasium for Denison University in Ohio. In addition, he erected numerous church and mission buildings and educated many individual pastors and missionaries. He was an active lay worker in the Mount Auburn Baptist Church in the suburb of Cincinnati where he had a mansion.

Doane was a man of medium height with a broad face, large, kindly blue eyes, a broad nose, thick lips and a neatly trimmed Vandyke beard. His personality has been described as "magnetic" and his manner as "cheerful, warm-hearted, and generous."[1] He was a very nervous man, fast-moving and hyperactive. As a businessman, he patented seventy inventions and so perfected the productivity of the woodworking machines he manufactured that in 1889 France named him a Chevalier in the famed Legion of Honor. And parallel to his business life, in his career as a musician he composed 2,300 hymns over a period of fifty-three years.

Doane and Fanny began to write hymns almost at once after their first meeting. A few days after he had given her the twenty dollars, he returned one evening and asked whether she could write him a poem using the phrase, "Pass Me Not, O Gentle Saviour." She said that she could and would, but she lacked suitable inspiration and therefore wrote nothing for several weeks. Then, in the early spring of 1868, she was speaking at religious services in a prison in Manhattan. She was receiving more and more requests to speak at the Y, at home missions, at churches, and at prisons, as the popularity of her hymns grew. During the course of the services, she heard one of the inmates cry out in a piteous voice, "Good Lord! Do not pass me by!" This provided Fanny with her needed inspiration, and when she retired that evening she wrote:

Pass me not, O gentle Saviour,
Hear my humble cry,
While on others Thou art smiling,
Do not pass me by.

Saviour, Saviour,
Hear my humble cry,
While on others Thou art calling,
Do not pass me by.[2]

She sent the words to Doane, who soon wrote a melody. The hymn was sung a few days later at the very prison where Fanny had been inspired and where she was still holding services. It made a profound impression on the prisoners, to the extent that not a few of them were converted on the spot. Fanny herself was so moved by the prisoners' reaction that she fell down in a swoon and had to be carried out.[3]

On April 30, Doane again appeared at Fanny's flat on Varick Street. He had a favor to ask of his blind friend, and this time he gave her not a title but a tune. "I have exactly forty minutes," he said, "before I must meet a train for Cincinnati. I have a tune for you. See if it says anything to you. Perhaps you can commit it to memory and then compose a poem to match it." He proceeded to hum a simple, plaintive melody.

After hearing it but once, Fanny clapped her hands, as was her wont whenever anything pleased her, and said, "Why, that says, 'Safe in the arms of Jesus!'" She could best write when the tunes "said" something to her.

She excused herself, promising to return in a few minutes. Scurrying to the other room of her tiny apartment, she knelt on the floor, as was her custom before composing a hymn, and asked God for inspiration. Seeing that his servant Doane was in a hurry, God saw fit to grant it quickly. Within a half hour Fanny had a complete poem. During that time she claimed that she was "wholly unconscious" of her surroundings and of everything except the hymn which formed itself, without any exertion on her part, in her mind. She always claimed that the hymn was not her own doing but was entirely the work of the "Blessed Holy Spirit." Returning to Doane, she quickly dictated:

Safe in the arms of Jesus,
Safe on His gentle breast,
There, by His love o'ershaded,
Sweetly my soul shall rest.
Hark! 'tis the voice of angels,
Borne in a song to me,
Over the fields of glory,
Over the jasper sea.

Chorus:

Safe in the arms of Jesus,
Safe on His gentle breast,
There, by His love o'ershaded,
Sweetly my soul shall rest.

Safe in the arms of Jesus,
Safe from corroding care,
Safe from the world's temptations,
Sin cannot harm me there.
Free from the blight of sorrow,
Free from my doubts and fears,
Only a few more trials,
Only a few more tears.

Jesus! My heart's dear refuge,
Jesus has died for me;
Firm on the Rock of Ages
Ever my trust shall be.
Here let me wait with patience,

Wait till the night is o'er,
Wait till I see the morning
Break on the golden shore.

Doane was enthusiastic and took the hymn back to Cincinnati, where he used it at a Sunday school convention a few days later. It became an instant success. After Biglow and Main included it in a hymnal three years later, it was widely sung all over the country.

Fanny always had a special attachment to "Safe in the Arms of Jesus." She claimed that she had written it "for dead relatives," and also for mothers who had lost children. Could it have been inspired by the memory of her dead child? At any rate, whenever she was comforting a mother who had lost a child, she would usually say, "Remember, my dear, your darling cherub is 'safe in the arms of Jesus.'" Perhaps that hymn consoled its author as much as it did the countless others who came to sing it.

The following year, Doane invited Fanny to his home in Auburn for the first of many visits. While there she was invited to address a group of workingmen in Cincinnati. Toward the end of her talk she had an overwhelming sensation that "some mother's boy" in the audience there "must be rescued that night or not at all." She then pleaded urgently, "If there is a dear boy here tonight who has perchance wandered away from his mother's home and his mother's teaching, would he please come to me at the close of the service?"

Sure enough, a young man of about eighteen came to her and asked, "Did you mean me?" going on to say, "I promised my mother to meet her in heaven, but the way I have been living, I don't think that will be possible now." Fanny prayed earnestly over the youth, and "he finally arose with a new light in his eyes and exclaimed in triumph, 'Now I can meet my mother in heaven, for now I have found her God!'"[4]

Doane had recently asked Fanny to write a hymn on "Rescue the Perishing"—a subject for home missions—and when she returned to her room that night she could think of nothing else but the words "rescue the perishing." Before she went to bed, she had composed a complete hymn, beginning,

Rescue the perishing,
Care for the dying,
Snatch them in pity from sin and the grave;
Weep o'er the erring one,
Lift up the fallen,
Tell them of Jesus the mighty to save.[5]

The next day she recited it to Doane, who immediately gave it a rousing and stirring tune. Published the next year in his Songs of Devotion (along with

104

"Pass Me Not"), it soon became the virtual battle cry of home mission workers all over the country.[6]

Biglow and Main of New York and the John Church Company of Cincinnati were among the nation's largest publishers of hymns. And from the late 1860s, Fanny completely dominated the hymnals published by the New York firm. In the hymnals that Biglow and Main published in the next two decades, Fanny invariably contributed between one third and one half of the selections. So prolific was her writing that the editors had to induce her to use pen names in order to disguise the fact that they depended to such a large extent on one person to supply the lyrics. In the 1860s and 1870s, besides signing her name as "Fannie," "F.A.N.," "F.J.C.," "Fanny Van Alstyne," "Mrs. Alexander Van Alstyne," and "Mrs. Van A.," she was using such frankly weird appellations as "L.L.A.," "D.D.," "D.D.A.," "J.W.W.," "G.W.W.," "J.F.O.," "##," "###," "*," and "The Children's Friend." In the 1880s and 1890s, she adopted a bewildering array of pseudonyms, among which were "Carrie Hawthorne," "Carrie Bell," "Louise W. Tilden," "Lillian G. Frances," "Grace Frances," "Leah Carleton," "Mrs. Edna Forest," "Mrs. Kate Smiling," "Mrs. L. C. Prentice," "Maud Marion," "Cora Adrienne," "Minnie B. Lowry," "Ryan A. Dykes," "Alice Armstrong," "Alice Monteith," "H. N. Lincoln," "Frank Gould," "James Black," "Catherine Bethune," "Lizzie Edmunds," "Sallie Martin," "Rose Atherton," "Eleanor Craddock," and "Flora Dayton."[7] The use of pseudonyms was not limited to Fanny Crosby; many of her friends used them. Ira Sankey also used the confusing pseudonym "Rian A. (or Ryan A.) Dykes." George Coles Stebbins often wrote simply as "George Coles." Charles H. Gabriel, who was to set many of Fanny's poems to music in the early 1900s, had seventeen noms de plume. But none of her friends could match Fanny's fanciful collection of 204 different pen names!

Indeed, Fanny was in great demand by all those composers who wrote hymns, and she had no trouble meeting those demands. In forty-seven years, she would furnish Biglow and Main alone with 5,959[8] hymns, to say nothing of the number she contributed to other publishers. However, of the nearly six thousand poems she submitted to the New York firm, only about two thousand were published, which means that she supplied them with nearly three times as many hymns as were needed. When a subject was suggested, she often wrote several poems, allowing the composer to choose the one most appropriate for his intentions. Naturally, by writing so much, the quality of her verse suffered and she produced much that was jejune and banal. But it was at this time that she was also producing some of her most popular songs. "Dark Is the Night and Cold the Wind Is Blowing" first appeared in Theodore Perkins' *Sabbath Carols* in 1868. It became quite popular and was used by Moody in his early evangelical work in Chicago. The next year Robert Lowry and Howard Doane issued a hymnal titled *Bright Jewels* that contained two hymns by Fanny that achieved immense popularity. "Praise Him! Praise Him!" immediately came into favor despite its mediocre lyrics and its uninteresting tune by an obscure musician named Chester Allen. "Jesus, Keep Me Near the Cross," set to music by Doane, was first published in that same collection and quickly found a place in the hearts of worshipers all over the country. In 1870 "Pass Me Not" and "Rescue the Perishing" were published in Doane's *Songs of Devotion*. In 1871, Lowry and Doane issued *Pure Gold*, which contained "Safe in the Arms of Jesus," which quickly came into enormous popular favor, and "The Bright Forever." This last hymn, set to music by Hugh Main, was on the subject of the life to come, and it became very popular. Two years later came Lowry and Doane's *Royal Diadem,* which contained two hymns, "Jesus, I Love Thee" and "Only a Step to Jesus," both with music by Doane, that attained a moderate success.

Fanny also continued to write for composers not officially affiliated with Biglow and Main. As we have seen, she wrote for Philip Phillips and contributed heavily to his *Musical Leaves*, published in 1868. In 1869, she contributed more than twenty hymns to Phoebe Knapp, who compiled *Notes of Joy*. John Robson Sweney, a Philadelphia songwriter whom Fanny was yet to meet, also published various of her hymns in his hymnals. By the early 1870s Fanny was well on her way to becoming the queen of hymn writers.

In writing hymns Fanny often matched her poems to familiar tunes, as she did in the case of "We Thank Thee, Our Father," written to the melody of the famous Portuguese Hymn (*Adeste Fidelis*), and "We Praise Thee, We Bless Thee," which she matched with the popular tune *Verlassen bini i* by an Austrian songwriter, Thomas Koschat. She set some poems to popular Scottish and Welsh airs and also used tunes by Stephen Foster. "Our Loved Ones Gone Before" was set to the tune of "Swanee River," and "Sorrow Shall Come Again No More" was written for the melody of "Hard Times Shall Come Again No More." "Speed Away!" was written for a melody by an American musician, I. B. Woodbury (1819–1858).

Being a classical musician of the first caliber, Fanny was also eminently capable of writing her own music. Privately, she improvised on the piano, composing many compositions said to have been of great beauty but which she refused to have written down or published. She also wrote some hymn tunes, but few of these were published either. One exception was a spring carol that was included in her 1903 autobiography. More than any of her other published efforts, this hymn best illustrates her musical talents. Here is a tune of great beauty and refinement, much more harmonically sophisticated than most of the efforts of Doane and Lowry and other contemporaries. Her musical line does not drop, as does that of most of her musical colleagues, requiring the use of a tenor or bass counter for several beats. On the contrary, her line flows smoothly.

However, Fanny was no more willing to set her own poems to music as she was to have her more sophisticated compositions put to paper. For one thing, she felt that the tunes she liked to compose were too difficult for the common worshiper, and for this reason she deferred, with regard to melodies, to her colleagues who composed simpler, more straightforward tunes. This was probably part of the reason for the fate of the hymnal that she and Van compiled at this time. All the hymns in that collection were written by husband and wife. Biglow and Main rejected it because it was felt by the directors that the public did not care for hymnals with all the selections by only two people. However, since both Fanny and her husband were skilled musicians, it is fair to ask whether part of the reason for the rejections was not the fact that their hymns were too difficult and sophisticated for the popular taste of the day. In any event, the only hymns ever published for which she supplied the music as well as the words were "Jesus, Dear, I Come to Thee," "The Blood-Washed Throng," which was included in her 1906 autobiography, and the spring carol. So it was by deliberate effort that Fanny wrote melodies of elementary simplicity. It was also by deliberate effort that she wrote poems that fell far short of the literary standard she was capable of attaining.

Although she was by far the guiding light of the lyrical staff of Biglow and Main, she was not by any means the only poet associated with the firm. The group of writers included William J. Stevenson, Josephine Pollard, and Kate Cameron. Beside Fanny Crosby, perhaps the best known of the Biglow and Main poets was Anna Bartlett Warner, who was born the same year as Fanny and died only a month before her. She gained the distinction of writing the world's most popular hymn, "Jesus Loves Me." Mrs. Mary Ann Kidder (1819-1905) Fanny first met as a writer for the New York Ledger. Born in Massachusetts, she was stricken blind as a teen-ager but was miraculously healed several years later. So complete was the cure that to the time of her death she never needed glasses. Although her religious beliefs were vague and broad and she considered herself "a deeder, not a creeder," she wrote several successful hymns, including the popular "We Shall Sleep, But Not Forever." Another author remembered for one work was Annie Sherwood Hawks (1835-1918), a Brooklyn housewife who was a parishioner at Robert Lowry's Hanson Place Baptist Church. She wrote four hundred hymns, and her "I Need Thee Every Hour" was one of the most popular hymns of its day and is still a great favorite in many religious circles. Another talented poet at Biglow and Main was Mrs. Elizabeth Payson Prentiss (1818-1878), an insomniac who wrote hymns on nights when she had trouble sleeping. Among them was the beloved "More Love to Thee, O Christ," which Doane set to one of his better tunes. Then there was an aging invalid, Lydia Baxter (1809-1874), a spinster Baptist who wrote "Take the Name of Jesus with You" and "There Is a Gate That Stands Ajar."

Little is known about some of the men who wrote the music to Fanny's words. Of Chester Allen (1838-1878) who wrote the music to "Praise Him! Praise Him!" and several less successful hymns, we know nothing else. Silas Vail (1818-1884) was a hatter who wrote music as a hobby; the composer of the melody of Mary Ann Kidder's "We Shall Sleep, But Not Forever," he also wrote the tune to Fanny's "Thou, My Everlasting Portion," which was published in Lowry and Doane's *Songs of Grace and Glory* in 1874. Theodore E. Perkins (b.1831) published several of Fanny's hymns in his songbooks *The Shining Star* and *Sabbath Carols*. A Baptist, he was long noted as a voice instructor at Princeton, Lafayette, and Colgate and at Crozer Seminary. Theodore Frelinghuysen Seward (1835-1902), who was one of the first men to collect and arrange Negro spirituals in Biglow and Main's *Jubilee Songs*, taking the songs down directly from former slaves, wrote some music in addition and provided settings for some of Fanny's hymns. More prominent, however, was Robert Lowry, who set many of Fanny's poems to music, including "Goodnight! Till We Meet in the Morning!" "Breaking Away," "'Twill All Be Over Soon," "Thine the Glory," and the Christmas carol, "Never Shone a Star So Fair." Of the hymns by Fanny for which he provided musical settings, by far the most successful was "All the Way My Saviour Leads Me," published in 1875.

Lowry, who was six years younger than Fanny, was a Baptist minister well known for his "brilliant and interesting" sermons. "Very few men," wrote a contemporary, Jacob Hall, "had greater ability in painting pictures from imagination. He could thrill an audience with his vivid descriptions, inspiring them with the same thoughts that inspired him."[9] Despite this extraordinary descriptive talent, however, music was Lowry's first love. Although he held the distinguished pulpit of the Hanson Place Baptist Church in Brooklyn, Lowry always said that he could reach more people through hymns than through sermons. He began to write tunes as a boy, and by the time he became associated with Bradbury and with Biglow and Main he had already written several popular hymns. He was more than a dilettante in music, for he did research, of sorts, in musical theory, attempting to reduce music to a mathematical basis. Using the established fact that the note of middle C has 256 vibrations per second, Lowry prepared a scale and went to work on the rule of three. After much calculation and experimentation, he concluded that he had carried his researches to the point where he could determine—that his idea was nonsense.[10]

Despite his great love of music and the honorary doctorate in music awarded by his alma mater, Bucknell, Lowry's skills as a composer were almost as limited as those of Doane and some of his other contemporaries. Although he wrote hymns of all types, Lowry was best with hymns that called for a martial, brass-band style, like "Shall We Gather at the River?" Some of his hymns are so simple musically that they can be accompanied by a tambourine. He was a great believer in "the big chorus," and if a hymn was submitted to him without a chorus he would often add one or try to make the last lines of the poem into a sort of refrain, as was the case with "All the Way My Saviour Leads Me." He was aware of the importance of the words in the composition of a successful hymn. A catchy tune was not enough to guarantee the success of a hymn, and he found Fanny's lyrics especially suited to the composition of Christian hymnody. A hymn, he felt, needed "something which is readily apprehended by the Christian consciousness, coming forth from the experience of the writer, and clothed in strong and inspiring words."[11] While Lowry found this quality in Fanny's verse, nevertheless he often had trouble with her lyrics. Lowry was best at writing march tunes of the type popular in secular songs of the Civil War, but most of Fanny's poems were not suited to martial settings. Moreover, Lowry was often at a loss for what to do with some of her lines. Although Fanny's poems are simple as poems go, they tend to be complicated for Sunday school hymns or gospel songs. And Lowry often found his style hampered by complex poetry.

As a person, Lowry was a pleasant and jolly man, noted for his sense of humor and enormous beard which obscured most of his ruggedly handsome face. Known as the "Good Doctor," he was an intellectual and Fanny loved to have him read poetry to her. He was sensitive to the quality of his music, and it always rankled him that he could succeed only in the genre of what he frankly acknowledged as "brass-band music." However, he was said to have been an excellent judge of music and verse, even if his own so often fell short of his expectations. When it came to editing hymnals, his word was respected by poet and composer alike as to what changes should be made in a text or a tune to make it more singable. Even Fanny often deferred to his judgment. She wrote, "His ear was trained to detect the minutest metrical fault,"[12] and she was not at all averse to taking his suggestions as to how certain of her poems could be slightly altered in order to become more effective.

Fanny wrote almost no hymns for Sylvester Main, a kind and gentle man whom Fanny knew as a "faithful counselor and guide."[13] He was more of a business director than an active composer in his firm. However, he and Fanny did collaborate at least once, in 1868. One day, Fanny heard him hum a tune in his office. "Oh, Mr. Main," she said, "that is beautiful. And if you let me, I am going to write a hymn for it."

"Well, if you think it is worth it, you may do so," he said.[14]

So Fanny wrote "I Come to Thee," which, with Vet Main's music, became quite popular.

Vet's son, Hugh, then an assistant to his father, set a great many of Fanny's hymns to music. Born while his father was running a "singing school" in his native Ridgefield, Hubert Platt Main began his adult life as a clerk in a clothing store. However, by the time he was in his late twenties, he was a member of his father's publishing firm. In 1869, with the hymnal, *The Victory*, he began a career during which he was to compile and edit nearly thirty books of hymns and secular songs and write the music to over a thousand lyrics.

Hugh was a short, thin man with heavy eyelids and a huge, drooping mustache. He had a dry wit and loved to write comic verse.

Now Hugh Main was not an "outrageously pious" man, as he said. The few surviving letters we have from him to Fanny Crosby do not ooze piety as do those of Doane and some of their other colleagues. He belonged to the Methodist Church but apparently had at least some doubts about salvation and the hereafter. As late as 1920, when he was over eighty, he remarked to George Stebbins, another hymn writer, on the death of the famous gospel singer, Charles M. Alexander, "I wish I could be as certain of my salvation as he was of his!" This rather horrified his friend, who wrote him a long letter telling how the Christian could and should have certainty about his eternal destiny.[15] Hugh Main was also a hard-driving businessman and, like Lowry, was an intellectual and a student of classical music. He became one of the foremost authorities on church music, ancient and modern, and amassed a huge musical library. By the time he died, his home in Newark contained one of the largest collections of hymnals in the United States. He was also a great lover of the music of Richard Wagner, whom he considered the greatest musical genius of all history.

Hugh Main was a much better musician than Lowry or Doane, and like Fanny he was capable of writing complicated and sophisticated tunes. Yet in writing hymns, he chose to mask his talent in composing melodies in the popular style, for he believed in "music for the masses." He knew that from the standpoint of classical music, his tunes and those of his contemporaries were trash. Yet he felt that the average person had to have a type of music for worship that could be understood and enjoyed. He felt church music ought to be of the same type that is popular on the street, where the tune is of such a nature that the person singing it can predict what is coming next. Yet even in this genre, Main was more skilled than his friends Lowry and Doane. He was able, by means of harmony, to get around the unrelieved bounciness that beset the music of his colleagues. Whereas Doane and Lowry could write marches and lullabies but little else, Main was proficient in many idioms. He could deal more skillfully with complicated, reflective poems, and one of these, "Hold Thou My Hand," was quite popular.

As we have seen, Van composed the melodies for some of his wife's hymns. Besides the hymn collection that was never published, Van provided several tunes for Phoebe Knapp's *Notes of Joy* (1869). He also provided a melody for his wife's "Stay Thee, Weary Child," published in *Pure Gold* in

1871. Although he was a trained musician, preferring the "wordless classics" of the seventeenth- and the eighteenth-century masters, he, like Hugh Main, condescended to write pop tunes on at least a few occasions.

Another man who set several of Fanny's poems to music was William F. Sherwin (1826–1888), who gained immortality by writing the tunes to the poems of Mary Artemisia Lathbury, "Break Thou the Bread of Life" and "Day Is Dying in the West." He also provided music to such poems as "Awake, the Trumpet Is Sounding," "I Know of a Jewel," and "The Brightest Day of All." No poem of hers for which he supplied the tune ever achieved the enduring success of some of those she wrote for Doane, Main, and Lowry. However, it was through Sherwin that it was possible for Fanny to make a friendship she would always deeply cherish.

Born in December 1836, Frances Ridley Havergal was almost seventeen years Fanny's junior, but the frail, precocious daughter of William Havergal, a clergyman and hymn writer, had been writing poetry since she was seven years old and had early distinguished herself in the field of hymnology. Well known in England, her simple, direct hymns had endeared themselves to Christian worshipers before Fanny Crosby began writing hymns for Bradbury. A trained singer and musician, Miss Havergal, like Fanny, sometimes wrote both words and music, and apparently she did it very well. Fanny considered Miss Havergal's hymns superior to her own. The English lady is famous for "Who Is on the Lord's Side?" and "Take My Life and Let It Be Consecrated, Lord, to Thee." Although she lacked the informality and emotional warmth of her American counterpart, Miss Havergal wrote verse that was more stately— "grander," to use a favorite adjective of hers—and less sentimental, although not lacking in emotional pathos. By the sixties her hymns were very popular in England, and, through Sherwin and others with whom she corresponded, they were published in America, where they slowly gained popularity.

Fanny's hymns, in like fashion, were beginning to make themselves known in the British Isles, and Miss Havergal came greatly to love and admire the new hymns attributed to Fanny Crosby. She knew nothing, however, about their author except the name. Therefore, in the spring of 1872, she wrote to Sherwin asking about Fanny, whom Sherwin described as "a blind lady whose eyes can see splendidly in the sunshine of God's love." Miss Havergal found Sherwin's description "delicious" and immediately wrote Fanny a verse greeting, "A Seeing Heart." Fanny was truly nonplussed when Sherwin read her the poem and always considered it the greatest tribute ever paid her. Fanny and Frances began to correspond regularly, and, although they were never able to meet on earth, they became mutual admirers and friends by correspondence.

The following year, the famous hymn "Blessed Assurance" was written. Fanny had already written many hymns for Phoebe Knapp, as we have seen,

111

including "Labor for Good," "Our Sabbath Home," "Pray Without Ceasing," "God Is with Me Every Day," and others. But none equaled in popularity this hymn which she wrote one day at the Knapp Mansion. Phoebe said that she wanted to play Fanny a tune which she had recently composed and thought appropriate for a hymn. The two women went into the music room, and Phoebe played what Fanny later described as one of the finest hymn tunes that she had ever heard. Immediately, she clapped her hands and cried, "Why, that says 'Blessed Assurance!'" Within a short time, she composed the words, which, joined to the tune, would become one of her greatest hits.

The year 1873 also marked an end and a beginning. It was an end for the work of Sylvester Main. The relationship that began in the 1830s in Ridgefield, Connecticut, ended for Fanny when her beloved friend and counselor died at the age of fifty-six. A pious man, Vet had no terror of death, and his last words to his family were, "The dear Lord is about to give me rest. If you love me, do not weep, but rejoice." [16] The beginning was for the work of Dwight L. Moody, who would later figure greatly in Fanny's life. Along with his baritone soloist, Ira D. Sankey, Moody began a series of evangelical meetings in the British Isles, during which thousands were apparently led to the Christian faith. Even Alexandra, the Princess of Wales, admitted to being "greatly helped" by Moody's preaching. Through Sankey's heartrending singing, the British public fell in love with the Sunday school hymn, which was now coming to be known as the "gospel hymn." Sankey used many of Fanny Crosby's hymns, and they became immediate favorites, with "Pass Me Not, O Gentle Saviour" gaining sensational popularity. Through the medium of Sankey's singing, Fanny Crosby's name was becoming a household word in Great Britain.

The following year Fanny was introduced to a tall man with golden hair and beard and a Herculean physique who had, of late, been setting the religious world on fire with his splendid hymns. Philip P. Bliss was the other leading light in American hymnody. Unlike Fanny, Bliss almost always wrote his own tunes and always edited his own hymnbooks, which were published by the John Church Company. Only occasionally did he compose tunes for other people's poems. He had a particular warm and winning personality, was always sunny and smiling, and claimed never to be depressed. Born in 1838, Bliss had little formal musical training but nevertheless gained fame as a music teacher and hymn singer. In 1871, his first hymnbook, *The Charm,* was published, followed by *The Tree* in 1872, *Sunshine* in 1873, and *Gospel Songs* in 1874. His hymns became so popular that it was partly from the title of the last-named hymnal that what had previously been called the Sunday school hymn gradually became known as the gospel song or gospel hymn. Bliss was truly a great hymn writer. He wrote the immensely popular march hymn "Hold the Fort," which, along with "Pass Me Not," spread through the British Isles like wildfire, as well as "Only an Armour-Bearer" and "Let the Lower Lights Be Burning."

Bliss possessed a musical talent far superior to that of any of his contemporaries in the gospel-hymn business, with the possible exception of Ira Sankey. Moreover, Bliss's bass voice was one of great richness and power. D. L. Moody realized that he could be of great value in evangelical work, and he wrote urging Bliss to become a full-time evangelist. He wanted to couple him with a thirty-four-year-old poet and former jeweler named Daniel Webster Whittle, affectionately known as Major, after his rank in the Civil War. Whittle, like Moody, was a layman and an excellent preacher. According to Moody's plans, Whittle was to preach and Bliss to sing. It was a hard decision for Bliss to make, for he was just getting to the point in life where he could live comfortably from his royalties. Full-time evangelical work would mean less time to devote to the work he loved best, that of writing hymns, and it would also mean less income. Nevertheless, Bliss accepted Moody's urgings as God's will and cheerfully undertook his new labors.

The same year, Ira Sankey suggested that Bliss and he merge their hymn collections. Sankey had compiled a collection in England known as *Sacred Songs and Solos* which was tremendously popular. The two men combined the hymns in this collection with those in Bliss's *Gospel Songs* to create *Gospel Hymns and Sacred Songs*, which would be published jointly by the John Church Company and by Biglow and Main the following year. It was at the beginning of his association with Biglow and Main that Fanny became acquainted with Bliss. She admired his musicianship and perhaps hoped for the opportunity to collaborate with him. However, Bliss was then involved with merging his collection with Sankey's and was not looking for any new poems to set to music.

That same year, Fanny was engaged in a speaking tour that took her as far as Cincinnati. While speaking in crowded churches and missions in that city, she was a guest at the Doanes' mansion, where another of her most successful hymns was born. One evening, Fanny and Doane were talking about the nearness of God. The sun was setting and the evening shadows were gathering. Fanny could see enough to appreciate the beauty and wonder of the scene, which she felt showed forth the glorious hand of God. She was almost in ecstasy when she retired, and before she lay down she composed the words:

I am Thine, O Lord,
I have heard Thy voice,
And it told Thy love to me;
But I long to rise in the arms of faith,
And be closer drawn to Thee.

Chorus:

Draw me nearer, nearer, blessed Lord,
To the cross where Thou hast died;

113

Draw me nearer, nearer, nearer, blessed Lord,
To Thy precious, bleeding side. [17]

She recited it to Doane the next morning, and he quickly composed a tune. Published the next year in *Brightest and Best,* the hymn immediately became a great favorite. Indeed, that hymnal produced a bumper crop of hits for Fanny. Also published for the first time in that collection were "All the Way My Saviour Leads Me," with music by Lowry; "Saviour, More Than Life to Me" and "To God Be the Glory," with music by Doane; and "Yes, There Is Pardon for You," an invitational hymn with a setting provided by Hugh Main. All these hymns became very popular, although one of them attained favor only belatedly. The straightforward, objective "To God Be the Glory," with its simple statement of the Christian faith, was scarcely noticed when it was published and was soon forgotten, only to be rediscovered and popularized by Billy Graham in the 1950s.

In March 1875 Fanny was fifty-five years old. She and Van were now living on the East Side at 82 East Ninth Street, near the offices of Biglow and Main. That year Fanny's friend Henry Ward Beecher, whom she considered the foremost "pulpit orator of the century," was involved in a shocking scandal, in which the wife of a supposed friend accused him of committing adultery with her. Fanny was one of many who backed Beecher, sympathizing with him and deploring "the bitter persecution" that the man of God was undergoing. When Beecher was eventually exonerated, she would claim that "like the Hebrew children [he] came out of the flames unhurt." [18] Whether or not that was the case, a far more important event occurred in the religious world of New York that year. Moody and Sankey came to Brooklyn to conduct an evangelical campaign.

CHAPTER 11
DAVID AND JONATHAN

As early as 7 A.M. on October 24, 1875, the streets were full of people in the vicinity of the Brooklyn Rink. By 9 A.M., when Moody appeared on the platform, the huge building was packed with 7,000 people—most of them young.

The *New York Times* described Moody as a "well-built man, with a smiling face, a small, shapely head, small features, a full brown beard, and a red face, indicative of jollity and good humor."[1] "Let us open with the twenty-fourth hymn," he said.

At once, he was joined on the platform by a "square-built, solid-looking man with a smiling face, and dark, curly hair, dark moustache, and side whiskers."[2] Ira D. Sankey sat down at the little reed organ, or harmonium, and bade the audience, "Please rise and sing heartily!" The audience rose and turned to hymn number twenty-four in Sankey and Bliss's new *Gospel Hymns and Sacred Songs,* which sold for two cents at the Rink. They joined in singing "Rejoice and Be Glad" by the Scottish hymn writer Horatius Bonar. The hymn closed amid shouts of "Amen" by the audience.

Moody leaped to his feet, threw his hands into the air, and shouted, "Let us unite in prayer." Quickly the chorus of Amens died down, and a Dr. Budinger, a local pastor, rose to pray. When he finished, Moody again sprang to his feet and said, "Let us continue the worship by singing the eighty-seventh hymn."

Sankey at the organ, added, "Let us all rise and sing heartily." The congregation, with increasing enthusiasm, sang "Lord, I Hear of Showers of Blessing."

When the hymn and the consequent exclamations were finished, Moody once again sprang to his feet. "I will read for you a part of the thirteenth chapter of Numbers, beginning at the twenty-fifth verse." He commenced to read, in his characteristic rapid style and with his Yankee twang, the chapter which describes how the Israelites reached the land of Canaan. Moses had dispatched spies, who now reported that the "land of promise" was flowing with milk and honey. Nevertheless, they were terrified at the great size and ferocious appearance of the natives.

"A strange kind of report, ain't it?" said the muscular New Englander. "I never heard tell of such a report as that being made in Congress. Did you? A land 'flowing with milk and honey,' yet one that 'eateth up the people'! There was not much danger that the Israelites would starve there! They saw 'great giants,' yet it was a land that 'eateth up the people.'"[3]

Moody read a dozen more verses, then asked Sankey to sing "Here I Am! Send Me!" It was the first time that New Yorkers had heard the voice that melted the heart of all England. Soon he had the people swaying their bodies and sobbing, as his glorious baritone resounded through the huge auditorium. By the time the last note fell, there was a "loud murmur."

Moody strode up to the lectern again, to preach on the text, "Let us go up at once and possess it, for we are well able to overcome it." He talked about a revival in New York City. His sermon was punctuated by exclamations of "Yes!" and "Amen!" from the audience. When he was able to continue, Moody concluded that "it is the unbelief inside the Church," rather than outside of it, that is able to hinder a revival. He went on to criticize the unbelief of the established churches which, he said, was hindering the work of God. He compared those who had doubted that a new revival was possible in New York to those Israelites who feared to enter the Promised Land for fear of its inhabitants. Cries of "Amen!" made Moody pause for a few seconds before he delivered his clinching statement that "when we *believe*, we are able to overcome giants and walls and everything!" The audience went wild, shouting, "Amen! Amen! Bless the Lord!" Moody continued, interspersing his exhortations with pithy epigrams, such as:

"A lie generally travels farther than the truth. It is an old saying that a lie will go around the world before the truth can get on his boots to follow him. The world always seems to rejoice when anything goes wrong with the Church."

He continued to exhort the people to believe and have the faith that, through God, all things were possible—even the conversion of wicked New York. He closed:

"If I had the voice of angels, I would like to ask the 40,000 ministers, 'Shall we go up to take the land at once?' If we do, we have got to get to work! We have to give way to the Lord. We have to bid farewell to the world—to stop parties and festivals and lectures!"

To this advice—so strange to modern man, even the modern religious man—came a mighty chorus of approving Amens. Moody went on to ask each of the local ministers who sat on the platform with him if he was ready.

"Mr. Budinger, are you ready?"

"Yes."

"Mr. Cuyler, are you ready?"

"Yes."

"Mr. Stuart, are you ready?"

"Yes."

The audience then exploded into salvos of "Yes!" "Amen!" and "Hurrah!"

"Thank God," cried the flushed and sweating evangelist, "for the manifestations of His Spirit. We *will* get up *at once* and *take the land!* . . . Oh! My God! May Thy Spirit descend upon us this morning! Mayst Thou use this according to Thy will for good." The sermon closed amid deafening shouts. The enthusiasm of the people was fanned to an even more frantic pitch by Sankey's rendition of Philip Bliss's "Only an Armour-Bearer." After Dr. Theodore Ledyard Cuyler pronounced the benediction, bands of youths burst forth from the Rink and marched down Fulton Street, arm in arm, singing Bliss's "Hold the Fort, for I Am Coming."[4]

The next afternoon, the entire area of the Rink was packed with people, many of whom had come from Manhattan, crossing the East River on heavily laden ferries. Whether Fanny Crosby was among them we do not know. If she came, it was most likely with Phoebe Knapp, who appeared at all the evangelical meetings that occurred in or near New York. At any rate, by three o'clock, Vanderbilt and Clermont Avenues from DeKalb to Myrtle Avenue were completely filled with struggling men and women waiting to get into the rink to hear the man who preached and the man who sang like an angel. The minute the doors were thrown open, seven thousand men and women fought their way, "crushing, tearing, panting, to the available seats."[5] When they were seated, an equal number of people were left out in the cold—literally.

Sankey began the afternoon meeting by leading the audience in singing Fanny Crosby's beloved "Safe in the Arms of Jesus." The *Times* reported that it was "sung with unusual effect."[6] After two more hymns, Dr. Talmadge, another local pastor, offered a prayer, in which he thanked God for all the people "saved" at the meeting on the previous day, Moody read the great Resurrection passage from 1 Corinthians 15, and Sankey, after a prayer, sang his most famous hymn, "The Ninety and Nine," which had made a terrific sensation in England, where the singer had composed the music to a poem by Elizabeth Clephone. The hymn was received with near-hysteria.

Moody then preached a sermon about death and resurrection, recounting how "before my sins were put away, death was a horrid monster," but how "the child of God has nothing to fear," concluding,

"My brethren, if you could have been
at that tomb where Christ was buried,

117

you would have seen Death laughing, and
you would have heard him say, 'I've got
him now!' But wait awhile . . . Christ
burst his bonds and rose again! I pity
the man who knows nothing of the Son of
God! I know, and I want everyone else
to know, that there is a Voice to be
heard by and by. The dead will hear
His Voice, and there will be a rising
of the dead."[7]

The meeting closed amid hysteria and the singing of "There Is a Fountain
Filled with Blood."

Moody and Sankey plunged Brooklyn and New York into a revival of great
dimensions, actually not new but simply a later phase of the revival which had
begun in the late 1850s. They drew on the religious enthusiasm already
present and raised it to fever pitch. How many were actually "saved" from
outright unbelief or indifference is debatable. From the number of Amens and
Praise Gods that were shouted at the Brooklyn Rink, it seems certain that a
large percentage of those who made up the throng were devoted church
people who were just as much concerned as Moody and Sankey in fostering a
revival among the indifferent. But it is also certain that some people were
indeed moved from actual unbelief as a result of the meetings.

Who were these men who had made such a profound effect in Scotland
and England and did so much to spread the hymns of Fanny Crosby over the
English-speaking world? Who were these men with whom Fanny Crosby
would later become so intimate?

Dwight Lyman Ryther Moody was an uneducated backwoodsman from
northern Massachusetts. Born February 5, 1837, he was reared as a Unitarian.
In his late teens, while working in a shoe store in Boston, he was converted to
orthodox Trinitarian Congregationalism. Later, in Chicago, the aggressive
young man could easily have made a fortune as a shoe salesman, but he
decided that he could best serve God by selling the gospel instead. During the
1860s, as a YMCA worker, he did much to help the poor boys of Chicago's
slums. So successful was he at this work that he was called upon to hold
revival meetings and eventually was invited to hold evangelistic meetings, or
"campaigns" (as in the Christian's "war" against the legions of Satan) in
Britain. It was owing to their success there that Moody and his musician friend
Ira Sankey became international celebrities. Moody was never ordained, but
even so, by the time of his return from Europe, many Protestant clergymen
and laymen looked to him as their spiritual leader. Until his death he was
perhaps the most important and influential figure in the American Protestant
churches.

118

Moody's appeal was not based on personal appearance. Five foot eight inches tall, at thirty-eight he still weighed a solid, muscular 245 pounds and showed no signs of the enormous corpulence that would soon overtake him. But he had a small bullet head with coarse, rather unattractive features, which usually were almost obscured by a gigantic beard. Although he believed in short hair, he believed that a man was somehow undignified without a beard. Moody spoke with a heavy New England brogue that many who heard him for the first time found hard to understand. He also spoke very rapidly; it was said that he pronounced the word Jerusalem in one syllable. He also made no bones about the fact that he spoke ungrammatically and often made mincemeat of the queen's English.

"You have no grammar!" remarked someone.

"Well," said the Yankee, "I wish you, with your grammar, would try to save men as I am trying to do without it!"[8] Although he sent both of his sons to Yale, he did not idolize education. "An educated rascal is the meanest kind of rascal," he maintained.[9] He would not "read any book unless it will help me to understand the Book" and poured contempt on biblical commentaries. "I pore over the pages [of the Bible] not through the specs of some learned commentator, but with my own eyes."[10]

Nevertheless Moody, who spent several hours a day in prayer and was said by one of his associates to have been in "constant communion with God," was loved and respected not only by the ignorant but by many members of the intelligentsia. An interesting, dramatic speaker, he had a knack of presenting the teachings of Christ vividly and in such a way as to appeal to those who were turned off by formal, erudite sermons. Whatever the defects in his education, nobody could say that he lacked sincerity, which was often the case with many better trained pulpit orators.

Moody was not at all skilled in music. He could play no instrument and sang abominably. He blamed this on the thickness of his "beefsteak" lips, but undoubtedly it was because he was just not musical. He loved to hear music, however, and realized that it was a very important element of evangelization. Like Fanny, he believed that the gospel could be sung into the consciousness of people who were not so easily moved by preaching. Therefore, he made it a point to give as much time to his song service as he did to preaching.

Early in his career Moody desired a partner to "sing the gospel" while he preached it, and he found such a person in 1870. In that year he was addressing a YMCA convention in Indianapolis, Indiana. He found the singing abominable until an obscure revenue official from western Pennsylvania was persuaded to sing. His rendition of "There Is a Fountain Filled with Blood" held the audience spellbound. As soon as the service was over, Moody hunted up the singer, Ira D. Sankey, and when he was introduced told him, "I've been looking for you the past eight years!" He insisted that Sankey give up his job and join him in Chicago at once. Sankey, who had a wife and two children, was

119

shocked by the demands of the audacious stranger and protested, but Moody was adamant and succeeded in getting Sankey to agree at least to think over the proposition.[11]

After Sankey had returned to Pennsylvania, Moody continued to badger him until he gave in, resigned from his job, and went with his family to Chicago, where he became an inseparable part of Moody's evangelical work. The two men became devoted friends as well as professional colleagues and were so attached to each other that Fanny Crosby came to refer to them as David and Jonathan, referring to the friendship of the future King David of Israel with the son of King Saul. Sankey, until his voice failed, was given equal billing with Moody, for the evangelist felt that the singer was just as important as the preacher. "Mr. Moody will preach, and Mr. Sankey will sing the gospel," it was usually announced.

Ira David Sankey was born in Edinburg in western Pennsylvania on August 28, 1840. Like Moody, he came from a poor family and had almost no formal education. He fought for the Union in the Civil War and often, while in the army, led the singing in the religious services. From childhood he had a great love for music, and by the time he had grown to manhood his phenomenal singing voice had attracted much attention. While working as a revenue agent, he gained local attention as a soloist in the Methodist Church in Newcastle, of which he and his wife, Fanny, were members. Sankey was five feet ten inches tall. His weight of 220 pounds was considered ideal by the people of his day, who did not have the modern mania for slimness. Considered quite dashing, Sankey was suave and polished, in contrast to his rather rough-hewn friend, and loved fine clothes, especially frock coats and gray silk top hats. He wore the fashionable mutton-chop whiskers. More mercurial in disposition than Moody, Sankey was an effusive, emotional man, usually very jovial and good-natured but easily becoming irritable and depressed. He was also somewhat pompous, quite garrulous, and given to rather overdone mannerisms.

Sankey apparently possessed a truly beautiful voice. When he was in England, Sims Reeves, a famous operatic tenor, commented that Sankey had the potential to be one of the world's finest opera singers.[12] Paul D. Moody, the younger son of D.L., too young to have heard Sankey at his best, observed, "I have been told many, many times by those who remembered him in his prime that his voice was the most moving and compelling that they ever heard."[13] Indeed, the New York Times observed that Sankey's voice was "wonderful," and "a rare combination of power and sweetness."[14] But Sankey had no vocal training, and after a few years of campaigning with Moody his voice was ruined. It showed the first signs of decline in a huskiness that was manifest in early 1876, and by the time he was forty his once-magnificent voice was an utter wreck. We have no recording of the majesty of his singing, and the few records he made were cut when he was nearly sixty, revealing nothing but a loud, hoarse, booming shell.

120

These were the men who in the fall of 1875 took New York by storm. Moody and Sankey were different in some ways from the run-of-the-mill evangelists of their day. They were less emotional, for one thing. The Amens and Hallelujahs and the shrieks and sobs at the Rink were a far cry from many of the revivals of the day, when people were known to embrace red-hot stoves and throw themselves on their hands and knees and imitate the cries of animals. By comparison, the campaigns of Moody and Sankey were restrained. At this point in his career Moody emphasized hell much less than did many of the fire-breathing evangelists of the time, and when he did mention it, it was usually obliquely. Although Moody vigorously opposed the theory of evolution as taught by the followers of Darwin, he was less strict about other things. Although he did not himself smoke, drink, play cards, or even go to the theater, he never preached against these things to any great extent, as many of his contemporaries did. He also had a concern for social justice. He had striven to improve the physical as well as the spiritual lot of the urchins in the Chicago slums, as much as he could.

Moody also favored integration. The black faces that dotted the audience and even the platform at the Rink startled some New Yorkers and made Moody's campaigns a different story, ethnically, from the earlier revivals in the late 1850s, when Negroes were often made to sit in the balconies and attics of the participating churches in New York. Among the ministers whom Moody invited to share the platform was Henry Highland Garnet (1815–1882), an eminent Negro Presbyterian pastor who had some ten years before given an address in Congress on the occasion of Lincoln's Emancipation Proclamation. The following year, Moody would run into great trouble with his integrationist policies. In Augusta, Georgia, he aroused the "contempt and abhorrence" of the white citizens of that city by refusing to separate the races. He allowed Negroes to "mingle indiscriminately with whites" until the citizens erected barriers. Moody violently objected. When one of the pastors told him that it was "impossible for the blacks and whites to mingle, even in religious meetings,"[15] Moody responded contemptuously, "I see you have not gotten over your rebellious feelings yet!" The same thing happened in Chattanooga, Tennessee, where at first his sponsors refused to permit Negroes to attend his meetings at all and relented only to the extent that they sanctioned a separate series of meetings for their colored citizens. Moody soon became persona non grata in the South, branded as a Black Republican and a Negrophile and accused of coming south with the expressed purpose of "changing the relation of the white and black race."[16]

The revival grew under Moody's preaching and Sankey's singing in the fall of 1875. They left in November to go to Philadelphia for a campaign there, but returned for a series in Manhattan in February. Here they met at the Hippodrome, the site later occupied by Madison Square Garden. Fanny, who with Van had moved back to the West Side and had a room in a tenement at

224 Hudson Street, almost certainly attended many of these meetings. The revivals at the Hippodrome were received as wildly as those at the Brooklyn Rink had been. Once more the scene of the meetings was pandemonium. Pickpockets mingled in the crowds; the streets for blocks around were impassable; on the congested sidewalks, boys hawked copies of *Gospel Hymns and Sacred Songs*, as well as biographies and pictures of Moody and Sankey. Moody protested this sale of photographs, saying from the lectern, "These photographs aren't our photographs. They ain't any more like us than they are like you. I ain't had a photograph taken in eight years. If you buy of these people, the sinners will say, 'We don't want anything to do with these meetings. Those fellows are only speculators.'" Indeed, Moody and Sankey were becoming objects of veneration. Like medieval holy men, they were held in such awe by the pious that anything belonging to them or representing them was considered somehow sacred or numinous.

It should be pointed out, however, that the revivals of Moody and Sankey were not the only expression of the generally deepened religious fervor of the day. Much of the religious enthusiasm of the time did not show a traditionally Christian face, for while this was the epoch of the camp meeting and the Bible-thumping evangelist, it was also the day of the medium, the seance, and the spirit rapper. Evangelical Christians had to contend with a rampant obsession with the occult as much as with outright unbelief.

This was the heyday of Madame Elena Petrovna Blavatsky, the founder of the Theosophical Society, who toured America and Europe teaching "secret doctrines" and working sensational miracles through familiar spirits. It was the heyday of Margaret, Kate, and Leah Fox, who claimed to interpret rappings of the spirits of the dead at the seances they held throughout the land. Seances in general were very popular then. As early as 1863, President Lincoln had held a seance in the White House, consulting the spirits of Washington, Franklin, Lafayette, and other deceased worthies.[17] Many of these were conducted superficially like church services. Strange things were attested at these sessions. For instance, in Memphis, Tennessee, many witnesses testified to having seen George Washington "materialised in power." Seeing two American flags in the room, the first President seized one and waved it vigorously and paraded back and forth with it, while the people cheered and shouted, "Glory to God! It is really our Washington!"[18]

Fanny was introduced to Moody and Sankey while they were in New York in 1876, and from then on her future was indissolubly connected with theirs. It was through their meetings that many of her hymns were introduced to a mass audience. And Moody and Sankey were eager for Fanny to supply them with hymns, for like most of their contemporaries they recognized her as one of the greatest contemporary hymn writers and found her hymns indispensable to their work. From this year dates Fanny's collaboration with Sankey, who began to fill his subsequent editions of *Gospel Hymns and Sacred Songs* with her efforts. Collaborating with Biglow and Main, he obtained the rights to many hymns she had already written, but he also engaged her to write new ones and began to write the melodies to many of her poems. Although untrained, and with a style nearly as simple and limited as that of Lowry and Doane, he was often capable of writing melodies of a heart-rending sweetness.

Supplying hymns not only for the Sunday school writers but also for the evangelists, Fanny was as active as she had ever been in her life. She spent several days each week at the offices of Biglow and Main, was active in Christian work among the poor and among prisoners, and often spent her evenings directing activities in her tenement houses. Moreover, she was now receiving many invitations to speak or preach and was traveling a great deal. One remarkable thing about her travels is that she journeyed alone, scorning the offers of well-meaning friends to accompany her on her speaking trips. She would not allow blindness to hinder her almost constant round of activity and refused to allow people to treat her like an invalid.

CHAPTER 12
THE QUEEN OF GOSPEL SONG

Any hopes Fanny may have been entertaining for collaborating with Philip Bliss were dashed forever shortly after Christmas of 1876. Bliss had a premonition of his approaching end, and at an evangelical meeting at Rome, N.Y., on December 28, he remarked to his audience, "I may not pass this way again," and sang the eerily prophetic "I'm Going Home To-Morrow."

Leaving their two little boys in Avon, New York, with relatives, Philip and Lucy Bliss boarded a Pacific Express train of the Lake Shore Railroad, which they hoped to take to Chicago, where they would join Moody, Sankey, and Whittle in an evangelical campaign. At eight o'clock that night a terrific snowstorm was in progress, and it was bitter cold as the eleven-car train crept out of the Ashtabula, Ohio, station. They were passing over an iron bridge that spanned a shallow creek when the structure collapsed, and in a second that seemed like hours to the 160 horrified passengers, the cars plummeted seventy feet and smashed into the creek bed, where, amid the crushed and splintered wreckage, the injured lay in all stages of mutilation among the dead and dying. Within five minutes, fire began to sweep the shattered ruins of the coaches, and panic broke loose among those trapped in the wreckage as well as those trying to free them. Those men who had escaped unhurt went back into the wreck to try to free their wives and children. Among these was Philip Bliss, who found that Lucy was caught fast in the ironwork of the wrecked seats. As the flames rapidly swept the shattered car, the other men urged Bliss to save his own life, since there was no way for him to rescue his wife. Bliss refused. "If I cannot save her, I will perish with her," he cried, and plunged into the flames.[1]

The death of Bliss "cast a cloud" over Fanny's spirit, as well as over those of all his other friends in New York. (His partner, Major Whittle, however, when he heard that his best friend had been burnt to cinders, gloried that Bliss had been "translated" like Enoch, the Old Testament patriarch who "walked with God, and was not.") Soon Fanny and her colleagues at Biglow and Main were involved in the project of editing Philip Bliss's last hymns, a venture jointly undertaken with John Church in Cincinnati. Many of Bliss's last hymns were incomplete poems which his partner, Whittle, was given the sad task to complete. The collection was published later that year under the title *Welcome Tidings*.

Fanny did not confine all her literary efforts to sacred songs. Her mother still lived, and Fanny wrote poems to celebrate her birthday and also to honor her sisters on their wedding anniversaries. She wrote poems for church and Sunday school anniversaries as well as for encampments of the Grand Army of the Republic. And she continued to write secular songs. The same year that she contributed to *Welcome Tidings*, she wrote words for Hugh Main's music to produce a love song called, "O When Are You Coming to Me Again?":

O when are you coming to me again?
I'm waiting with heart so true,
And wishfully chiding the long, long hours
That keep me away from you.
The cricket is chirping,
'Tis evening now,
The time that we love so well;
Then meet me alone, by the brook, mine own,
The brook in the leafy dell.[2]

Although she had grown increasingly religious over the past two decades, Fanny was still by no means averse to writing love lyrics.

Fanny was occupied not only with hymn writing but also with speaking engagements that often took her away from New York. Her talks, like her hymns, were simple, direct, and personal, and this quality of intimacy, combined with the love and joy that she came to radiate in middle life, made her a popular speaker. On some occasions, it has been reported that the lines wrapped around an entire city block as people hoped, often vainly, to get into the church or hall where she was speaking. Although most of her church talks were during afternoon and evening services, she occasionally took the pulpit to deliver the Sunday sermon in those Methodist churches which permitted women speakers and even ordained them as ministers.

Fanny would take the podium and greet her audience with her famous greeting, "God bless your dear hearts, I'm so happy to be with you!" Then, always holding a little book in her hands which many thought contained, in braille, the text of her address but which only served, she said, to give her security, she would say something similar to this:

My friends! I am shut out of the world, and shut in with my Lord! I have served Him as I could. As I have listened to the remarks made to-night [by the person who introduced her], I have thought, "Not unto me, O Lord, but unto Thee, be all the glory!" The Lord is the sunshine of my soul. I do not want to love for myself, but for Him. I remember my grandmother, as I knelt by her chair in which she rocked me to sleep and taught me to pray that if it was His will, to give me what I wanted, but if the Lord did not want me to have the things, it is best not to.

My friends! It is so good to be loved! Loved by God's own people! The memory of this meeting will never fade from my mind! When I go home and look into my Father's face and see the sunshine of His smile, my feelings will be like the tender affection and gratitude that glows in my heart now for you.[3]

Short, rambling, but sincere and inspiring—such was the character of her address. She almost always recited one or more of her poems, however, and sometimes she would compose one spontaneously for the occasion, and these were recited with great effect on the audience. She always closed with the Mizpah benediction: "May the Lord watch between me and thee, when we are absent, one from the other." There was a warmth, an aura of holiness that her presence radiated that cannot be captured in the transcribed word, something that transcended the brevity and simplicity of her remarks and was enough to incite people from all walks of life to stand all day in stifling heat or freezing cold to hear her. She spoke with tremendous effect, communicating her sense of joy to believers who were despondent, arousing the lukewarm to a greater sense of commitment, and inciting the agnostic or indifferent to make the decision to become a Christian. Sometimes there were several conversions when she spoke. Although she spoke to fewer people and received, partly through her own insistence, less publicity than some of her friends, in many ways Fanny Crosby was becoming one of the most effective evangelists of her day.

Though a very little woman, Fanny had seemingly boundless energy. She was never strong and always somewhat delicate, but on the other hand she was never seriously ill. Even in extreme old age, she would tire out people twenty and thirty years her junior. But even she needed a vacation at least once a year, and so in the summer of 1877 she attended the camp meeting at Ocean Grove, New Jersey. The Ocean Grove Camp Meeting Association of the Methodist Episcopal Church had come into being eight years earlier, when pastors from the New York, Philadelphia, and Trenton areas felt a need for a summer resort, but one "free from the fashion and folly"[4] and the lewd amusements and vulgarities that blighted most secular amusement parks. They wanted a resort where, along with recreation, they could also hold religious exercises. Accordingly, a tract of land was bought along the Jersey coast and a Methodist resort built where the faithful could come to swim, fish, and wander along the beach but also hear the Word of God proclaimed in three or more services that were to be offered each day. Preachers of all denominations spoke at the Ocean Grove retreat. In those days the vacationers rented tents which were often so small that one was obliged to enter on his hands and knees.

Fanny had heard of Ocean Grove but had never had the opportunity to go, for she never had the money to rent a tent. But in 1877 she was the "honored guest" of friends, probably the Knapps. Fanny made the two-hour trip by train, alone. As usual, she made friends on the train, and a kind passenger escorted her to her friends' tent. Fanny described this first trip to Ocean Grove in a long, enthusiastic poem. An anonymous preacher had once remarked, "If you want to hear such singing as you can hear nowhere else this side of heaven, then go to a live camp meeting at Ocean Grove. The singing alone is enough to sweep down the powers of hell!"[5] Fanny agreed with him, for she wrote:

That very night—the morrow—O, what joy!
    The very hills with gladness rang;
We felt that we had almost reached
    The "Beulah Land" of which we sang.
To see those cottages and tents
    Where praise ascended to the sky
Was bliss; ah, more—'twas heaven below;
    In such a scene how sweet to die![6]

She heard

    . . . the word of Life proclaimed,
We heard the deep and fervent prayer,
We heard the hearts so filled with love
    They scarce another drop could bear.[7]

The highlight of the camp meeting was the evening Surf Meeting. At sunset, the faithful trooped down to the beach, where they were led in a moving vesper service, and although she could see but a few faint hues of the sunset, Fanny was just as moved as her sighted friends.

It was here that Fanny made some important contacts. The song leader at Ocean Grove was John Robson Sweney. A stout, balding man with heavy-lidded eyes and a mustache and goatee, Sweney was already well known, both as a bandleader and a hymn writer. Born December 31, 1837, the same year as Moody, Sweney had studied vocal music and had been in charge of the band of the Delaware Regiment during the Civil War. His feet were frozen, and he suffered for the rest of his life from the effects of the injury. After the war he organized Sweney's Cornet Band in Philadelphia and taught music at the

Pennsylvania Music Academy. By 1877 he was a famous and popular bandleader, composer, and song leader. A Presbyterian, he led the singing for the Methodists at Ocean Grove and also in other evangelical camp meetings around the country. "Sweney knows how to make a congregation sing," was the remark most frequently made of him. He specialized in light, bouncy, rollicking tunes. His melodies were often composed of long strings of eighth notes. At the time, he was famed as the composer of the music to Edgar Page Stites's "Beulah Land," which Fanny mentioned in her poem. He also wrote a musical setting for Frances Ridley Havergal's touching poem "After." He had already published several hymnals, including *Gems of Praise,* which included "Blessed Assurance" and a few other poems by Fanny. But now he met her for the first time and was very interested in getting her to supply the words for more of his tunes.

So was William James Kirkpatrick, Sweney's friend and colleague. (So close a friend of Sweney's was he that when Sweney died, many years later, Kirkpatrick married his widow.) A jolly man, born in Duncannon, near Harrisburg, Pennsylvania, in 1838, he had extensive musical training in his youth including vocal music, the pipe organ, harmony, theory, and composition. Expert with the flute, violin, fife, and cello, as well as the organ, the "Professor," as he was called, was much better trained as a musician than many of his hymn-writing contemporaries. After a stint in the army, he moved to Philadelphia, where he became a successful furniture dealer, composing music on the side. He was, like Theodore F. Seward, especially interested in Negro spirituals and not only collected them but wrote them himself. A composer whose music possessed a "melodiousness that appeals to popular taste,"[8] Kirkpatrick, who was currently music director at the Grace Methodist Episcopal Church, had recently joined with Sweney to publish books of hymns for a Philadelphia firm. A devout Methodist since his conversion at the age of seventeen, he was a happy, vivacious, warm man who, having worked extensively with Negro spirituals, loved to imitate the Negro dialect. He wore a beard and mustache so dense as to totally obscure his mouth and lips and make the lower half of his face scarcely distinguishable from that of a fox terrier. He had absolutely no hair on top of his head, save for a thin fringe. He wore thick wire-rim spectacles. Fanny and he became especially good friends. Fanny, with her strong sense of humor, much enjoyed the company of "Kirkie," who would in the future have her frequently as a guest in his home in Germantown, while Fanny would supply Sweney and Kirkpatrick with nearly a thousand hymns for the books that they edited. It was also in this period that Fanny began to supply Ira Sankey with poems for his *Gospel Hymns,* which in the next decade would run to six volumes.

About this time, in New York, Fanny came to meet still another composer, a six-foot-tall, gaunt, ascetic-looking man with pince-nez spectacles and a neat goatee. Quiet, gentle, and restrained, George Coles Stebbins was of a quite different type from the gregarious Kirkpatrick. Born on a farm in Orleans County, New York, in February 1846, Stebbins had for many years been a music director in various churches, and despite the fact that as a musician he was largely self-taught, he acquired a considerable reputation as a choirmaster. He was serving as music director at Tremont Temple Baptist Church in Boston in 1876 when Moody called him to evangelistic work. Stebbins readily responded to Moody's call and was paired with a preacher with the auspiciously appropriate name of George Pentecost. Since that time, he had been a full-time evangelical song leader and soloist. Over the next few decades, Stebbins would set many of Fanny's poems to music. He did not always do a good job, however, for his style was frequently monotonous, awkward, and unmelodic. He rarely changed chords or harmony and often sacrificed the melodic line to the chords. He did, however, write some very appealing music, such as "There Is a Green Hill Far Away," "An Evening Prayer," "Out of My Bondage, Sorrow, and Night," and "I've Found a Friend, Oh, Such a Friend." His best work was done with poets other than Fanny Crosby. However, with her, although he produced much of mediocre quality, he did manage nevertheless to achieve success with some of her poems. "Jesus Is Calling," written in 1883, became moderately popular, and "Saved by Grace," written about a decade later, became enormously so. Stebbins also arranged as a duet a hymn Fanny had written in 1876 for Doane, "Though Your Sins Be As Scarlet." In its original form it had been overlooked, but after Stebbins rearranged it and sang it with his wife in evangelical meetings, it gained considerable popularity.

By this time, Fanny had created most of her most famous hymns. She had, in a period of nine years, written "Safe in the Arms of Jesus," "Blessed Assurance," "Pass Me Not, O Gentle Saviour," "Jesus, Keep Me Near the Cross," "I Am Thine, O Lord," "All the Way My Saviour Leads Me," "Close to Thee," "Praise Him! Praise Him!," "To God Be the Glory," "Every Day and Hour," and "Rescue the Perishing." These hymns comprise the overwhelming majority of her hits. In later years, with two or three possible exceptions, none of her hymns would equal in popularity those she wrote in the first decade of her career. Why was this? Had she written herself out? Most likely, yes. Fanny Crosby had said everything that she had to say, and almost everything she would produce in the future was simply a paraphrase of something that she had written earlier.

But Fanny was by no means washed up as a hymn writer. Even her paraphrases attained a moderate degree of popularity and often were superior to most of the lyrics of the majority of her contemporaries. Fanny was in ever-increasing demand by musicians for lyrics, and a large number of her later hymns became moderately popular, even if they did not equal some of her earlier works in their appeal. Two hymns, for instance, which Fanny wrote in the late 1870s and were published in Lowry and Doane's *Good as Gold* in 1880, were in this category. "Hide Thou Me," with music by Lowry, and "'Tis the Blessed Hour of Prayer," with a setting by Doane, were quite successful, even though they never ingrained themselves into the hearts of worshipers to the extent that "Safe in the Arms of Jesus," "Pass Me Not," "Blessed Assurance," and other hits of her earlier period did.

> In Thy cleft, O Rock of Ages,
>   Hide Thou me;
> When the fitful tempest rages,
>   Hide Thou me;
> Where no mortal arm can sever
> From my heart Thy love forever,
> Hide me, O Thou Rock of Ages,
>   Safe in Thee.[9]

The sentiments and ideas are of similar quality to those of many of her earlier successes, but the trouble is that they were to be found in hymns of hers that were already quite popular. "Hide Thou Me" is in many ways a recapitulation of much of what she said in "Safe in the Arms of Jesus."

That her current hymns were not, as a rule, attaining the popularity of some of her earlier ones did not trouble Fanny. She had the assurance that she was doing the Lord's work and felt certain that her hymns would be helpful to some people. If they were the means of leading just one person to Christ, she was content. But one thing that did bother her was that many of what she considered her best poems were not set to music. Frequently she complained that her musician friends ignored her best and set to music her worst lyrics. Unfortunately, few of these unused lyrics have survived. The ones that have were certainly too complicated to be adequately treated by the musicians who usually set her work to music. Such lyrics would not fit well with "music for the masses."

It was at this time that Fanny's friend by correspondence, Frances Havergal, died. Her name had become a household word in America through Sankey's *Gospel Hymns*, which published many of her works. In the spring of 1879, however, Miss Havergal fell gravely ill at her home in Casswell, Swansea, Wales, and died on June 3, 1879, calling, "Come, Lord Jesus! Come and fetch me. Oh, Run! Run!" Fanny was nearly sixty and had outlived both of those friends who, with her, had spearheaded the lyrical wing of the gospel hymn movement. Bliss, who was just as much a loss as a musician as he was as a poet, was dead at thirty-eight. And now Miss Havergal was dead at forty-two. Their premature deaths left Fanny unrivaled as the "queen of gospel hymn writers," as she was now known. There were many in her court, such as the

Rev. W. O. Cushing, Eben Rexford, John Clements, and, most outstandingly, Daniel W. Whittle and Eliza Edmunds Hewitt. But none of them equaled her in fame or esteem, and until her death Fanny Crosby was the patron saint of hymnody for evangelical Protestants.

Fanny regularly made trips north to Bridgeport, where her mother and sisters lived. On May 31, 1879, Mercy Morris completed her eightieth year, but she was still alert and vigorous and, indeed, looked scarcely older than her eldest daughter. She still had three of her four children, as well as William Morris, the stepson who had chosen to stay with her rather than accompany his father to the West. But Mercy had outlived most of her own generation. Her sister Theda had succumbed to a heart attack in 1876, leaving only the other sister, Polly, who had recently come to Bridgeport from Allentown, Pennsylvania.

Mercy still made her home with her daughter Carolyn, who, five years before, after the death of her first husband, had married an epileptic tin peddler named Joshua Leland Rider. Fanny's other sister, Julia, lived nearby, working as a dressmaker to support her disabled husband and his dropsical brother George, who lived with them. She and Byron had celebrated their twentieth anniversary a year before, but the last decade had been rough going. Byron was able to work as a shirt cutter only occasionally, and often he was not able to do anything. He was never able to return to the coach-lamp business which had seemed to offer his life so much promise before the war.

The stepbrother, William Morris, a shoemaker, still lived on Brook Island Avenue with his children, Laura Frances, Florence, and Albert. But he was in the last stages of tuberculosis. His oldest son, Walter, had already succumbed at twenty to the "white plague" in 1876, but the father would linger until November 7, 1880.

In contrast, Fanny at sixty was more active than most women or men at forty. She had only recently begun what became a second career, parallel to her hymn writing, as a home mission worker. She now spent several days a week in the missions of New York's Bowery district.

CHAPTER 13
RESCUING THE PERISHING

The plight of the thousands who lived in New York's tenements had long been a concern of many Christian people who were determined to do something to help the miserable inhabitants. For years, dedicated individuals had toiled to help the unfortunate masses in the morass of Manhattan's slums, but with little obvious effect. In the early 1880s, Fanny Crosby was living in a dismal flat at 9 Frankfort Street, on the Lower East Side. It was near, if not in, one of Manhattan's worst slums. Just a few blocks away stretched the notorious Bowery, which was then—and still is—one of America's most depressing places.

The Bowery was both a haunt for hopeless alcoholics and the main artery of a thriving commercial area, red light district, and pornographic center. Here were innumerable taverns, dance halls, and sordid shops where one could buy all manner of filthy pictures and literature. There were "concert halls" which specialized in the cheapest and most degrading burlesque shows and "dime museums" in which the curious could view the grossest indecencies. The streets swarmed with Italian organ grinders, harpers, and keepers of dancing bears. Bedraggled prostitutes strutted to and fro. Along the way one's horrified eyes could see human wrecks made that way by the Civil War—men without arms, legs, eyes, or noses, whose only livelihood was begging. Vendors sold hot corn on the cob and raw oysters sprinkled with pepper sauce. The peak of business was between ten and eleven at night, when, by the light of turpentine torches, the vendors did a great business among workingmen who were just getting off the job after a fourteen- or sixteen-hour day.

Indeed, the neighborhood was so terrible that people from better areas of the city would hire carriages and, taking a detective for a guide, ride through the area for some sordid sight-seeing. In this district, in the words of a social worker, "almost every door led to a dive or dance hall. Sounds of revelry, clinking glasses, curses, and fighting would issue forth until broad daylight."[1] The area was full of various "resorts" known as "The Fleabag," "The Hell Hole," or "The Billy Goat," which were haunted by "women so worn, raddled, and hideous that their appeal to men was inconceivable."[2] There was one place where admission was charged to see a man named Jack the Rat bite the head off a living rat.[3]

Christian workers had long toiled in this district with little results. The John Street Methodist Church, which was nearby, encouraged its laymen to work among the wretched in the Bowery district. However, they often met with frustration; for every man or woman who decided to go straight, there were fifty who daily seemed to sink into worse debauchery and degradation.

The 1870s had seen the establishment of home missions in which a full-time team of Christian workers ministered to the down and out. One of the first and most important was the Water Street Mission, located near the East River, almost under the shadow of the still-incomplete Brooklyn Bridge. This mission was founded by a remarkable man, Jeremiah McAuley, born in Kerry, Ireland, about 1839. Coming from a broken home, he was never given any education and remained practically illiterate until the day of his death. At fourteen, he was sent to live with relatives in New York City, where he quickly became a hoodlum and member of a street gang that robbed and terrorized passersby. At the age of nineteen he was convicted mistakenly of highway robbery and sentenced to fifteen years at Sing Sing Penitentiary. He had been there for five years before he could establish his innocence and obtain freedom. During his term in prison, however, he had been converted from nominal Roman Catholicism to fervent Methodism through the efforts of Orville "Awful" Gardner, the prizefighter who had been converted at the beginning of the revivals and who had devoted his life to working with prisoners. After discharge, without any Christian friends to give him moral support, Jeremiah, or Jerry, as everyone called him, once again slipped back into the life of a drifter and bum. After several attempts, however, he finally reformed, and from his late twenties he led a blameless life.

McAuley became a devoted member of the John Street Methodist Church. He also became rabidly anti-Catholic. Sensitive about the fact that the church had done nothing for him when he really needed it, he turned violently against his old religion. As a mission worker, he continued to excoriate the Roman Church until the day of his death. "I never read of the Mass or Confession in the Bible," he would say. "It is a most degrading thing to bow down before a fellow man to worship him!" Directing his remarks to the Roman clergy, he cried, "Your people are afraid of you! You will lie to benefit the Church, but God has said, 'All liars shall have their part in the lake that burns with fire and brimstone!' "[4]

Whatever his grudge against the Roman Church, McAuley was concerned very much about men who were caught in a plight similar to his former state. He therefore founded, in October 1872, the Water Street Mission. Ten years later, he opened the Cremorne-McAuley Mission on West 32nd Street, near what is now the Avenue of the Americas. In this mission, a three-story building with a chapel, a kitchen, and living quarters, the homeless and unemployed were fed and clothed. The men shared meals with Jerry and his wife, Maria, upstairs. Apart from the religious services, where McAuley or some outside speaker would urge the men to enter into a personal relationship with Christ, the guests were not prodded or coerced into religion. Some mission workers tried to make the men promise to become Christians even before giving them food or clothing, but not the McAuleys. It became a saying around their missions that "We hit our men with beefsteaks before we hit them with the Gospel."[5] The men were not questioned, nor were they scolded or reproved for their past life. Sam Hadley, who was to take over the mission after McAuley's death, said, "Our sovereign remedy is Divine Love."[6] The prison authorities came to know McAuley's work, and when a man had served his term at Sing Sing, he was usually advised, "You had better go down and see McAuley at the Water Street Mission." There, jobs were found and moral support was given.

After returning to New York from Maspeth, Long Island, Fanny Crosby gradually became involved in mission work. In the 1870s, she heard about McAuley and made frequent visits to the mission. She was much impressed with McAuley. "As a speaker, he used simple language, but his manner was so impressive that all men were drawn to him."[7] She also became acquainted with other rescue missions. In 1879 the Rev. Albert Rulifson had founded the Bowery Mission, which was located on Bowery Street, and in the early 1880s the hymn writer became a regular visitor there. She also frequently appeared at Mrs. E. M. Whittemore's Door of Hope, an establishment for "fallen women." These creatures were much more despised than male derelicts because, in Sam Hadley's words, women "are naturally higher than men, and they have to fall lower, and then sink into the depths of degradation in order to keep down, or their conscience would drive them to suicide."[8]

Fanny was not a passive spectator. Often she would be asked to give the address, and she would tell of the joy it gave to walk in the light of Christ and urge the men to come forward in token of their decision to give their lives to Christ. More often, however, she would simply go and sit in the audience, mingling among the men or women. Her conversational counseling was immensely successful. In an address to the First Methodist Church in Bridgeport many years later, she described her method:

During twenty-five years in mission-work, I have seen those of whom you would say, "Why, we cannot do anything." You don't know what you can do until you try. I have sat down by people who had no hope, and yet that Divine Principle of Love was brought to them, and they have wept tears.

Continuing, she told of an experience which was typical of her work in the rescue missions: "I remember once I met a man who came into the church and
134

sat down right in front of me. It was in the Bowery Mission. He sat down right in front of me, and the Holy Spirit prompted me to speak to him."9

"Are you fond of music?" she asked him.

"Yes."

"Wouldn't you like to stay to our evening services?"

"No."

"Well," said Fanny, "will you allow me to come and sit down by you and talk to you?"

"Yes, I would like to have you."

So Fanny slid out of her chair and sat down beside the rough, bedraggled man. They talked for a long time on various subjects related to the man's interests. Finally, Fanny turned the conversation to religion by saying, "Do you know what are the sweetest words in our language or any other?"

"Why, no! I don't know that I do. Will you tell me what they are?"

"Yes, the sweetest words in our language or any other are mother, home, and heaven."

That started the man to thinking. He was quiet for a while, lost in thought. Then he said, "My mother was a Christian," and was silent again.

Fanny knew then that her comments had touched him. The service began, and Pastor Rulifson preached on "Mother's Influence." (Apparently Fanny knew the topic beforehand and had planned her conversation with the man accordingly.) After the service, she said to her newly made friend, "Now, when the invitation is given to go to the altar, will you go?" At no time had she "proselytized" him, lecturing him on the Christian religion or the eternal consequences of not making a decision to follow Christ.

After she asked him to go to the altar, the man hesitated for a moment. "Will you go with me?"

"Yes," she replied. "I will go with you."

So she took his arm and together they walked to the altar, where "he was hopefully converted. He had yielded to the Holy Spirit, yielded to his better feeling, and given himself to God."10

Her approach was similar when she delivered the address. On one occasion at the Bowery Mission, she closed her remarks with "If there is a man present who has gone as far as he can go, he is the person with whom I want to shake hands."

Sure enough, a man appeared. Fanny asked him, when the meeting was over, whether he did not wish "to come out and live a Christian life."

"Aw! What's the difference?" asked the man. "I ain't got no friends. Nobody cares for me."

"You're mistaken!" replied Fanny. "For the Lord Jesus cares for you—and others care too! Unless I had a deep interest in your soul's welfare, I certainly would not be here talking with you on this subject." She gave him several passages of scripture. The man seemed to be interested and said that he

135

would come the next evening and sign the pledge not to use alcohol. Would she come with him?

"Yes," she said. "I will be here again tomorrow. But although I don't want to discourage you for signing the pledge, it seems to me that the best pledge you can give is to yield yourself to God."

The man reappeared the next evening, "and, before the close of the meeting, we saw the new light in his eyes and felt the change in his voice."[11]

After she was sixty, Fanny considered her chief occupation that of a home mission worker.[12] In many ways, hymn writing was but an extension of her mission work, and many of her hymns were written expressly for use in missions. This explains the fact that a large percentage of her hymns either urge one to make a decision, describe the joys of a relationship with Jesus, or offer the broken and downcast the hope of a better world. Of her mission work, she said, "It is the most wonderful work in the world, and it gives such an opportunity for love. That is all people want—love."[13] Indeed, love was the hallmark of her work, and the way she went about it was evidence of this. She never served in any official or employed capacity and gave her time freely, without asking for a cent of remuneration.

"Don't tell a man he is a sinner," she always insisted. "You can't save a man by telling him of his sins. He knows them already. Tell him there is pardon and love waiting for him. Win his confidence and make him understand that you believe in him, and never give him up!"[14] Those were her guidelines for mission. She wrote:

> I could give more than one instance where men have been reclaimed, after a long struggle and many attempts at reformation, because someone spoke a kind word to them, even at what appeared to be the last moment. I have also known many others who turned away from a meeting simply because the cheering word had not been spoken, nor the helping hand extended. Never to chide the erring has been my policy, for I firmly believe that harsh words only serve to harden hearts that might otherwise be softened into repentance.[15]

She did not believe in pointing out people's faults to them. "Kindness in this world," she said, "will do much to help others, not only to come into the light, but to grow in grace, day by day. There are many timid souls whom we jostle morning and evening, as we pass them by. But if only a kind word were spoken, they might become fully persuaded [to become Christians]."[16]

Fanny was diligent not to hurt anyone's feelings in her mission work. All the men with whom she worked were "my boys." Of the trainmen with whom she worked closely through the YMCA for many years, she said, "They are all my boys! And I love them all!" Of the men with whom she worked at the Bowery and Water Street missions, most of whom reeked of alcohol and tobacco, swarmed with vermin, and had gone for weeks without a bath, she said, "Not one of them was ever ugly to me."[17] Like her friend Father Mathew, of the Capuchin Order, she felt, "If they are bad, then, poor souls, they need help all the more." In mission work and in her evangelism, public and private, Fanny Crosby believed that "Love counts more than anything else. It is wonderful!"[18]

The Bowery Mission, which was sponsored by the periodical *The Christian Herald*, was Fanny's pet mission, and she spent more time there than in any other. She was the speaker on sixteen occasions for the annual anniversary service, when all those converted and rehabilitated by its ministry appeared as guests of honor. Besides frequently working with the McAuleys at the Water Street and Cremorne missions and with Mrs. Whittemore at the Door of Hope, she was also active in the Railroad Branch of the YMCA. Significantly, it was through a kind word that she spoke one day that her work was begun there.

In 1880, Fanny was entering a surface car when she happened to step on the conductor's foot. "Oh, conductor," she cried, "I know that I have hurt you, but I did not intend to. Will you please forgive me?"

The conductor, accustomed to having people step on his feet without a second thought about it, was deeply moved, especially so when he realized that she was blind and really had a valid excuse. "Lady, you didn't hurt me at all. And if you had, you made it up by speaking a kind word."

Fanny was struck by the impression a simple word of kindness had made on this streetcar conductor, and the incident was still on her mind when, a few weeks later, she was invited to the home of her friend William Rock, who was president of the New York Surface Car Line.

A pious man, Rock was concerned about his employees. These men had a hard lot, working seven days a week, and, given the nature of their jobs, they received few kind words and little fellowship but much abuse from irate and testy riders. Because of the work and the wages, the Surface Line employees tended to be a gruff, surly lot. Rock, however, felt that some provision should be made for their spiritual welfare and consulted Fanny. Accordingly, "it was agreed that the room where they waited for the trolleys be fixed up, each Sunday morning a service lasting one hour be conducted in the interest of the conductors and drivers." Rock asked Fanny to conduct the services, and she gladly consented. So, in a "dingy little room made cheerful with a bit of red carpet and a few flowers and plants," she began the mission with her "railroad boys."[19] Here, as always, her sermons were of love and consolation.

Fanny's work with the streetcar conductors and bus drivers made a great impression in New York. The following year, a delegation called on her from the newly formed Railroad Branch of the YMCA, centered across the Hudson at Hoboken, New Jersey. They asked her to become a regular lecturer for their organization, and for the rest of her active life she undertook speaking tours in which she addressed men in YMCAs all over the East Coast. She was just as dedicated to the railroad men as she was to the Bowery bums. They too were "my boys," and over the years, she "adopted" six hundred of them.

Fanny was also active in Temperance work. She felt strongly that half the battle for the soul of the down-and-out man was won if a way could be found to stop him from drinking. She had seen what a curse the regular consumption of beer, wine, and whiskey was from living in the tenements of Lower Manhattan, where so many of the residents were constantly drunk. She had seen alcoholism in all its horrors at the missions on Water Street and on the Bowery. And she had experienced its effects in working with the railroad men and streetcar conductors. She knew how it led to disastrous marital problems and broken homes. Because of what she had witnessed, Fanny was totally against the use of alcohol. Perhaps there was nothing wrong with it in itself, and perhaps certain people could use it in moderation, but she felt so many people could not that it was a far better thing to practice and encourage total abstinence. Her solution to the problem of alcoholism was the temperance pledge. If one never used liquor, there was no danger of becoming a slave to it. The good that beer, whiskey, and wine might do in the way of nourishment and pleasure could be obtained just as well by the consumption of nonintoxicating beverages, and the evils connected with John Barleycorn were so strong as to outweigh by tenfold any good purpose it might serve. So, to Fanny, alcohol—all kinds and every form—was a curse. She never used it, and she heartily discouraged others from doing so. She never identified abstinence with Christian faith, or equated signing the pledge with a religious commitment. She did believe, however, that total abstinence in the use of alcoholic beverages was a goal which any intelligent Christian should aim for—not merely for himself, but for others. For even if a given individual could drink in moderation, his example would be detrimental to those about him who could not. Therefore, for the sake of the potential alcoholic, she felt it was a good thing for even the man who could drink temperately to abstain.

Fanny was not alone in this sentiment. Moody felt the same way, as did most of the religious leaders of that day. As we have seen in the case of Theobald Mathew, temperance, in the form of total abstinence, had long been popular in the Roman Catholic Church. But, among those who worked in the missions, those who had seen the full effects of alcoholism, this feeling was especially strong. Jerry McAuley and his associate, Sam Hadley, were both recovered alcoholics, and they were "dead against" all liquid intoxicants. There was much concern for alcoholics and alcoholism in those days, and there was much obsession with the fact that the first drink often brings addiction. Lydia Sigourney had years before written a heartrending poem, "Only This Once," which tells how a young man decides to try liquor for the first time and becomes hooked on the first drink. Young people should be encouraged never to take that first sip. Sam Hadley liked to tell the story of Little Mamie, who is sent to the tavern to get some beer for her mother and who for curiosity's sake begins to "sip the deadly stuff," immediately gets hooked, and ends up committing suicide. Biglow and Main published many temperance hymns in those years, including an entire temperance hymnal, *The Tidal Wave,* with songs by Fanny Crosby, Annie Hawks, Josephine Pollard, Robert Lowry, and others.

Temperance, then, was but one of the many causes to which Fanny gave herself in the sixth decade of her life. But all her activities were inextricably linked to the hymn writing by which she sang her faith and her ideas into the hearts of thousands.

CHAPTER 14
"THE VALLEY OF SILENCE"

Fanny wrote most of her hymns after midnight; only then did she have the absolute silence required for perfect concentration. The constant shuffle of feet on the rickety wooden floors, the strident babble of several languages piercing the insubstantial walls, and the shouts, curses, and imprecations of drunken and quarreling tenants absolutely precluded any mental work. Since Fanny was never much of a sleeper, the lateness of the hour did not bother her. Also, it was really the only time that she had to work on hymns. Her entire days and evenings were occupied either at Biglow and Main, in social work, or, increasingly now, in public appearances.

Fanny Crosby's hymn writing was inextricably connected with her mysticism. When the noises of the tenement had died away and she sat alone, Fanny entered into prayer and arrived at a meditative state that she often referred to as "The Valley of Silence." Here she believed she entered into direct communion with the spiritual world, often feeling her soul sallying forth from her body in mystic and ethereal reverie. In the rapture and ecstasy of "Deep Meditation," as she called it, Fanny often felt she could hear the unearthly harmonies of "the Celestial Choirs." In this state she claimed she felt the presence, not only of Christ and his saints and angels but also of her relatives and friends who had "passed beyond the silent vale." In meditation, she often received inspiration to write her hymns. As she wrote in a poem toward the end of her life:

> In the hush of the Valley of Silence,
> I dream all the songs that I sing,
> And the music floats down the dim valley
> Till each finds a word for a wing,
> That, to men, like the dove of the Deluge,
> The message of peace they may bring.[1]

Sometimes, however, her soul was flooded with inspiration so powerful that she could not "find words beautiful enough, or thoughts deep enough, for expression."[2] Much of her mystical experience could not be captured by language:

... far on the deep, there are billows
That never shall break on the beach;
And I have heard wings in the silence
That never shall float into speech;
I have dreamed dreams in the Valley
Too lofty for language to reach.[3]

These songs for which she could find no words, she could sing only in spirit.

While it was in the Valley of Silence that many of her hymns did "find a word for a wing," many of them received initial inspiration from events in the material world. Fanny was frequently given a topic on which to write a hymn by one of her musician friends, such as "The Morning Land," "The Blessed Feast," or "Trust in the Promise." Fanny would keep these subjects in mind as she went about her affairs, sometimes for days, weeks, or months, until something happened to interest her in writing about it. For instance, the death of a friend might lead to a hymn such as "The Morning Land." Something that went on at the missions might draw her to the subject "The Blessed Feast." We have seen how the dramatic conversion of a young boy after a talk she had given led her to write "Rescue the Perishing."

One day in 1874, Fanny was at a loss as to how she would pay her rent so she decided to pray for it. Just then a man appeared whom she had never met, who left at once after pressing a ten-dollar bill into her hand—the exact amount needed to pay the rent. This inspired her to write a hymn on a topic Lowry had given her: "All the Way My Saviour Leads Me." That night, the words flowed into her head:

All the way my Saviour leads me;
What have I to ask beside?
Can I doubt His tender mercy
Who through life has been my guide?

Fanny did not necessarily have to be given a theme in advance. A chance remark or an event could also serve as inspiration. Fanny was staying with the Doanes in Cincinnati when a twilight talk had led her to write, "I Am Thine, O Lord." Ira Sankey once told Fanny about a miner who had come forward in one of the campaigns in England. He begged to be prayed for. For some reason, the leader of the inquiry meeting which followed the regular meeting suggested that the miner come again the next night. Perhaps it was getting late, and the leader wanted to get home. But the miner cried piteously, "No! It must be settled tonight! Tomorrow may be too late!" Moved by his importunity, the leader gave in to his request. He was prayed over and left the meeting "saved." The next day there was an explosion in the mine where he worked, and he was one of those who perished. The story moved Fanny so much that she composed a hymn the day she heard about the incident called "Shall I Be Saved To-Night?"[4]

On another occasion, Fanny was the guest of William and Sara Kirkpatrick at their home in Germantown, Pennsylvania. Along with some other guests, they were discussing the transitory nature of earthly life. "How soon we grow weary of earthly pleasures, however bright they may be," mused Fanny.

"Well," said the Professor, "we are . . . never weary of the grand old song!"

Immediately, Fanny seized upon the rhythm of the words as ideal for a hymn and startled everybody by suddenly crying, "But what comes next?" Her host paused, somewhat confused. "Why, glory to God, Hallelujah!" continued Fanny. She insisted that Kirkie seat himself at the piano, to compose an appropriate tune to the words she dictated on the spot:

We are never, never weary of the grand old song,
Glory to God, hallelujah!
We can sing it in the Spirit as we march along,
Glory to God, hallelujah![5]

Another time Fanny was talking to one of her neighbors, who complained bitterly of his poverty. "If I had wealth I would be able to do just what I wish to do; and I would be able to make an appearance in the world."

Fanny replied, "Well, take the world, but give me Jesus." She was here inspired by her own words to write a hymn with that title.[6]

Still another hymn was born when Fanny was visiting a dying friend who was in excruciating pain but remarked, "It's all right. It's only a little way on to my home."[7] This inspired Fanny to write:

'Tis only a little way on to my home,
And there in its sunshine forever I'll roam;
While all the day long, I journey with song,
O Beautiful Eden-land, thou art my home.[8]

Kirkie was leaving Fanny's flat one day after an all too brief visit. "Oh, dear, it's nothing but meeting and parting in this world, isn't it?" she remarked.

The jovial Professor replied, "Well, I will not say, as Bliss did, 'Meet me at the fountain,' but I *will* say, 'Where the tree of life is blooming, meet me there.'" This inspired Fanny to write a hymn entitled "Meet Me There," for which Kirkpatrick supplied the music.[9]

One day, somewhat later than the period we are now discussing, shortly after Fanny's mother had died, the poet had a vision of her departed parent in which Mercy spoke to her from "beyond the river." That night, Fanny was moved to compose:

142

Over the river they call me,
Friends that are dear to my heart,
Soon I shall meet them in glory,
Never, no never to part.[10]

In the year 1874, Fanny was undergoing a spell of deep depression. One day she cried out to God, "Dear Lord, hold my hand!" The result was that "almost at once, the sweet peace that comes of perfect assurance returned to my heart, and my gratitude for the evidence of answered prayer sang itself into the lines of the hymn":

Hold Thou my hand, so weak am I and helpless
I dare not take one step without Thy aid;
Hold Thou my hand, for then, oh, loving Saviour,
No dread of ill shall make my soul afraid.[11]

Sometimes, as we have seen in the case of "Blessed Assurance," "Safe in the Arms of Jesus," and others, a composer would play a tune and ask her to write words to it. Fanny would listen, and if the tune "said something," she could write a hymn. It was very important, however, what the tune "said." After she listened to it once or twice, she might tell the composer, "No, I cannot write any words for this. This tune does not *say* anything."[12]

No one should have the impression that Fanny felt actual inspiration for every hymn she composed. She might have desired this, but Biglow and Main required her to write on many topics which did not inspire her at all. She was expected to supply a certain quota of hymns whether she felt like writing or not, although she confessed that "there are some days, or at least hours, when I could not compose a hymn if all the world were laid at my feet as a promised recompense."[13]

In order to meet a deadline or fulfill a commitment, Fanny often had to force herself to write anyway. "Give me a New Year's hymn," Doane might demand on December 30. "Fan, I'd like you to compose twenty selections for my Easter collection," Hugh Main might have said, "and I'd like them in two weeks." "I'd like three invitational hymns for my services," Jerry McAuley might have asked of her. Since Fanny seldom refused, in such instances, she would have to "build a mood—or try to draw one around me."[14]

Hymn writing was difficult if she had no inspiration. She would "pray to God to give me the thoughts and feelings wherewith to write my hymn." Then, "after a time—perhaps not unmingled with struggle—the ideas . . . come."[15] Indeed, most of the hymns that she wrote—perhaps the vast majority—were not those for which she was inspired or which came out of a mystical experience, but rather those which she had to force herself to write. These too were usually written at night, perhaps after those for which she had really been inspired.

143

When she was writing hymns, Fanny had the peculiar habit of holding a little book upside down in front of her face, just as she carried such a book whenever she spoke in public. This was a ritual, apparently like that of a baseball pitcher who will not shave the day he pitches, or the prima donna who will not go onstage unless she kisses her mother's picture. For Fanny, it was a superstitious habit similar to her practice of always carrying a miniature silk American flag. Holding the book upside down before eyes so clouded that "were all the letters suns" she could not read them, served no practical purpose, but, she said, "words seem to come more promptly when the little volume is in my grasp."[16] The contents of the little book seemed to be of less importance to her than the size and shape. Often she used a Bible, a prayerbook, a psaltery, or even a completely secular book. She liked a book small enough so that her long, slender fingers could easily fit around it.

When she was trying to compose a hymn for which she was not inspired, she prayed, and when she was "sure that I am in condition to reach the minds and hearts of my constituency and sing them something worthy for them to hear," she "cast about, for a few minutes, as to the measure, and possibly, the tune."[17] She often took a popular tune, such as "Sweet Hour of Prayer" or "Stand Up, Stand Up for Jesus," and used it as the model on which to construct her verses. It was very important that the verses be singable. "Much more depends on matching the verses with some tune than might at first be the case," she said. A hymn had to be constructed in such a way as to provide it with maximum singability. How she constructed the meter and placed the accents was very important. "For if there is a false accent or a mistake in metre, the hymn cannot stand much chance of proving a success; or, at least, its possibilities are very much lessened. Among the millions of hymns that have been sung and forgotten, many, no doubt, contain deep and pious thought and feeling, but have been crippled or killed by the roughness of some line, or the irregularity of one or more measures."[18]

If no tune were already provided, or if she did not think of one already existing on which to hang the words, she had to be careful to construct her verses "in such a manner that the composer of the music may readily grasp the spirit of the poem and compose notes that will perfect the expression of the poet's meaning."[19] This was a problem, for, as we have seen, many of the men who set her words to music were amateurs and were not able to set just any poem to music—at least in such a way as to express the thought adequately. There was no problem of this sort when a tune was provided, as Fanny was a master versifier and had no trouble composing verses for suitable tunes, so she preferred to have a tune rather than a topic. In that way, she could be sure of a successful hymn. If the tune was good, she could write a good poem; if it was bad, she could reject it. But if she were given a topic or thought and wrote a good poem, she could not be sure that it would be given a good tune.

144

When a hymn came from divine inspiration, the poem came to Fanny as a whole, and quite rapidly. Otherwise, it came slower, but still comparatively quickly. Her hymns often came by stanzas and, in many instances, verse by verse. When she was not inspired, Fanny often had to labor for hours in order to get a satisfactory poem. With the poem "The Bright Forever," she labored two days without being able to get up a single line. Then, suddenly, as if by magic, "almost in a twinkling, the words came, stanza by stanza, as fast as I could memorize them."[20] Usually, however, she completed the first draft of a hymn in a single night, often after two or three hours. After she finished the first draft, if she had the time, Fanny "let it lie for a few days in the writing-desk of my mind, so to speak, until I have the leisure to prune it, to read through it with the eyes of my memory, and, in other ways, mould it into as presentable shape as possible."[21] Within a few days, therefore, after Fanny first set to work, her complete poem was ready. But she did not always have the time to prune and revise as she was often under great pressure from publishers to provide a certain amount of poems within a short time. For some reason, she thought that she had to compose two or three poems for every topic or tune, and this made the pressure greater. So, the large majority of Fanny's nine thousand hymns were written in great haste and, as the hymnologist John Julian characterized them, they were rather "weak and poor." However, on those rare occasions when Fanny was inspired and had the leisure to take her time, the hymns were often of excellent quality.

During these years of major writing, Fanny dictated her lines to a secretary. Hugh Main described her very unusual methods of work: "She has her hymns written down for her and will dictate to 2 persons at once, or 2 lines of one poem to one person, and 2 lines of another hymn to another person and never forgets herself."[22]

Many people marveled at Fanny's wonderful memory. People were dumbfounded at her ability to commit a seemingly limitless number of hymns to memory and dictate them without any apparent difficulty, one right after another. But whenever people made a great deal of this apparent "talent," Fanny would give them a lecture, maintaining that she was simply using a gift—memory—which God gives to everyone, but which most people who have eyes lose through laziness. She would excoriate "memorandum-tablets and carefully-kept journals and ledgers" as destructive to "the books of the mind." These memory books were "just as real and tangible as those of the desk and library-shelves—if only we will use them enough to keep their binding flexible, and their pages free from dust." She would usually conclude the little harangue with the warning, "Do not let go to decay and ruin those vast interior regions of thought and feeling, good brother or sister! Your memory would be much to you if you were ever deprived of some of the organs of sense that so distract you from deep and continued thought."[23]

For each hymn Fanny was paid a dollar or two by Biglow and Main and most other publishing houses. No matter how successful the hymn might turn out to be, she would get nothing more. The words were the exclusive property of the composer and no one else could set them to music. George Stebbins once wanted to write a more appealing tune to one of Fanny's hymns which had been set to music (of sorts) by Howard Doane, but Ira Sankey had to inform him that Hugh Main asserted that the words belonged to Doane and could not be used for other tunes. In most instances even the composer made comparatively little money from the hymn; it was the publishing company that received most of the profits. Through the years many people felt that Fanny was being exploited and she was urged to at least insist on being paid a higher price for her services, but she demurred, saying she felt that in writing hymns she was doing a favor for her friends. More important, she was doing God's work, and her recompense was the number of souls that were being led to God through the hymns.

CHAPTER 15
TO WIN A MILLION MEN

If there had been a rating for popular songs in the last two decades of the nineteenth century, several of Fanny's hymns would certainly have been in the Top Ten. For nearly a decade "Safe in the Arms of Jesus" had been a universal favorite and within another twenty years it would be translated into more than two hundred languages and sung the world over. "Blessed Assurance" also had attained immense popularity. Ira Sankey testified that it was "one of the most popular and useful"[1] of all the hymns that he and Moody used in their campaigns.

The number-one hit of their meetings was "Pass Me Not, O Gentle Saviour," of which Sankey wrote, "No other hymn in our collection was more popular than this at our meetings in London in 1874. It was sung every day at Her Majesty's Theatre in Pall Mall." It also was translated into several languages.[2] After the return of the evangelists to the states, "Pass Me Not" continued to be the most popular hymn of the campaigns. Dr. E. I. Dakin, a prominent New York Baptist clergyman, claimed of the hymn that it was "credited with bringing more people to Christ than any other hymn."[3] "Rescue the Perishing" and "Jesus, Keep Me Near the Cross," as well as "I Am Thine, O Lord" and "All the Way My Saviour Leads Me" were likewise tremendous hits.

The hymns were popular not only in religious circles but in secular ones as well, and they became just as popular as "Silver Threads Among the Gold," "When You and I Were Young, Maggie," and "In the Good Old Summer-Time." It was perhaps through their universal appeal that by her sixth decade Fanny was beginning to realize her ambition of winning a million men to Christ through the agency of hymns. Reports abounded of how people previously indifferent to religion were moved to the point of conversion by her simple but earnest lyrics.

Fanny was eager to hear of news of conversions wrought through her hymns, not for the sake of pride in achievement but because she felt that it was evidence of the workings of God. "God has given me a wonderful work to do," she said, "a work that has brought me untold blessing and great joy. When word is brought to me, as it is from time to time, of some wandering soul being brought home through one of my hymns, my heart thrills with joy, and I give thanks to God for giving me a share in the glorious work of saving human souls."[4] Fanny's hymns served not only to convert the indifferent and unbelieving but also were said to have been a great comfort and consolation to those who already believed. "You have been the means of cheering tens of thousands trudging along the highways of life," Ira Sankey once wrote her.[5] We have many examples of how Fanny's hymns affected various individuals, and through these "stories of the hymns" one can see clearly how they touched people's hearts and consciousness.

Sankey said "Safe in the Arms of Jesus" was a song by which so many "weary travelers . . . having reached the end of their earthly pilgrimage, have fallen sweetly to rest." This hymn was famous not only for the conversions it precipitated but for the comfort it gave to the dying and bereaved. The Rev. Dr. John Hall (1829–1898), for years the pastor of New York's Fifth Avenue Presbyterian Church, remarked that in his experience it gave more "peace and satisfaction to mothers who have lost their children than any other hymn I have ever known."[6] He also knew it to give consolation to the dying. He was fond of telling how a dying child once bade him sing the song to her.

One day a woman came up to Fanny after church and cried, "Oh, thank God I found you. I have prayed that I might see you before I die. 'Safe in the Arms of Jesus' was the last thing my mother said before she went home!"[7] A similar account was given to Ira Sankey when he and Moody were holding a series of meetings in Glasgow, Scotland, in 1885. At the end of the meeting, Sankey was accosted by an ancient crone who related, in graphic detail, the lingering death of a spinster daughter who had been converted in the evangelist's first campaign some ten years earlier. "Maggie" had asked her mother to open her hymnbook to her favorite hymn, "Safe in the Arms of Jesus," saying that she wanted to sing the song once more before she died. Although to all appearances she was too weak to sing, she managed to get through the first stanza before being overcome with exhaustion. She died a few minutes later, crying, "Jesus, I am coming!" The old woman told Sankey to thank Fanny Crosby for having written the hymn: "When ye gang back to America, gie her mie love and tell her an auld Scotswoman sends her blessing."[8]

Another story about "Safe in the Arms of Jesus" and how it brought solace to travelers near the end of their earthly pilgrimage concerns a little English girl named Mary. She was only six, but she loved that plaintive hymn and was continually singing it. One day she sang it to her father, looking so wistful and pensive that he asked her, "What are you thinking of, darling?"

"I want to go and be with Jesus."

The father was startled. "But what shall I do without you? You are my only little girl!"

148

"Very well, then, I won't go just yet, though I would like to."

But not long afterward, she suddenly became ill with a disease "of a most malignant type." Just before she lost consciousness, she told her brother, "Look here, Willie, I can find my own hymn myself now, 'Safe in the Arms of Jesus.'" She showed the hymn to Willie, and asked if they should sing it. Willie agreed, but poor little Mary found that she had not the strength to sing anymore. "No, I can't sing with my head this way."[9]

"Safe in the Arms of Jesus," though it was famous for the frequency with which it was muttered by dying tongues, also led to conversions and gave great consolation to many in time of personal crisis. An eminent pastor in Richmond, Virginia, attributed his conversion to hearing it. Countess Schimmelmann, who was imprisoned for her religious faith, claimed that the only thing that kept her going in solitary confinement was the hymn "Safe in the Arms of Jesus," which she sang over and over in German.

"Blessed Assurance" also had great effect. There is a story about a teenage boy who was afflicted with an incurable malady and was confined in a hospital. He was said to have converted fourteen fellow patients by his singing of "Blessed Assurance." Eventually, he was sent home to die. As the last moment approached, he sang fervently, "Safe in the Arms of Jesus." Just as his soul was departing, he cried out, "Ma, I hear the voice of angels! Ma, there are the fields of glory! Ma, there is the jasper sea!"

"Rescue the Perishing" led to many conversions, and, although it is directed toward Christians rather than to Christ and is intended to stir them up toward the winning of unconverted souls, it acted as a missionary in many instances. Its very words, apart from any human agency, seemingly led to conversions. An alcoholic, altogether down and out, aimlessly wandering the Bowery's streets, passed the Water Street Mission one day and heard the worshipers singing "Rescue the Perishing, Care for the Dying." He was first attracted to the lilting, forceful tune and went inside to hear it better. When the hymn was over, he "broke down in contrition."

"I was ready to perish, Mrs. Crosby," he later told Fanny, "but that hymn— that hymn, by the grace of God, that hymn saved me!" When he gave that testimony in a public meeting, the audience burst into tears![10]

A New York doctor who had become addicted to the bottle was stumbling along the Bowery when he heard a chorus of women singing "Rescue the Perishing." Presently he saw that they were marching in procession, and who should be leading and singing the very loudest but his own mother! More than that, he was affected by the words of the song and was so moved by them— and also, undoubtedly, by his mother's concern—that he was converted.

An Englishman wrote to Sankey, attributing "my conversion, through the grace of God, to one verse of that precious hymn, 'Rescue the Perishing.'" He told the singer that "I was very far from my Saviour, and living without a hope in Jesus. Yet I was very fond of singing hymns, and one day I came across this beautiful piece." When he had sung the words

Touched by a loving heart,
Wakened by kindness,
Chords that were broken will vibrate once more,

"I fell upon my knees and gave my heart to the Lord Jesus Christ. From that hour I have followed Him, Who, through this verse, touched my heart and made it vibrate with His praises ever since!"[11]

One evening at the Bowery Mission, a drunken man staggered in, "intoxicated, his face unwashed and unshaven, and his clothes soiled and torn." The hymn "Rescue the Perishing" was being sung and made a great impression on the poor wretch. Then the speaker referred in the course of his sermon to certain experiences he had during the Civil War, and mentioned the name of the company with which he served. After the service, the drunkard, agitated, reeled up to the speaker and sputtered, "Do you remember the name of the captain of your company at that time?" The speaker said he did and quoted the name. "You are right," said the bum, emotionally. "I am that man! I was your captain! Now, look at me to-day and see what a wreck I am! I have lost everything in the world that I had—through drink—and I don't know where to go! Can you save your old captain?" The drunken veteran was converted that evening and afterward became a devoted mission worker. He gave many a lecture telling about his conversion experience and attributing his change of heart to the hymn "Rescue the Perishing."[12]

"Pass Me Not" was likewise said to have led to many conversions. A prominent Englishman who wished to remain anonymous confessed to Sankey that he found salvation through the words of that hymn. Sankey wrote of him that "he had been very much opposed to our meetings, and his opposition was not lessened when he saw his wife converted." However, on the last day of the meetings, he agreed to attend with her as "a sort of concession," and that very afternoon the Englishman was so moved by the words of "Pass Me Not" that he felt "touched by the Spirit of God." He afterward became a devoted worker—as a result of the hymn, he said, and not, evidently, because of his wife's power of persuasion![13] A prominent New Jersey businessman told Fanny that he had been converted by the words of "Pass Me Not" and was still so fond of the hymn that he kept a copy of it with him wherever he went. There is also a story of a tugboatman who was converted by hearing that same hymn sung at a chapel onshore. Right on the tug, he called out, "Lord, do not pass me by!"

Many persons also were moved by some of Fanny's lesser-known works. In the early 1870s, Fanny was with Howard Doane on a trolley when the inspiration suddenly came. Right then she wrote a hymn beginning:

Jesus, I love Thee, Thou art to me
Dearer than ever mortal can be;
Jesus, I love Thee, Saviour Divine,
Earth has no friendship constant as Thine;
Thou wilt forgive me when I am wrong,
Thou art my comfort, Thou art my song!
Jesus, I love Thee, yes, Thou art mine.
Living or dying, still I am Thine![14]

Doane was moved and set the words to music that evening. The hymn was among those published in *Royal Diadem* in 1873 and became moderately popular. Moody and Sankey also used it during their campaigns in Britain. A British Methodist pastor used it as an invitational hymn during an evening service several years later. Between verses of the hymn, he urged "all those who really loved Jesus" to rise during the singing and remain standing. After each succeeding verse, he pleaded again. Finally, after the last verse, he said, "Now, if there is anyone here who is not a Christian and feels·they ought to be, if there is anybody who wants Jesus to love them—I want those people to stand." A visitor arose and "surrendered herself fully to the Lord." She became one of the most devoted and faithful members that congregation had ever known. She always felt that it was the words to Fanny Crosby's hymn that had first enlightened her soul, and she wanted others to know and share the joy that she felt in Jesus Christ. She was such an energetic and effective witness that before her death a year later she had led twenty-four persons to make a personal commitment to Christ and join the church. On her deathbed she asked her pastor to thank Fanny Crosby for writing the hymn.[15]

Another hymn of moderate popularity, "Only a Step to Jesus," was responsible for another conversion, this time in the southern United States. It seems that there was a country squire who, though completely indifferent in matters of faith, loved to listen to hymns. One night this squire happened to be in town and decided that, before he went home, he would stop by the local church, where a prayer meeting was in progress, and take in a couple of those beautiful hymns. He heard just one, "Only a Step to Jesus." It moved him so greatly that he could not put it from his mind. The words of the song repeated themselves over and over in his head. He dreamed about them that night and they were in his consciousness when he awoke, and he began to think about their meaning and to examine his life. Soon he was a committed believer. He went to the church where he had heard "Only a Step to Jesus" and related his experience. Many of the faithful, who had never expected this man to display even the slightest interest in religion, wept openly as he testified to a newfound faith.[16]

A famous story is told in connection with "Saved by Grace," which Fanny wrote in the 1890s. Around 1900, the staid and smoky atmosphere of a

Pittsburgh Anglican church was jolted when suddenly a woman, apparently on an impulse, went forward to "testify," an unheard of thing in an Anglican Mass. Before the chasubled priests, gaping thurifers and candle bearers and acolytes, and shocked parishioners on their knees with prayerbook in hand, the woman began to tell about her checkered life. "About two years ago, I was in Chicago." She had been a chorus girl and a woman of easy virtue, and was "on my way to Ferris Wheel Park to spend the afternoon in revelry," when she happened on an open-air meeting conducted by a Methodist congregation.

> I stopped through curiosity, as I believed, to listen; but now I know that God arrested my footsteps there. They were singing "Saved by Grace."
> ... Recollections of my childhood days came trooping into my soul, and I remembered that in all the years of my absence, my mother, until her death nine years ago, had been praying for me.

The woman was converted, "and falling on my knees on the curbstone, I asked the Father's pardon. Then and there I received it and I left the place with a peace which has never forsaken me." The rector descended from the high altar and "with tears in his eyes, approached the speaker, bidding her Godspeed." Parishioners spoke of the feeling being so intense that they imagined themselves in a Methodist meeting. Some said that "the Lord Jesus and His Mother have been here."[17]

There are many other stories told about the profound effect made by Fanny Crosby's hymns. What was there about these simple hymns, set to even more simple tunes, that affected so many so deeply? Fanny explained it in terms of the action of the Holy Spirit. Whenever she wrote a hymn, she prayed that God would use it to lead many souls to him. She prayed that she might be the means of saving a million men through her hymns. And so, whenever she heard of numerous conversions occurring, apparently as a result of the singing of her hymns, she attributed it in part to supernatural means. She said that inasmuch as the hymns were consecrated to the purpose of winning souls, God chose to work miracles through them.

When one looks at many of these hymns as poetry, one might agree that there must have been some miraculous element connected with their tremendous effect. However, although the hymns were not, by Fanny's own admission, first-rate literature, yet they did contain elements that gripped the imagination. There was something in them eminently capable of producing a great emotional effect.

One of the qualities that enhanced Fanny's hymns was their simplicity. She had a knack of setting forth ideas in a clear, straightforward way. The hymns were usually simple enough for a child to understand, yet not as pedantic or trite as most hymns of the time, and she achieved a vividness through the use of familiar phrases and cliches. While "sylvan bowers" and "vernal flowers" make for the worst of poetry, expressions of this nature made for very successful hymnody. People singing hymns could absorb stock, shopworn, and tritely familiar figures of speech more quickly than the original images of first-rate poetry. This may indeed make for bad poetry but, according to Fanny's thinking, hymnody was not "pure" poetry but had a more utilitarian purpose—to facilitate worship. This utilitarian function was best served by the familiar figure of speech rather than the novel and the intricate. So Fanny filled hymns with such familiar and shopworn phrases as "Rock of Ages," "saved by grace," "golden shore," and "bleeding side." She chose images and phrases which were familiar to most worshipers and which tended to evoke consoling or pious thoughts. Much of her imagery was scriptural: "living bread" (John 6:35), waters "gushing from the rock" (Numbers 20:11), "my Father's house above" (John 14:2), "the angel reapers" gathering in the harvest (Matthew 13:39), the "pearly gate" (Revelation 21:21), the "banquet" prepared by Jesus (Matthew 22:1–14), the "rest that remaineth for me" (Hebrews 4:9), and "the Good Shepherd" (John 10:11). One could go through all of Fanny's hymns (indeed, a lifetime task!) and find a book, chapter, and verse of scripture for ninety-five out of one hundred of the allusions. Indeed, one of her hymns, "Though Your Sins Be as Scarlet," is simply a paraphrase of Isaiah 1:18. One curious exception to this was Fanny's use of "summerland," which comes from spiritualism and refers to the dwelling-place of the happy dead.

Fanny also enhanced the effectiveness of her hymns through a power to elicit emotions. Perhaps it was owing to their emotional power that her hymns were so dear to the hearts of those who sang them. This is inherent in Fanny's very definition of a hymn: "A song of the heart addressed to God." Fanny had the knack of saying things in such a way as to elicit the maximum emotional response. In hymns she related everything she said to the worshiper's own experience, and thus her hymns are very personalistic. "Now there is pardon for *you*," "Pass *me* not," "*I* come to Thee, *I* come to Thee" are typical expressions. Often writers are said to put their stories in the first person so that readers can more intimately identify with the characters. Likewise, Fanny wrote most of her hymns in the first person so that those who sang them might become more intimately involved in their thought. When Christians sing a hymn, they are addressing God or singing of some aspect of their relationship to him. Why then, Fanny believed, should a hymn be objective, impersonal, and cold? Instead, it should be subjective and personal, relating to the worshiper's own experience. It should be intimate and warm.

One of the most striking things about Fanny Crosby's hymns is the familiarity with which the Savior is addressed. She uses the "familiar and fondling epithets" so decried by Lowell Mason when she was a child. Even today this is an aspect of her hymnody that many find objectionable. Some people have speculated that because of this quality "Miss" Crosby was channeling unfulfilled sexual passions into her hymns. Typical of this attitude is a passage from C. M. Smith's *How to Become a Bishop Without Being Religious,* which says rather sarcastically:

It has been said that, had Miss Crosby, through some misguided impulse, have gotten married, she never would have written this and other inspiring hymns. How grateful we are that she sublimated her normal human inclinations which were then able to burst through into matchless religious poetry. Her case illustrates, beyond doubt, the validity of the celibate life for certain religious vocations.[18]

But in truth we know absolutely nothing about Fanny's sexual life; one would assume that these "normal human inclinations" were fulfilled by her husband, with whom she lived throughout the period that she was writing her best-known hymns. She had a child and there is no reason to assume that she was sexually repressed.

There are better explanations for her way of addressing Christ than attributing this characteristic to unfulfilled sexual desires. Her belief in a strong, intensely personal relationship to God is one. It must also be remembered that Fanny lived in a very emotional age, when affection was more openly acknowledged than in the present day. Victorian letters abound with references to "adored Papa," "sweet Mother," "beloved friend," and "precious sister." It will be recalled how the minister pumping the organ when Doane first played "More Like Jesus" was so overcome by emotion that he came and threw both arms around his friend's neck. Tears rolled down Sankey's cheeks whenever he sang. When President Garfield was fatally shot in 1881, he was walking arm in arm with his Secretary of State.[19] It was an age when even men wept profusely in public. The frenzy manifested in religious services of even many of the established denominations, so incomprehensible today, reflected the heightened emotionalism of the age. This was an age of abundant physical gestures and flowery epithets, and Fanny was a particularly demonstrative person. Partly because she was blind, no doubt, physical contact meant a lot to her. She was always hugging and kissing, and greeted everyone with the words, "God bless your dear heart! I'm so happy to see you!" In conversation, she was similarly gushy. The Bowery bums and the railroad men were "my boys," Carrie and Jule were "my precious, darling sisters," Kirkpatrick was "Kirkie." Her friend Adelbert White was "dear Deacon" or "darling Hezekiah." Since Fanny addressed relatives and companions in emotionally affectionate language, it was very natural for her to address her Savior in like manner. After all, she loved him more than anyone else. Fanny felt that if one truly loved Jesus, emotions toward him and for him should not be suppressed like lust or rage but be fully expressed. If any emotions were involved in the act of loving Christ, why should they not be fully expressed in hymnody? And certainly a good Christian should have emotions connected with the love of Christ!

In addition to her use of emotions, Fanny enhanced the effectiveness of her hymns by the use of repetitions. In them, she tends to repeat a key phrase, word, or figure of speech throughout the hymn. This is the same sort of psychology that many modern advertising people use when they flash a slogan on and off so fast that the viewer is not aware of reading the words "Buy Sudso"—although the subconscious perceives it. Although she probably never heard of these psychological mechanisms, Fanny used the same strategy in hymns. In "Safe in the Arms of Jesus," for instance, in three stanzas the word "safe" is repeated five times and is found twice in the chorus, so that, in the course of the hymn, it is repeated eleven times. The worshiper is not really aware that "safe" is being repeated over and over again. But when he sings the hymn, "safe" implants itself so inexorably in his unresisting mind that his consciousness absorbs the content of the word, and when he is through singing it, he feels better, not the less because his subconscious is now telling him that he is "safe" in Jesus' arms. So the success of Fanny's hymns, although according to her they were due chiefly to supernatural Providence, was partly attributable to their construction. Through their simplicity, their use of familiar phrases, their personalism, their emotionalism, and their repetitiveness, her hymns were able to have an extraordinary effect upon people.

What about the tunes to the hymns? Some people have claimed that the success of Fanny's hymns resulted more from the tunes than the words, but it would seem that the various accounts of conversions through her hymns would tend to disprove that. In most instances, it was the words which struck the hearer; the tune was only a vehicle. Lowry often stated that the words were usually more important than the music in terms of the effect a hymn would have on the hearer. And we have seen how many of the tunes provided for Fanny's hymns tended to detract rather than enhance them. It was clearly the words that were most important in the gospel hymns, especially those which Fanny Crosby wrote. Often the tune did serve to enhance the words, as C. M. Smith had observed of the tune of "Blessed Assurance," writing facetiously:

> The music is . . . easily remembered even by a backward member of the Jukes family after one hearing. It has a syrupy quality about it, with the added advantage that it lends itself to loud and raucous congregational singing—a combination which is difficult to come by in a hymn and hard to beat for purposes of public worship. Belted out by a church-full of

enthusiastic Christians, with everyone unleashing a few extra decibels on the refrain, it will lift even the most stolid clod in the congregation out of his grubby, materialistic, unimaginative, uninspiring, everyday concerns and transport him to the Elysian fields of spiritual bliss.[20]

Although this author ridicules the tune, he is nevertheless right about its purpose. The tune served to furnish a musical setting for the words so simple that even the most backward and unmusical could readily remember it. It was intended to induce enthusiastic and fervent congregational singing, to help worshipers forget about their everyday troubles and be transported "to the Elysian fields of spiritual bliss."

Even in her own day, Fanny's hymns were criticized as being substandard as poetry as well as music, but this did not trouble her, for she was writing not for the critics but for common people. And she knew that this was the type of hymn the common person could best understand. When a hymnist disparaged "gospel hymns" to Sam Hadley, the social worker replied:

If you strike out the simple old Gospel songs, you take away, for some persons, the very backbone of religious music. Such songs may not be the best of poetry or written to the best music, but they embody a simple Christian faith. They ... touch the heart and bring consolation ... to countless thousands who could not be reached by the combined choirs of the earth singing their *Te Deums* and *Stabat Maters,* glorious though they be. I have seen too many hardened sinners thrilled to tears and brought to repentance through these songs to wish to see them discarded.[21]

CHAPTER 16
DRUNKS, OPERETTAS, AND CONVENTIONS

With the opening of the Brooklyn Bridge on May 24, 1883, Brooklyn and Lower Manhattan were linked closely together, making it fairly easy for those who worked in busy New York City to commute to the more suburban city of Brooklyn. Many people started to buy or build homes across the East River. Among those who obtained homes in Brooklyn in the early eighties were George Coles Stebbins and his wife and son, who moved from Chicago to a house at 19 Verana Place in what is now the Bedford-Stuyvesant section. Around the same time, Ira Sankey brought his wife and sons, also from Chicago, and settled in a large, beautiful frame house at 148 South Oxford Street. Fanny now had the opportunity to know both families more intimately. She became friendly with the gentle, quiet Stebbins, who became one of her "most devoted and precious friends." Of him she said, "If ever there was a man of high honour and culture of character, it is Mr. Stebbins. He has filled up every nook of my life with his goodness."[1]

Fanny was frequently a guest at the Stebbins home, but more often the two met at the Sankeys' home. The highly strung, effusive singer was very similar in temperament to Fanny, and he soon became "my never-failing friend."[2] During the next decade and a half, she was a regular and welcome guest in the Sankeys' spacious parlor. Next to Moody, Fanny was perhaps Sankey's closest friend. "I was with him so much,"[3] she mused years later, after his death.

Sankey and Fanny came to write an increasing number of hymns together, many of them at the reed organ in Sankey's parlor. Among them were "What a Gathering," about the Second Coming; "Waiting for Thy Coming," on the same subject; "Descend, O Flame," Fanny's homey, personalistic version of the Latin hymn, *Veni Spiritus Sanctus;* "We Praise Thee, We Bless Thee," a rather formal, classical hymn of rare grace and beauty; "Oh, Serve the Lord," written for "public worship"; and scores of others. Sankey set Fanny's poems to his simple but plaintively melodious airs.

Fanny came to know and like Ira's wife, who was also named Frances. A quiet, retiring woman, Frances Sankey was seldom seen in public and took no part in her husband's career, but devoted her time to making a home for him and their sons, Harry, Edward, and Allan. She was considered by her husband's friends a paragon of graciousness and goodness. However, Fanny was closer to Ira, and in the area of religious and theological affairs the two were confidants. Along with Phoebe Knapp, Sankey was probably Fanny's closest friend at this time.

In 1883 or 1884, Fanny moved from Frankfort Street in Lower Manhattan uptown to First Avenue and 79th Street. Now too far away to attend the John Street Methodist Church, as she had for the past several years, she began to go regularly to the Cornell Memorial Church on 76th Street and eventually became a member. It was the first church she had ever officially joined. We know Fanny was—and remained—a person who did not like being bound to one congregation, let alone one denomination, and loved to visit different churches for services. Now perhaps she felt she was at an age when it was wise to be officially affiliated with a congregation, if for no other reason than to be assured of having a clergyman to conduct her burial services!

Whether Fanny was still with Van at this time is a good question, but it is certain that he no longer figured prominently in her life. As of 1882, the couple was still together, but owing to the differing interests and circles of friends with which they had entered their late marriage, and perhaps compounded by a dimunition of physical passion due to advancing years, the two blind musicians were growing apart. There was apparently no overt rancor between Fanny and Van, but they were less and less in each other's company and tended to pursue their own lives and careers. Gradually the relationship was, by their mutual consent, downgraded from that of husband and wife to one of simply good friends. Although she and Van continued to love each other—according to Fanny—they more and more gravitated to other friends. Fanny tended to look to Ira Sankey and Phoebe Knapp for intellectual and spiritual companionship, while Van became fast friends with the family of Harriss Underhill, a New York publisher. There was no hint of infidelity, simply a seeking of support and companionship elsewhere.

Hugh and Louise Main were also good friends of Fanny, and on March 24, 1884, they held the first of the annual Fanny Crosby Birthday Parties that were to become a yearly tradition at the offices of Biglow and Main on Ninth Street and Madison Avenue. After twenty years and some three thousand hymns, Hugh thought that Fanny was more than due an annual tribute of some sort, so he arranged a gala banquet to be held on her sixty-fourth birthday. A sumptuous table was spread at the office, prepared by the wives of the members of the publishing firm. As many of Fanny's friends were there as were able to come, and the highlight of the evening was a reading of birthday poems which friends had written in her honor. Since Fanny appreciated greetings in verse form, Main, Sankey, Kirkpatrick, Lowry, Doane, and others

158

tried their best to put their good wishes into poetical form. Hugh Main composed a comic poem, and Fanny was so delighted with it that at subsequent celebrations every year thereafter she looked for this humorous poem as the high point of the festivities.

In October 1884 Moody came to New York, to lead, along with Sankey, a "Christian convention" on evangelism. They held meetings at Theodore Ledyard Cuyler's Lafayette Avenue Presbyterian Church in Brooklyn, only a short distance from Sankey's home. Moody was concerned about the personal evangelism of church members and realized that he and Sankey could not do the job alone by public preaching and singing. If there was to be any kind of meaningful revival, laymen had to do their part, so Moody suggested that individual churches have revivals at regular intervals, in which the minister would preach on ten consecutive evenings, after which the parishioners would go out to their friends and neighbors, inviting them to come to the ensuing services. Moody's comments were widely publicized in the New York papers, but there is no evidence that any church people took his advice.

Fanny continued to write hymns. Not only did she write for Sankey but also, of course, for Biglow and Main. She contributed a heavy percentage of the hymns in *Our Glad Hosanna*, published in 1882, *Joyful Days* (1884), and *Glad Refrain* (1886), all edited by Lowry and Doane. She was perhaps writing her most successful hymns at this time for Kirkpatrick and Sweney, and among the many she contributed to *Songs of Redeeming Love* (1882) and *Glad Hallelujahs* (1887) were "Tell Me the Story of Jesus," "Redeemed, O How I Love to Proclaim It," "We Are Never Weary of the Grand Old Song," and

Take the world, but give me Jesus,
All its joys are but a name,
But His love abideth ever,
Through eternal years the same.[4]

By far the most successful hymn she wrote for them was "He Hideth My Soul in the Cleft of the Rock," for which Kirkie provided the music.

Fanny continued her work in the missions, although she lost a good friend in Jerry McAuley. The Irishman had never been well, and his labors at the mission put his fragile health under a terrific strain. By his mid-forties, he was suffering from tuberculosis. The end came unexpectedly when he was stricken with a severe hemorrhage of the lungs on October 18, 1884, and died within minutes, pointing toward heaven and telling his wife, "It's all right up there."[5] Soon afterward, S. Hopkins Hadley took his place as the director of the Water Street Mission. Born the scion of a distinguished family in 1842, Sam, as he was known to his friends, became an alcoholic in his twenties but had reformed at forty to become an ideal Christian. In early 1886, he took over McAuley's work and Fanny came to know and admire him, although she was better acquainted with his brother.

In 1886, Henry Harrison Hadley was forty-five years old and an alcoholic. An officer in the Union Army, he had a distinguished war record and was generally known as the Colonel. He had first sold insurance and then studied law but, although he built a thriving practice, he was always a heavy drinker and soon became completely addicted. Losing his law practice, Hadley went into journalism, publishing a weekly paper in Upper Manhattan called *The Uptown News*. He was very much concerned with social issues, including alcoholism, and had, in fact, organized the Businessmen's Society for the Encouragement of Moderation, an organization that was instrumental in having public water fountains installed all over Manhattan in an effort to encourage city employees to drink water rather than booze. At first the Colonel thought he too could learn to drink in moderation, but he was forced to conclude that for people of his type a "moderation society" was useless. He had managed to stay off the bottle for a while, but in trying to drink socially he became addicted again.

The Colonel first met Fanny when she put into verse an incident reported in his newspaper concerning a judge who released a prostitute from prison after pleas by her small son. Hadley soon asked Fanny to write poems espousing the Temperance cause and, in the spring of 1886, to write a series of poems to be published every other week. The first urged businessmen not to drink during their working hours. The next urged them to refrain from drinking altogether for twenty-four hours. The third bade them give up the habit entirely. Fanny was condemned for this by various Christian workers who believed, as she put it, "in taking a whole loaf of bread or none at all." Although taken to task for not advising the adoption of abstinence once and forever, Fanny persisted, feeling that if a man could arrive at freedom from alcohol in steps, it was fine, just so long as the goal was attained. She could very well see Hadley's point that some men can give up the bottle only gradually—or not at all.

Unfortunately the Colonel soon found that he himself could not give up the bottle, gradually or otherwise. His drinking grew rapidly worse, and by the summer he was taking more than forty drinks per day. Fanny tried her best to counsel him. The Colonel was a nominal Anglican but was something of a freethinker, with "original ideas on religion."[6] At any rate, Hadley, who "never tried to force his views on others," talked quite openly and amicably with Fanny. Although intensely devout, Fanny was the kind of person with whom one could apparently speak for hours without a loss of temper, even given a pronounced disagreement. After weeks, she got Hadley to the point of admitting, "I guess you are right. Perhaps I shall see it as you do . . . some day."

Fanny left New York in July to go to Ocean Grove, as usual, and after that she was with Ira and Fanny Sankey in Northfield, Massachusetts. After her return, when she next visited the Water Street Mission, she was informed that Colonel Hadley had been converted. Yet Fanny heard nothing from the Colonel, and he made no effort to contact her. She found this quite unusual, as she usually saw him frequently, and she began to wonder if the Colonel had "returned to his evil habits."

Finally, at nine o'clock one October night, Hadley rang Fanny's doorbell, calling repeatedly, "I have found the Lord!"

She invited him in, saying, "Bless you, Colonel Hadley! You come right upstairs and tell me all about it!"[7]

Hadley obliged and spent the evening telling Fanny about his conversion. One midnight, after a day on which he had taken fifty-three drinks, Hadley solemnly vowed never to touch the bottle again. Within a day, he was "trembling in every nerve" and sought out his brother at his mission. Staying for the service, he was impressed by the testimony of a recovered alcoholic and prayed to God not so much to take away his "appetite for drink" but to enable him to bear "this thirst as long as I live" in gratitude for Christ dying for him on the cross. He left the meeting in a state of euphoria and awoke the next morning singing. He never again felt a desire for strong drink—or for tobacco either![8]

Fanny was delighted with his story but had one question. "Why did you wait so long to tell me?"

"Oh," said the Colonel, "I wanted to be sure that I would hold out."[9] And hold out against unbelief and alcoholism he did. Before he died sixteen years later, Henry Harrison Hadley founded sixty rescue missions and became an internationally known Christian lecturer.

Fanny was delighted that autumn of 1886, not only by the conversion of her editor friend but by the things that she had seen happening in Northfield, Massachusetts, that summer. It was in 1879 that D. L. Moody held the first of the Northfield Christian Workers' Conferences that became an annual affair in his hometown. Moody liked to spend the summer in study and relaxation at Northfield, where he owned a fine home. As energetic as he was, however, he found that he could not relax for long, and soon he was conducting public Bible readings in his dining room, inviting everyone in the area who was interested. There were so many people that not everyone could get in the house, and the porch was crowded with people who were obliged to look through the window to follow the proceedings. Encouraged by the interest displayed in these informal gatherings, Moody decided that it might be a good

161

idea for Christian workers to meet together for a week each summer in that rustic paradise, to pray and study scripture and find greater strength to perform their service in Christian work.

The first of these retreats for Christian workers was held in September 1879, on the grounds of the girls' school, or seminary, which he had recently established. Moody called the meetings with the object "not so much to study the Bible (though the Scriptures will be searched daily for instructions and promises) as for solemn self-consecration, for pleading God's promises, and waiting upon Him for a fresh anointment of power from on high."[10] Three hundred people attended that first retreat. Accommodated in the dormitory of the Northfield Seminary, they met for ten days, studying "the doctrine of the Holy Spirit" and praying for various Christian institutions.

By the mid-eighties, the summer convention was a yearly event. The Rev. H. B. Hartzler, a friend of Moody's, likened these meetings to "the Jerusalem Pentecost." Indeed, there were "devout men out of every nation under heaven" in attendance. "Pastors and evangelists, professors and editors, elders and deacons, devout women and earnest youth" all met "with one accord in one place."[11]

Although Fanny had heard of the meetings since their inception, it was not until 1886 that she attended. She stayed with the Sankeys at their summer home in Northfield and was very pleased by the convention.

There were meetings in tents and meetings in the seminary chapel. There was prayer and there was "testimony." In one of the tent meetings, "under common impulse," those attending the particular meeting "clasped one another's hands, stood in a circle, and entered a solemn covenant of consecration with God and one another." It was even proposed that they pledge themselves to pray daily for each other until death—until Moody objected on the grounds that this would soon become, not "the delightful privilege it is now, but an irksome duty."[12]

Moody wanted Fanny to speak from time to time, but she always refused. She never spoke at Ocean Grove, either. No doubt she came to these retreats with the intention of being the recipient of religious instruction, rather than the dispenser of it. The days she spent here and at the New Jersey campground were her vacation, her only respite from the constant round of talks and addresses that she was now obliged to give during the year. She did compose a few hymns there, however. Vacation or no vacation, she could not resist the promptings of the Holy Ghost.

In the summer of 1886, Sankey induced her to write a hymn, albeit not without difficulty. He played a tune one day and urged, "Why not write a poem for this tune tonight?" She refused. Fanny was alone at the house while the Sankeys were out for a drive. That afternoon, a number of students from the nearby boys' school called on her. Already Fanny had become a great favorite of the young people at the educational institutions at Northfield, and eventually she would be known as the foster mother of the boys at the Mt. Hermon School. She spent much of this particular afternoon talking with the boys, and when they left she felt under the compulsion to write a hymn. She sat down at the piano, played the tune Ira had suggested, and composed a poem so rapidly that it was complete and she was able to recite it by the time the Sankeys returned:

O Child of God, wait patiently,
When dark thy path may be;
And let thy faith lean trustingly,
On Him who cares for thee;
And though the clouds hang drearily
Upon the brow of night,
Yet in the morning joy will come
And fill thy soul with light! [13]

Sankey used the hymn for the services that very night, and it immediately became a success. Years later, he wrote that "many a poor soul has been comforted by this simple hymn."[14] Fanny always liked it and commented, "I know that I have been permitted to do a little good here."[15]

That fall, Fanny's summer rest over, no longer was she breathing the "mountain air so sweet" of Northfield but New York's foul and smoky atmosphere. But she was happily at work on her hymns, as usual, and also on an operetta which would be produced the following year. Fanny had been engaged as librettist by Hart Pease Danks (1834–1903), a well-known composer of secular music, famous for his hit song, "Silver Threads Among the Gold." He had first met Fanny when Sankey had enlisted him to write tunes for some of her lyrics. Soon, however, he began to engage her services as a librettist. In the past few years, she had written the book to a cantata and a "juvenile operetta." Now he asked for another, and the operetta Zanie was produced the next year. Fanny's libretto was a sentimental Victorian tale about the love of an English nobleman for a "gypsy queen" who turns out to be the daughter of a wealthy American kidnapped as a baby. The one-act composition ends with Zanie—now known as Isadora—married to the nobleman.

Unlike many of her contemporaries, Fanny was not opposed to the theater. Moody and Sankey would never attend, but Fanny felt that as long as the content was wholesome or edifying, there was nothing wrong with a play or opera or popular music. Although she no longer wrote as many secular songs as she once did, she continued, over the years, to publish occasionally such popular songs as "Mother, I Dream of Thee" and "Grandma's Rocking Chair." The year after Zanie, she collaborated with Howard Doane in writing a totally secular Christmas cantata called *Santa Claus*. Apparently she had gotten some negative feedback from morally righteous friends because of her totally secular "operetta," so she styled this composition, which is of the same length as *Zanie*, a "cantata." An introduction explained that "this cantata has a religious sentiment pervading it, intending to illustrate the triumph of Right over Wrong."

While Fanny was busy writing librettos for operettas and cantatas, she was very much concerned with her family. Her sister Carrie was again a widow. Throughout their nine years of marriage, Lee Rider's epilepsy had grown progressively worse and he was forced to give up peddling tin about 1880, taking a job as a janitor in Union School in Bridgeport. By 1882, he was unable to work and Carrie had to nurse him night and day, until on December 27, 1883, he died at the early age of thirty-six. Carrie was not alone and idle, for she worked out her grief in providing a home for her aged mother, who still lived with her. Fanny was now more concerned with Jule and Byron.

Byron's health was failing. Suffering for several years with a heart condition and arthritis as well as from the effects of his wounds, Athington had been unable to work, and Jule had to work hard as a dressmaker. However, in the spring of 1887, despite his weakening heart, he decided to stay home no longer. He took a job with the coach-lamp firm of Bishop and Swift in New Haven, Connecticut, and forced himself to commute about fifty miles each day on the train. It was too much for him, and in the fall he had to resign because of declining health. He died on December 12 at age fifty.

Fanny felt the loss of her brothers-in-law very keenly. She was very fond of both Lee and Byron, both of whom she has described as being very devout. Within a month of Byron's death, she experienced still another loss. Her one surviving aunt, Polly Decker, dropped dead of a heart attack at age seventy. Polly was just two years Fanny's senior and had been more of a sister than an aunt to her in early childhood. Until she was five, Fanny had Polly as a constant playmate. After that the two girls grew apart and as adults they were still more distant, with Fanny spending most of her adult life in New York and Polly in Allentown, Pennsylvania. It was only in later years that Polly came to Bridgeport to be near her sister and nieces. Still, Fanny must have felt sad as one of the last links to her childhood was forever broken. From those long-vanished days in Gayville, only one figure still remained: "Mother Dear," still hale and hearty at eighty-eight. In the May of that year, on Mercy's eighty-ninth birthday, Fanny recited a poem at the annual celebration that Carrie and Jule arranged for their mother, which concludes:

Mother's birthday! God reward her
For her gentle, patient care,
May He light the path before her

Is the burden of our prayer;
And may all who now are gathered
On this happy eve so bright,
Meet at last beyond the river,
Where they never say "goodnight."[16]

On March 4, 1889, Grover Cleveland completed his term as President of the United States and with his twenty-five-year-old wife, Frances, moved into a home on Madison Avenue in New York. Soon afterward, he invited Fanny to come to see him. Thus, after an interval of thirty-five years, a friendship begun in the New York Institution for the Blind was renewed. From the time Grove and his brother William left the Institution, Fanny had heard nothing of her bright young protégé until 1882, when she heard that he was running for election as Governor of New York. She at once wrote him a letter of congratulations, and he responded warmly. Shortly after he became Governor, Fanny's friends gave her a benefit, and someone wrote Cleveland, asking him to come. Cleveland wrote, "I remember my old friend Fanny Crosby very well," and, regretting his inability to attend, sent her a sizable gift of money instead.[17]

Now, Fanny and Cleveland met again. She was received kindly by her old friend, now grown bald and jowly, and by his beautiful young wife, Frankie. Cleveland asked why she had not written him since he had become President.

"Well," replied Fanny, "I neglected you for so many years, it just did not seem the right thing to open a correspondence with you then, because it might look as though I wanted to court favor."[18]

Cleveland chided her for that attitude, insisting that they now regularly keep in touch. "I would rather have a letter from you than all the encomiums."[19]

Fanny was still writing hymns. In 1889, she contributed forty of them to Lowry and Doane's *Bright Array,* but none achieved any degree of popularity. Fanny was now almost totally written out. Everything she produced was probably the fifth or sixth paraphrase of something she had written years before. Moreover, the quality of her hymns was deteriorating. "O Child of God, Wait Patiently" and a few others that she wrote for Sankey, who was less demanding than Doane and Lowry, were exceptions among an output in the late 1880s which was growing increasingly jejune and insipid. But Biglow and Main wanted more and more hymns, and Fanny supplied them, even though she wrote them, as it were, out of the thin air. Biglow and Main even insisted that she write paraphrases of such popular hymns by other authors as "Wonderful Words of Life" (Bliss) and "Showers of Blessing" (Whittle). But her versions of these were quickly forgotten.

Fanny wrote so many hymns, and most of them so rapidly and mechanically, that she often could not remember what she had written and what she had not. She sometimes could not even recognize her own hymns when they were sung, and an embarrassing situation occurred at Northfield about this time. Sankey had used a hymn that she had written him, entitled, "Hide Me, O My Saviour." At dinner, in front of guests, she asked Ira, "Where did you get that?" Ira, thinking that she was joking, laughingly passed off the remark. The whole company laughed, and Fanny was puzzled. That evening, it was sung again, and this time Fanny was determined to learn its author. "Now, Sankey, you must tell me who wrote 'Hide Me, O My Saviour.'"

Ira replied, "Really? You don't recall who wrote that hymn? You ought to, for you are the culprit!"[20]

Even though she was writing few hymns of any quality at this time, so great was the work that Fanny had accomplished in the field of hymnody in the past that she was able to rest on her laurels. Even though she wrote perhaps no more than a half-dozen good hymns in the next quarter century, on the strength of her past achievements and also her growing activity and reputation as a preacher and lecturer, her fame continued to grow immensely. And although her most effective contributions in future would be in the pulpit or lectern, she was always known as "the hymn writer" and "the queen of gospel song."

CHAPTER 17
THE "HEART'S SONG"

The same month that Fanny celebrated her seventieth birthday brought Moody back to New York for his first major campaign since 1876. The decade and a half since he and Sankey had taken New York by storm had produced many changes. Always thickset, Moody had grown stupendously fat. Someone commented that he could "lay his Bible on the book-rest which nature had provided him, which he carried with him wherever he went, between the two buttons of his waistcoat."[1] He was so stout that he had to have clothes specially made and either wear loafers or have one of his sons tie his shoes.[2] With his enormous white beard and ruddy complexion, he looked remarkably like Santa Claus.

Time had altered not only Moody's appearance but also his audiences. He no longer had to engage the largest halls, for his middle-aged and elderly listeners could be accommodated at local churches. The fact that his audiences were composed almost entirely of people already "saved" disappointed the evangelist, who complained bitterly that his meetings were attended only by "chronic attenders of religious meetings, who crowd everybody else out." He groused that he seemed to be looking at the same faces that had greeted him over a decade before. "Why, they look as if they had been running to religious meetings for the past twenty years."[3] Sankey did not accompany Moody this time. Although he was not yet fifty, the baritone's once-golden voice was now almost completely a thing of the past, and he sang only occasionally. Tenor George Stebbins served as soloist and song leader.

In the "Bible-readings," as he called his meetings, Moody spoke of the declining interest of religion in America. Truly, the revival which had begun in the 1850s and peaked in the 1870s had completely run its course, and Moody was very concerned. He wondered how religion could be made more palatable to the young, and from the pulpit of the Marble Collegiate Church in 1890 he urged ministers to give shorter sermons and to inject greater pep into their services. And, by all means, he said, clergymen should not arrogate to themselves the pretentious title "Reverend," for that was reserved for Christ. A minister should be content to be known as "Mister," like any other man.[4] Moody came down hard on spiritualism, which was increasing in popularity as orthodox Christianity was diminishing. "I don't think it is becoming in a child of God to be . . . running after departed spirits." He went on to say that "I have received numbers of invitations to go to rooms where the gas was to be turned down and tables were to tip and chairs to jump about. I have always answered that as God had given me light, I have no desire to voluntarily enter into darkness."[5] As usual, he made liberal use of Fanny's hymns, especially "Blessed Assurance," now a hit tune.

Fanny attended but predictably refused all Moody's requests to speak or even to appear on the platform. Toward the end of the meetings, however, at the 23rd Street Dutch Reformed Church, Fanny, unable to find a seat because of the crowded condition of the church, was about to leave, when Moody's son Will told her that he would find her a seat. As young Moody led her into the chancel of the church and onto the platform as the people were singing "Blessed Assurance," Moody, Sr., stood up and raised his hand to interrupt the singing, shouting, "Praise the Lord, here comes the authoress!"[6] It was now too late for Fanny to avoid a seat on the platform, and she sat amid a thunderous ovation by the worshipers. Far from being enraged by this ruse, she took the incident in good humor.

May brought her to Bridgeport, and on the thirtieth she addressed a Decoration Day crowd in Seaside Park and recited a poem written for the local post of the Grand Army of the Republic. The appearance was such a success that she was invited to make it an annual event, and for the rest of her life the Decoration Day poem and address would be an institution in Bridgeport. At the age of ninety, she could still move the aging veterans and their families to tears.

The following day, Fanny helped her mother celebrate her ninety-first birthday. Mercy's birthday was always a gala affair for her adoring family, and the Morris clan made that celebration the highpoint of the year. Mercy, who lived with Carrie in an apartment on Washington Avenue, was still apparently in good health and in full possession of her faculties. Although now bereft of brother and sisters, stepson, and two sons-in-law, she was nevertheless joined on her natal day by a large host of relatives, including her three daughters, her granddaughter, Ida Leschon (Jule's daughter), and Ida's adopted son, James. Present as well were the children of William Morris—Albert, Laura Frances, and Florence—with their husbands and children. Fanny recited a poem that concluded:

God keep her still in health as now,
God spare our Mother Dear,
And with His richest blessings crown
Full many a coming year.[7]

However, God granted Mercy Crosby Morris but a few more days. That

168

summer she became painfully ill and was removed to a hospital, where her condition was pronounced hopeless. Although she was afflicted with great pain, Mercy's last days were "calm and beautiful—a blessing to all who knew her." After ninety-one years, she was ready for that world which contained so many more of her relatives and friends than the one in which she presently lingered. At sunset on September 1, with Fanny, Carrie, and Jule at her bedside, the end came and Mercy "passed peacefully from this world to a brighter home above."[8] The funeral was held at the home of Florence Morris Booth. Before the meager form was borne to Mountain Grove Cemetery, to be interred beside the remains of her daughter Wilhelmina, Fanny recited a poem that concluded:

We loved our tender mother
Far more than words can tell,
And while with deep emotion
We breathe our fond farewell,
We know her tranquil spirit
Has reached the longed-for shore,
And now with joy is greeting
The loved ones gone before.

Oh, Mother, we are coming,
The time will not be long
Till we shall clasp thy hand again
And join the blessed song.
The sheaf of wheat is garnered,
The sickle's work is done,
And everlasting glory
Through Christ her soul has won.[9]

More than by the passing of her mother, Fanny was saddened by the conduct of her sisters. Mercy, who had come to Bridgeport fifty odd years before with nothing, had "a little something" when she died, thanks to a well-to-do brother and prosperous sisters, none of whom left any heirs. But as Mercy had left no will, Jule and Carrie applied for the estate, declaring themselves the "only heirs and next of kin." Whether Fanny knew what was going on at the time or not, she did not oppose or object, and the courts awarded the two sisters Mercy's entire estate. Fanny did not receive a penny, yet she accepted this without bitterness or rancor, feeling that it was better for a Christian to accept suffering and deprivation than to cause it in others. She might easily have gotten the money if she had gone to court, but she felt that God provided for her needs and that was enough.

The next year, Fanny again found her Muse and wrote two hymns that

169

achieved great success. Early that year, Sweney asked her to write "something tender and pathetic."[10] He enclosed, however, a tune that sounded anything but "tender and pathetic." It was a peppy, brass-bandish tune that sounded very much like "She'll Be Comin' 'Round the Mountain." Nevertheless, Fanny prayed that "appropriate words might be given me for this music."[11] Finally, she entered a "train of thought" that "brought me to the sweet consciousness that I will know my Saviour by the print of the nails in His hands."[12]

When my lifework is ended and I cross the swelling tide,
When the bright and glorious morning I shall see,
I shall know my Redeemer when I reach the other side,
And His smile will be the first to welcome me.

• • •

O, the dear ones in glory, how they beckon me to come,
And the parting at the river I recall;
To the sweet vales of Eden they will sing my welcome home,
But I long to meet my Saviour first of all.

Each stanza is reinforced by the chorus:

I shall know Him, I shall know Him,
And alone by His side I shall stand!
I shall know Him, I shall know Him,
By the print of the nails in His hand.[13]

The jingling tune, so reminiscent of a popular folksong, helped "My Saviour First of All" to popularity, although one wonders if almost any other kind of tune could not have better expressed the words Fanny wrote. Within a few years, almost everyone in England and America knew it.

Fanny felt that "My Saviour First of All" accomplished its greatest good through a single incident in England. It seems as if there was a self-proclaimed messiah who had a very large following and was wont to preach in the public parks. One day this man, who claimed that he was an incarnation of Christ, was preaching to a large crowd in London when a delegation of the Salvation Army appeared on the scene, singing, "I shall know Him, I shall know Him, by the print of the nails in His hand." One of them challenged the mountebank to show his hands to the throng. The fact that there was no print of nails on them exposed him as a fraud in the minds of many of his listeners, and he was never again a force for the church to contend with. Even the most devoted followers of the Enlightened One knew the hymn and began to sing along, without thinking. Gradually, however, the throng became aware of the sense of the words they were singing. And Fanny felt that in this she had been given a special blessing.

An even more popular hymn was born shortly thereafter. In March 1891, Fanny's cousin, Howard Crosby, the Presbyterian pastor, died of pneumonia at age sixty-five. Not long afterward, Lucius Biglow read her a pamphlet containing the text of Dr. Crosby's last message. It said no Christian need fear death: "If each of us is faithful to the grace which is given us by Christ, that same grace which teaches us how to live will also teach us how to die."[14] Fanny was moved by that last message and wrote a poem called "Some Day":

Some day my earthly house will fall,
I cannot tell how soon 'twill be,
But this I know, my All in All
Has now a place in heaven for me.

Some day the silver cord will break
And I no more as now shall sing,
But, oh, the joy when I awake
Within the Palace of the King.

Some day, when sets the golden sun
Beneath the rosy-tinted west,
My blessed Lord shall say, "Well done!"
And I shall enter into rest.

Some day—till then I'll watch and wait,
My lamp well-trimmed and burning bright,
That when my Saviour opens the gate
My soul to Him may speed its flight.[15]

Fanny wrote "Some Day" in a matter of minutes and under "divine inspiration," as she had "Safe in the Arms of Jesus" and her best hymns of the sixties and seventies. She put it in Biglow's hands, who paid her the usual two dollars and put it in his vault. For three years, "Some Day" seemed destined to be one of those poems that Fanny considered among her better efforts but which was not set to music. With slight variations, however, this poem was to become the well-known hymn "Saved by Grace."

Fanny had good reason to reflect on death that year. First her mother had died, then her cousin Howard, and in July she received word from Bridgeport that "the White-Robed Angel" had made off with her favorite grandniece, Clare Morris (Albert's daughter), after a bout with scarlet fever. She had not fully recovered from that blow when in September she learned that Joseph Knapp had died suddenly on shipboard while returning with Phoebe from a European vacation.

In October, Fanny had some good news, for a change. Along with the rest of the nation, she learned that Frankie Cleveland had given birth to a daughter, named Ruth. Fanny delighted in the joy of her old friend Grove and his wife, and sent a baptismal poem, dedicated to "the winsome Baby Ruth."

Despite griefs and troubles, Fanny was blessed with several excellent friends. There was Ira Sankey, her "never-failing friend." Then there was the beloved Phoebe Knapp, to whom she once wrote, "words . . . have not the power to speak what thou hast been and what thou art to me." With an income of $50,000 per year from her husband's estate, Phoebe moved into the luxurious Hotel Savoy in downtown Manhattan and had installed in her suite a pipe organ that cost $30,000. Howard Doane, too, was a faithful friend, and Fanny spent several weeks out of each year with his family. Now, in the 1890s, Fanny made two more great friendships.

At Cornell Memorial Church, she developed a close friendship with the assistant pastor, the Rev. Gerhard Johannes Schilling. A native of Germany, Schilling had been converted in Burma after being smitten by guilt for ordering statues of the Buddha for the natives from the glass factory in Germany of which he was the agent. Feeling that he could not in all conscience trade in idols and "graven images," he wired his company that he was not going to sell the glass Buddhas and was fired. Subsequently, he came to New York, where he met the pastor of Cornell Memorial when, singing hymns while candling eggs in the basement of the delicatessen where he was working, his voice seemed to drift up from the sidewalk into the ears of the passing cleric. When he told his story, the minister was so enthusiastic that he and his church financed Schilling's studies at divinity school. Schilling was forty years Fanny's junior and called her "Aunt," as did many people. In his carriage, Schilling picked up "Aunt Fanny" every Sunday and Wednesday evening for church. He came to know and love her hymns. In 1894, with his American wife, Schilling left for the mission field in Burma, where he translated the Bible and wrote hymns in the native dialect.[16] He claimed Fanny as his inspiration.

During this period Fanny also came to know Eliza Edmunds Hewitt. She first met Miss Hewitt at the Kirkpatricks' home in Germantown. Born in Philadelphia June 28, 1851, Eliza, or Lida as she was sometimes called, went to normal school and then taught for several years until she was stricken with a painful and incapacitating disease of the spinal cord. After several years in bed, she regained enough strength to become an active church worker. While teaching in the Sunday school of Olivet Presbyterian Church, she first began to write religious poems, and these attracted the attention of William Kirkpatrick, who, along with Sweney, set some of them to music. Later, moving to a different area of the city, she became affiliated with the Calvin Presbyterian Church, where she headed the primary department of the Sunday school. As the years went by, Eliza Hewitt supplied fifteen hundred hymns for Kirkpatrick and Sweney. By the mid-nineties, she was one of the grand duchesses in the court of Fanny Crosby, the acknowledged queen of the gospel hymn. Among Miss Hewitt's most successful hymns were "There Is Sunshine in My Soul" and "Will There Be Any Stars in My Crown?" Her lyrics, if less polished and refined than Fanny's, had the simplicity that was so essential to the gospel hymn, as well as a profound earnestness and sincerity and a subjective personalism. She was a homely woman with a huge nose, protuberant lips, and a bovine expression, but she had a warm personality. Fanny came to love Lida Hewitt well. She visited at her home on Redfield Avenue every time she went to Philadelphia, and the two had further fellowship when they attended the camp meetings at Ocean Grove.

Although the demand for hymns was not now as great as it had been earlier, Fanny still contributed to the hymnals of Biglow and Main and of Sweney and Kirkpatrick. In 1893, she contributed to Doane and Lowry's *Sunny Side Songs* and in 1895 to *Highest Praises*. In 1894 she contributed to Sweney and Kirkpatrick's *Songs of Love and Praise*. Most of the hymns she did write during this period received little attention, but one was moderately successful. Now practically a member of the Sankey family, Fanny was at Oxford Street when Stebbins called. He had come for Fanny's assistance.

"Fanny," Stebbins said, "I have a subject for a hymn and I would like you to write some verses for me. I think I have something both of us will enjoy."

"Good! What is it?" she asked.

Stebbins suggested the text from 1 Corinthians 2:9: "Eye hath not seen, nor ear heard, neither have entered into the heart of man, the things which God hath prepared for them that love Him." He had set that rather unmusical verse to music as a chorus and now asked Fanny to provide verse to the body of the hymn tune. Fanny went into another room and within minutes reentered the parlor. She had composed some verses:

They tell me of a land so fair,
Unseen by mortal eyes,
Where spring in fadeless beauty blooms
Beneath unclouded skies.

"Splendid, Fanny!" said Stebbins. "Give me some more like it." Within minutes, she returned with a verse which Stebbins found even more beautiful than the first:

They tell me of a land so fair,
Where all is light and song,

Where angel choirs their anthems join
With yonder sacred throng.

Stebbins asked for still another verse, and again within minutes Fanny had produced a verse, one that the composer found the most beautiful of all.

No radiant beams from sun or moon
Adorn that land so fair,
For He who sits upon the throne
Shines forth resplendent there.[17]

Largely because of the words, "Eye Hath Not Seen" achieved some popularity, but it is not particularly easy to sing, and this explains why it did not rival some of Fanny's lyrics which were set to slightly better tunes.

It was in 1894 that Stebbins was given the opportunity to set Fanny's "heart's song" to music. Fanny was spending the summer with the Sankeys in Northfield, Massachusetts. The Moodys were in Europe that particular summer, and the Bible conference was headed by Dr. Adoniram Judson Gordon, an eminent Baptist clergyman and writer. One of his lectures was on the subject of the Holy Spirit. After his address, Sankey came to Fanny and asked, "Will you say something? There is a request from the audience that you speak."

"Oh, Sankey, I cannot speak before such an array of talent!"

Gordon then added, "Fanny, do you speak to please man or to please God?"

That pricked her conscience. "Why, I hope to please God!" she replied.

"Well, then," said Gordon, "go out and do your duty."[18]

Taking her position at the lectern, Fanny made a few remarks; then she quoted her "heart's song," the poem "Some Day." When she finished there was not a dry eye in the auditorium.

"Where did you get that piece?" asked Sankey, excited. Fanny told him that she had submitted it to Biglow and Main three years before, but that no one had seen fit to set it to music. Sankey was now enthusiastic about finding it a musical setting. Fanny told him that she would, however, rather have "Some Day" remain without a tune. Perhaps she felt that no tune such as she was accustomed to being provided could do justice to the delicate sentiments. Sankey still could not rest.

Luckily for him, a newspaper reporter had been in the audience, and "Some Day" was printed in a periodical in England. Ira got hold of the poem and sent it to Stebbins, bidding him to write a tune for it. Apparently, he felt enough compunction about Fanny's request as not to write the tune himself.

Stebbins had Fanny provide a chorus: "And I shall see Him face to face, And tell the story—Saved by Grace." He set it to a slow tune, and although the music is not particularly delicate or melodic, Fanny's "Heart's Song" became a favorite among evangelical Christians the world over. It became a favorite of Moody's as soon as he heard it. It became one of the hit songs of the Gay Nineties and was on everybody's lips. It was to be Fanny's last truly popular hymn.

CHAPTER 18
"WHO IS MOODY?"

In the 1890s the raddled little woman who was the queen of the gospel song was a familiar figure along Manhattan's streets, where she was frequently recognized, perpetually smiling, as much as her ill-fitting dentures would permit her, and clinging to the hand of a companion. By now she was quite bent and stooped and wore a curly brown wig over her thin gray hair. The antiquity of her appearance was further emphasized by her habit of going about as one of her contemporaries put it, "garbed after a very ancient fashion." The style of her gowns and bonnets was that of the 1840s rather than that of the present day.[1] Although to the casual observer Fanny might appear to be eighty or more, anyone who spent even a few minutes in her company was forced to change their initial impression. Her energy, verve and vivacity, mental acuity, enjoyment of life, and sense of humor and fun were not that of a woman of seventy-five but thirty-five. Despite her ravaged face and wasted form, Fanny seriously contended that she felt no different than she had at sixteen.

Certainly, at an age when most people have long since retired, Fanny Crosby kept up a round of activity that would have exhausted many a person forty years her junior. Her activity increased and did not diminish with the passing years. She still provided Biglow and Main with two to three hymns per week and still satisfied the hymnic desires of Sweney and Kirkpatrick. She still worked tirelessly at reforming the drunkards, dope fiends, and other derelicts at the Bowery, Water Street, and Cremorne missions, as well as at the Door of Hope. Her time was constantly being booked for speeches and lectures for the Railroad Branch of the YMCA and at churches and grange halls in various towns and cities. During spare moments, she did not sit by the fire in a rocking chair but engaged in intellectually stimulating conversation or in musical activities with Ira, Phoebe, or other friends. Even then, she found that she could not do just one thing at a time. When she talked, she usually was knitting or sewing too, for she was nervous if her hands were not constantly occupied.

In 1896 Fanny moved to Brooklyn, taking a room alone in a rather poor section of town, at 683 Lafayette Avenue. She was, however, not far from the

Sankeys and Stebbinses, who regularly looked in on her. Van, too, was now living in Brooklyn, boarding with his friends the Underhills at 400 South Third Street in a fashionable apartment. Fanny frequently called on this "good friend," whom she still regarded with affection.

That year Fanny conceived a new ambition: to enter the foreign mission field. She had always been fascinated by the work of the foreign missionary, but her enthusiasm was further kindled in the spring of 1896 when Bishop William Taylor arrived in America and passed through New York en route to a Methodist convention in Omaha, Nebraska. Taylor, who was a year younger than Fanny, was another tremendously vital and active senior citizen. For many years, he ministered where, in the words of a favorite hymn of Fanny's "Afric's sunny fountains pour down their golden sand." Now in his mid-seventies, he was expected by the Methodist Church to retire. Taylor, however, hoped to receive permission at the Omaha convention to return to Africa one more time. During his stay in New York, this patriarchal figure, with a beard that extended to his abdomen and covered his entire chest, gave several lectures. Fanny attended one of them and was fascinated by Taylor's accounts of the exotic tribes of the Dark Continent. She felt a longing to go in person to bring the good news to those who lived "in sultry forests, where apes swing to and fro." Taylor, realizing her desire, asked her, "If you were thirty years younger, would you go with me to Africa?" She told him that she would indeed go "and help you plant missions." But even though she may have *felt* sixteen, she knew that she was *not* sixteen—or even sixty, for that matter—and so she contented herself to pray for the conversion of the Dark Continent. She visited with Taylor once more, after he had returned to New York from Omaha, where he had been granted permission to return to Africa.

"Well, Fanny," he said, with a smile, "I'm going once more."

Fanny replied that it was her prayer that the good bishop be spared to return to Africa "many times yet, if it be Our Father's will."

The hoary bishop, who was to retire a few years later, was so moved by the poet's enthusiasm that he laid his hand upon her bewigged head in benediction. It was then that Fanny saw "a vision of the multitudes to whom his ministry had been a benediction." It "came to my eyes with a strange power and pathos."[2] For the rest of her life, she prayed that God would raise up men and women to bring the gospel of Christ Jesus to Africa.

About the same time Bishop Taylor embarked for Darkest Africa, D. L. Moody arrived in Darkest Manhattan for the same purpose—to win the unbelieving to Christ. Christian workers were beginning to realize that there were just as many heathens on the streets of New York and Washington as there were on those of Timbuktu or Calcutta, and Moody promised his biggest campaign since 1876. But the almost rabid religious fervor that had so characterized the late 1850s and the subsequent two decades had subsided in

177

the eighties to the point that now, as the twentieth century approached, religious tepidity was prevalent. It was the "Gilded Age," when many devoted their lives to building fortunes; it was also a time when increasing numbers of discontented poor were coming to find their solace not in religion, as their fathers had, but in socialism, communism, and anarchism. Moody was welcomed with only a shadow of the enthusiasm that had greeted him in 1876. Reservations were expressed even by the local clergy. In late September, sixty-five ministers from New York and New Jersey, representing the Baptist, Methodist, Presbyterian, and other "evangelical" denominations, met to make arrangements for the campaigns. Some of the clergymen expressed grave reservations about Moody. One well-known minister maintained that there was no evidence that Moody's past campaigns had made any substantial or permanent increase in church attendance and expressed doubt as to whether the projected November campaign would be helpful or desirable for the local churches. Others were in agreement that, while some sort of religious "revival" in the New York area was desperately needed, it was questionable whether a revival à la Moody would fill the bill.[3] However, by a vote of 49 to 16, the clerics decided to support the efforts of the world-famed pulpit orator.

On November 8, the grizzled evangelist opened his campaign in the Carnegie Music Hall on West 57th Street. It was just after a tumultuous political campaign which had seen William McKinley defeat his Democratic rival, William Jennings Bryan, the "Silver-Tongued Orator," for the presidency. Moody had this in mind as he addressed his middle-aged, churchy audience. "I had intended to speak to the unconverted," he said, but, seeing that his audience was composed of the same old faces he had deplored in his 1890 "Bible Readings," he changed his mind:

I am going to talk to you church people. If we can get the church members on fire like these politicians have been for the last few months, they'll do the rest. There are a lot of Christians who are ashamed to show their colors. They don't want to be seen with tracts in their pockets! They are ashamed to do what the politicians do. There are forty million people in this country who don't go to church! We've got to take the church to them, then!

He continued, lamenting the fact that

there's more excitement in a whiskey shop in one day than there has been in your churches in twelve years! I'm just waiting for some politician to say I'm too enthusiastic. Would to God I had some of the enthusiasm they've had lately! I'd like to stir up the country as *they* have!

After making it perfectly clear that his hearers were more diligent in their worldly business than in their Christian faith, the snowy-bearded man from

178

Northfield lambasted his hearers for their lack of what we would today call social action—on a *personal* level. "Send your carriage out and give poor people a drive in the park once and a while and they'll call you an angel, I'll warrant."[4] Moody was not so much concerned with working to solve the evils of society as with individual men. Society could not be changed until individuals were.

In the next few days, Moody moved out into the local churches. He wanted these congregations to act as "fire-centers from which to spread the flames" of revival.[5] He had come to realize that, at least in big cities, he could win few to Christ through mass meetings. The giant auditoriums rented by his supporters tended to be filled largely with people who were already Christian, and not the indifferent or the "infidels" whom he desired to reach.[6] But he was convinced that every man and woman in New York City could be reached *if* he could get the cooperation of the local pastors and congregations. He needed the local pastors to go from house to house to witness to the occupants therein. He needed both pastors and people to hold small, intimate neighborhood "cottage meetings," for prayer, discussion, and devotion. Only in this way could a revival take place in modern times, Moody felt. But, even in the local churches, he got nothing but pious people.

The parishioners could not or would not go out among the highways and byways to encourage their unchurched friends and neighbors to come, but they flocked to hear Moody at his first "fire-center" meeting at the Marble Collegiate Church. Continual choruses of "Amen!" and "Hear! Hear!" greeted everything that Moody said. A reporter for the *New York Times* observed, moreover, that there were ten women to every man at the Moody meetings. Sankey, who had sung less frequently in late years, was with his old friend this time, but his charm had faded considerably. He was described by one observer as "an immense, bilious man with eyes surrounded by flaccid, pendent, baggy wrinkles." His gestures were "unctuous" and he rolled his eyes "in an affected manner" as he sang, in a ravaged voice, such old favorites as Fanny Crosby's "Blessed Assurance" and "Blessed Homeland," and such newer hymns of hers as "Eye Hath Not Seen" and "Saved by Grace." His deteriorated voice and Moody's impassioned preaching were not, however, able to win to Christ those who simply were not there.

Moody moved his meetings to Cooper Union, an educational institution in downtown Manhattan in whose Great Hall he undertook another series of mass meetings. Perhaps he would attract more "infidels" this time. Here the old man thundered against the "higher criticism" of the Bible, through which many pages of Holy Writ were being dismissed as spurious or explained away as myth or legend. He claimed that it was a "master stroke of the devil" to get men to question the story of Jonah and the Whale. He inveighed against new translations of the Bible and books "written by atheists and infidels," and railed against the Sunday papers which did "more to demoralize the church of

God than anything else!" He took them to task for encouraging crime by reporting murders, divorces, and football games![7]

On November 24, Moody induced Fanny Crosby to make an appearance and introduced her as the author of "Saved by Grace." Although, as usual, she refused to give a speech or sermon, she did appear on the platform and stood when Moody introduced her, and she was given a thunderous ovation.

But for Moody things went from bad to worse. After several mass meetings at Cooper Union, he carried the campaign to a second neighborhood center, as he had previously planned, this time "an old aristocratic brownstone church on 14th Street and Second Avenue."[8] The church was virtually empty and only a handful of people met his gaze as he lumbered onto the platform for the first address.

"Where are the people?" he asked, bewildered.

The pastor of the church shrugged his shoulders and said, drily, "On the streets."

Moody was angered, feeling that the pastor had not done his part in trying to recruit an audience. "Well," he roared, "why don't you go out and get them?" He held up the service until the minister and several other local clergymen could go out and round up some more people.

The frantic clergymen searched high and low, but nobody seemed interested. Finally two of them entered a local bar. To the men who stood about, they asked, sheepishly, "Don't you want to come up to the church on the corner of Second Avenue and hear Dwight L. Moody preach?"

"Who is Moody?" growled one of the men, who, like his companions, went on drinking.[9]

Dwight L. Moody, the man who never grew discouraged, had to admit "complete defeat" in his campaign of 1896 to bring the gospel to New York City. Like many of his friends who ran the rescue missions, he must have felt that somehow he was losing his grip on the masses. He certainly seems to have sensed that he was nearing the end of the road during those dark closing days of the campaign. Fanny's hymn "Saved by Grace" became a consolation to the old man, and he had it sung at nearly every service, sometimes three times a night. During the singing, the hoary preacher would sit with a far-off look in his eyes while tears ran copiously down his rubicund cheeks.

It was during this time that Dr. Lowry, grown white-haired and deaf, decided to do something to secure an income for Fanny's closing years. The demand for hymns and hymnals was growing less and less. He and Doane were working on what would prove to be their last joint effort, *The Royal Hymnal*. The good doctor anticipated that, in the coming years, Fanny would have considerably less work—and considerably less income. As it was, she never earned more than $400 per year, a small sum even for that uninflated time. So

Lowry decided to have Fanny publish another collection of poems, *Bells at Evening*. In addition to an excellent biographical sketch written by Lowry, it included poems from Fanny's three earlier volumes, now long since out of print. There were also later secular poems, and what Fanny considered to be the best of her hymns. *Bells at Evening*, with 224 pages, sold at fifty cents per copy, and Biglow and Main saw to it that all the profit went to Fanny. The volume sold nicely, and there were several editions.

There were some who felt that Fanny was still not sufficiently remunerated for her great work. Many thought that for all she had done to enhance the gospel of Christ, she should be well-to-do, as were many of her peers. Moody owned a fine house in Northfield. Sankey had a fine house in Brooklyn as well as a summer home in Northfield. Why shouldn't Fanny be as well off as her friends? Phoebe Knapp, probably Fanny's richest friend, was especially determined to do something. Unable to persuade Fanny to accept monetary gifts, she turned to other means. Mrs. Knapp approached the poet Will Carleton (1845-1912), author of many volumes of popular sentimental verse and editor of the magazine *Every Where*. He had known Fanny for several years and loved and admired her. Phoebe suggested that he take down from Fanny's dictation the story of her early life and publish it in serial form in *Every Where*, which Carleton consented to do. Part of the profit from these articles would, of course, go to Fanny. By this means Fanny's financial situation could improve without her feeling that she was receiving charity.

Carleton called on Fanny, who agreed to furnish the material for the articles. Carleton was appalled by the squalor in which the world-beloved hymn writer was living, "in one room, in a poor section of Brooklyn." While he had to confess that she was "not in actual want," her circumstances were not, in his estimation, in any way worthy of someone of such august reputation. He was appalled when she told him cheerfully that she received $2 apiece "for the hymns that were singing themselves into the hearts of thousands all over the world."[10] Carleton and his wife began inviting Fanny frequently to their home. "And sometimes here, sometimes there, sometimes in her own small quarters, or . . . in the corner of someone else's home," Carleton drew from Fanny's "detached narratives" an account of her life story.[11] Carleton then wrote the articles in the form in which he intended to publish them, reading them over to Fanny and securing her approval. Then, paying her $10 for each article, he published them in *Every Where* over a period of months.

Although the sales went well, Hugh Main, Howard Doane, and others in the firm of Biglow and Main were offended because Carleton implied and Phoebe Knapp insisted that they were not paying Fanny enough. Indignantly they pointed out that Fanny was receiving far more from *Bells at Evening* than from Carleton's articles. She would receive all the profits from the book that Lowry had issued but was paid merely $10 for each article that Carleton was writing, regardless of how many copies of the magazine were sold. Justifiedly, they pointed out that, far from helping Fanny financially, Carleton was hurting her by providing competition and cutting down the sales of a book which would benefit her far more than would the articles.

This was only the beginning of a quarrel that would reach a showdown between Doane and Main and Carleton and Mrs. Knapp within a few years. No one seemed to realize that Fanny was poor by choice. Although she appreciated the efforts of these friends in her behalf, Fanny in no way wanted to be wealthy. She could have insisted that Biglow and Main pay a larger fee for her hymns, for many hymn writers less celebrated than she charged a fee of up to $10 for their efforts, but she did not. She settled for the minimum and never set a price for her services as a speaker, often refusing honoraria. When forced to accept something in the way of remuneration, she always protested that she was being given too much. She had a horror of wealth almost equal to that of her namesake, Francis of Assisi. Nevertheless, the fact remains that what little she did accept she gave away almost as soon as she got it.

Alice Rector, her friend in later years in Bridgeport, recalled many years after her death that Fanny "could have been a rich woman had she cared to become one, but she poured out the wealth of her mind and heart solely to make others happier and better." Mrs. Rector recalled how Fanny gave away consistently a great percentage of everything she received. She would often give away all the money in her possession if she felt someone needed it. She would cite Proverbs 3:9-10 as the incentive for her style of life: "Honour the Lord with thy substance, and with the firstfruits of all thine increase: So shall thy barns be filled with plenty, and thy presses shall burst out with new wine." On this basis she justified giving away practically all she received, and praying for food, rent, or whatever she needed from day to day. "From the time I received the first check for my poems," she said many years later, "I made up my mind to open my hand wide to those who needed assistance."[12] Neither Phoebe nor Carleton nor Main nor Doane, in their own ways, could have made her rich. "Gold is good, in its place," she said, "but when it becomes our master, it places a crown of thorns upon the brow that crushes the strongest to the earth. Better a man without money than money without the man."[13]

Fanny's friends must have known that she could have been more affluent had she so chosen, but out of love for her so intense that it led them to quarrel among themselves, they were determined that Fanny live in style whether she liked it or not. Moody, too, got in on the act. He felt that his friend whose hymns had been so instrumental in making his campaigns a success in the past deserved something better than she had. Thus he proposed to Main that instead of paying her $2 for each hymn, he should pay her a regular weekly salary of $8, and Main consented. This brought in about $416 per annum, roughly the equivalent of what she had been receiving by being paid for each hymn. But Moody and Main knew that in coming years there would be fewer hymns published, and this new arrangement would make certain that Fanny would continue to receive the amount she had been getting for years, even though she would be asked to write fewer hymns. In the future, however, certain friends would renew their efforts to make Fanny more affluent than she wanted to be. The battle was not yet over.

Fanny's friends had good reason for their solicitude, for they feared that the day when she could no longer work was not far off, whatever the demand for hymns might be. After all, she was closer to eighty than seventy, and she looked terrible. The fact that she persisted in living alone worried not only friends but her family. The sisters in Bridgeport urged her to come north and make her home with them, but Fanny refused. During this period, in Northfield, she fell down the steps at Moody's house and was seriously cut. Shortly after recovery that winter, she suffered a heart attack in Brooklyn, and for a while her life hung in the balance. For days she was in a partial coma, more in the spiritual world than the physical. When she was herself again, she testified to seeing wonderful visions and vividly perceiving the spirits of her loved ones in the other world. She made a complete recovery, but, like Paul, was torn between a desire to "depart and be with Christ, for that is far better," and a desire to remain on earth and continue her work in behalf of humanity. Her friends and physicians urged rest, but she refused, saying she wanted to "die in harness" as her friend Henry Ward Beecher had done. [14] When she was no longer able to work, then let her die, but she would not sit around in a rocking chair, doing nothing. She wanted to work until she dropped, and she did—although it was to take nearly twenty years, by which time she would have outlived practically everyone who was so worried about her in the 1890s!

Fanny, in fact, resumed her former work load as soon as she could, continuing to work in the New York night missions. She also continued to travel in New England to lecture, still insisting that she needed no companion. In the summer of 1897, she revisited the scenes of her girlhood, perhaps for the first time since she had left to go to the Institution. She was invited to address the graduating women of the Drew Seminary in the town of Carmel, not too many miles from Gayville. Perhaps she had someone drive her to the cottage where she had been born and lived the first few years. At Drew, she delighted the audience with reminiscences about the locality in the days of her childhood. She recited poems and then spoke to the girls about her faith, appealing to them to put their lives in the hands of Christ. She closed with a poem dedicated in honor of the school.

In August she journeyed once more to central New York. Named poet laureate of the Chautauqua Circle at Tully Lake, she had consented to attend their summer Round Table and deliver at least one major poetic address. The

Chautauqua Assemblies were a system of adult education and entertainment that was popular in the late nineteenth and early twentieth century. They performed generally the same service that television does today. At Assembly Park at Tully Lake, which was about thirty miles south of Syracuse and one of about a hundred Chautauqua centers thriving at the time, audiences were instructed and entertained by speakers and performers from a diversity of fields. For instance, at the Round Table at Tully Lake at the turn of the century the inhabitants of the Syracuse area pooled their various talents to give such diverse presentations as a reading of the graveyard scene from *Hamlet*; a lecture by a Syracuse doctor on the eye, illustrated by "crayon drawings and practical experiments"; a lecture by a local lady on her recent trip to Japan; and a solo by a local tenor. Fanny, as a nationally known poet, was the star attraction of the Circle's summer program.[15]

Although the Chautauqua Society was affiliated with the Methodist Church, the programs, at least those in which Fanny appeared, were basically secular. Unlike her addresses in most other places, Fanny's presentations here were not religious in orientation. She was usually called upon to open or close the meetings with poems written expressly for the occasion. These showy poems delighted audiences who, like those who loved her recitations while she was the poet laureate of the Institution for the Blind, liked long, tinselly poems, loaded with learned allusions and florid metaphors. It must have taken quite a bit of time and effort for Fanny to create poems of this sort to recite at the Round Table meeting. But amazingly, in addition to her daily recitations there, Fanny spent the rest of her time at Tully Lake fulfilling speaking engagements in nearby communities. A week's itinerary recorded in a Syracuse newspaper in the early 1900s is an example of a typical summer's activity in Tully: Sunday evening Fanny spoke at the Rescue Mission in Syracuse; Monday she visited the State Fair and delivered a lecture at the Women's Pavilion; Tuesday she spoke at a nearby reservation of Onondaga Indians; Wednesday she recited a poem, written expressly for the occasion, at the Elmwood Grange; Thursday, she had no commitments, save to the Round Table, at which she recited daily anyway; Friday afternoon, she spoke at the Old Ladies Home at Syracuse; and Sunday she spoke at noon to the Chevaliers of the Goodwill Congregational Church and the same day delivered the sermon at the evening services there. It was certainly a schedule capable of killing a person of forty, let alone a woman well along in years and only recently recovered from a heart attack.

Somehow Fanny found some time for relaxation at Tully Lake. Eliza Hewitt annually attended the Round Table and was her companion there. Here Fanny enjoyed the friendship of a woman who was almost like a sister to her. Eliza was not pushy and domineering like her other close lady friend, Phoebe Knapp, but seems to have been of a gentle, soft-spoken disposition. Fanny spent, "many happy hours" with her, enjoying "one of the best things earth has to offer any mortal . . . the immortal friendship of kindred spirits."[16]

Fanny also found the time to strike up or renew other friendships at Tully Lake. Here, after at least sixty years, she enjoyed a reunion with Lucy Kingsbury, her old friend from the Institution. It was at Assembly Park that Fanny met in 1897 a high school student from the nearby town of Oran, New York. Henry Adelbert White wrote poetry and had long been interested in Fanny and her work. The venerable lady and the young boy quickly became great friends, and later, while attending Wesleyan College in Middlebury, Connecticut, he would make frequent trips to see the poet, who was then in Bridgeport. This bespectacled, clean-cut young man, sixty years Fanny's junior, would soon become one of her closest friends and confidants.

Fanny was never too busy to receive "pilgrims" who came to call. She stayed at the home of the John Roberts family in Tully, and her hosts realized that she needed time to prepare her poems, sermons, and other addresses, so they tried to shoo away the callers who continually sought her out during the evenings. But Fanny would not hear of it! She was never too busy to receive anybody who had come to see her. No matter whether she had a twelve- or fourteen-hour day crammed with lectures and interviews, no matter whether she was in the midst of writing a poem or lecture, she interrupted what she was doing to spend time with her callers. And this was her "summer vacation"! All this is more remarkable when we are reminded that she did all of this without pay! Her hosts paid railroad fares and provided meals and transportation and accommodations while she was in the area, but beyond that Fanny usually would not accept a penny for her services. Fanny was in growing demand as a speaker during this time for her popularity, like her activity, increased with the passing years. This was not the case, however, with many of her contemporaries.

In January 1898 Moody returned to New York for still another campaign. His meetings at Carnegie Hall were not so much geared to convert unbelievers as to enlighten and empower those who were already faithful. He had now concluded that in New York, at least, "mass evangelism" was fruitless if conducted with the aim of winning over the indifferent to Christ. It was the individual Christian who had to be the evangelist in the modern city, witnessing to the unbelieving who were their neighbors or co-workers. In the two-month campaign, Moody presented a star-studded cast before the New York public. Henry Van Dyke, eminent pastor of the Brick Presbyterian Church in New York and author of the beloved novel *The Other Wise Man* and the hymn "Joyful, Joyful, We Adore Thee," shared the platform with the portly evangelist and assisted him in many of the meetings. Oliver Otis Howard, the famous general and statesman and also a devoted Congregational layman, was on the platform and led the meeting in prayer on at least one occasion. The Glee Club of Yale University, where Moody's son Paul was a student, sang, and Booker T. Washington, the Negro rights leader, gave an address in which he said that the one thing Negroes could teach Whites was a simple faith. Moody also spoke, of course. He was now only sixty-one but looked over seventy. He had grown so unwieldy and dropsical that he moved with difficulty and often gasped for breath. He spoke much about death, apparently cognizant of the fact that he was nearing his own end.

At first, Moody's meetings were attended heavily but still, predictably, chiefly by old women who "sobbed convulsively" during most of the service. Sankey did not make an appearance, and his duties were now divided between Victor Benke, the young organist of the Bowery mission; J. H. Burke, a Chicago soloist; and stout, gray, and ailing John Sweney, himself but a year away from the grave. Fanny was not present either, or at least made no appearance on the platform, but she was there in the presence of her hymns, which were liberally sung at the meetings. Burke and Sweney sang "Eye Hath Not Seen" and "Though Your Sins Be As Scarlet" on several occasions. And Moody used "Saved by Grace" as much as he had in 1896. He loved to split the singing between the choir and audience and would direct the choir to sing "And I shall see Him face to face" and the galleries to respond with "And tell the story, saved by grace!"

The campaign closed on March 20 and Moody looked terribly weary. After a good beginning, his crowds had dwindled so that, during the last few meetings, he was speaking to a nearly empty hall. In May he returned to speak at the Hanson Place Baptist Church in Brooklyn, where Robert Lowry had once served as pastor. He came to raise funds for evangelical work he was initiating among the soldiers based in large numbers at Tampa, Florida, preparing to leave for Cuba and the now raging Spanish-American War. But Moody put himself in line for criticism when he sent Ira Sankey and Daniel Whittle, both of whom were just as old as he and in worse health, to minister to the soldiers, while he declined to go himself, on account of the heat. His efforts met with little success then or in August, when he returned to make another appeal at the Fifth Avenue Presbyterian Church.

While the popularity of other celebrities in the religious world of her generation declined, Fanny's continued to augment. This was perhaps owing to the fact that she spoke to small groups and could come across better as a personality than those preachers like Moody and Whittle, who appeared amid a sea of humanity in some cavernous auditorium. It may also have been due to her positive approach. As we have seen, the typical nineteenth-century preacher chided and scolded and threatened, while Fanny, assuming that her audience knew that they were sinners, offered a message of comfort and encouragement. Then too, she had something that Moody did not have which was capable of drawing the unchurched to meetings: her blindness. And, of course, a great deal of Fanny's appeal was due to her charisma and indefinable mystique, a mystique that overwhelmed all who met her. There were few who failed to come under her charm. It is amazing that of all the contemporary accounts which describe Fanny Crosby and her work, not one falls anything short of adulation for her as a person. Even those who bitterly criticized the quality of her hymns had to admit that as a person she possessed an irresistible charm and an indisputable holiness.

Years later a man who as a boy of eighteen had heard Fanny speak provided this striking account of "Aunt Fanny" and her profound effect. "She was dressed in black. In her hand she carried the accustomed little black book which she always used when speaking. Her eyes were sealed with dark glasses." Then "she lifted a frail little hand and in a voice as sweet as the songs of a bird, as calm with spiritual assurance as if angels had inspired her,"[17] she quoted several stanzas of "Redeemed, O How I Love to Proclaim It." That was the extent of her presentation. Yet the effect of this brief, simple, seemingly innocuous recitation was one of shattering profundity. "I can never get away from the spell that was cast over my soul by Fanny Crosby's quoting this," the anonymous man testified nearly a half century later. "My life was literally remade!"[18]

One reason, perhaps, why Fanny was so reluctant to speak at Ocean Grove, Northfield, or in Moody's campaigns was that she generally tended to steal the show from the star attraction and did not want to embarrass her friends. An incident of this nature occurred in 1898, when she was asked to make a few remarks at a revival held by evangelist William P. Hall at the Baptist Temple in Brooklyn. By simply telling the story of how she came to write "Saved by Grace" and by composing and reciting a little poem of six lines on the spot, she electrified her audience and completely eclipsed evangelist Hall, even though he preached a good sermon. Her spontaneity, candor, and sincerity all combined with her ability as a speaker and the holiness that she was said to radiate to bring about conversions wherever and whenever she spoke. Many of her contemporaries had their day and now their star had begun to set, but it was not so with Fanny. It seemed as if her charisma increased with the years and her effectiveness with her wrinkles and gray hairs.

CHAPTER 19
"NEVER GIVE UP"

The generation of hymn-tune composers who had helped Fanny create her greatest hits was beginning to pass from the scene. Chester Allen, Silas Vail, and William Sherwin were already dead. John Sweney suffered a stroke shortly after the Moody campaign and died on April 10, 1899. Next it was Lowry's turn to rest. Since the publication of *Bells at Evening*, his health had been in decline, and soon it was obvious that he was in his last sickness. Fanny went to Plainfield, New Jersey, to visit him at home, where he was bedfast and in pain. "We talked to-gether of many of the events of thirty years," she recalled.

Finally, the dying man turned the conversation to the thing that most concerned him—his approaching death. "Fanny," he whispered softly, "I am going to join those who have gone before—my work is now done."

Fanny, with a figurative lump growing in her throat, found herself unable to "speak with him concerning the parting" without betraying intense grief. "So I simply took his hand in mine and said quietly, 'I thank you, Dr. Lowry, for all that you have done for me.'" Then, echoing the words of the hymn they had written together years before, she said, "Good night, until we meet in the morning" and "silently went down the stairs, with the impression on my mind that the good man would soon be at rest from his labors, and so indeed it proved."[1] On November 25, the "Good Doctor" was gathered "with the saints at the river" of which he had sung.

A new generation of hymn writers was arising, however, and some of them composed in a style identical to that of their predecessors. Charles Hutchison Gabriel, born in Wilton, Iowa, in August 1856, was probably the hymn writer who can most aptly be called the true successor to Lowry, Doane, Sankey, Sweney, and Kirkpatrick. His hymns were very simple and had "the old Methodist swing." He was completely self-taught, and in the words of Jacob Hall, a contemporary hymn writer, he was therefore "little hampered by purely scholastic rules of form, and hence [was] free to produce many effects and contrasts which other composers are apt to lose."[2] Gabriel's music was "seldom difficult or severe" and was quite easy to sing. Like Lowry, he often wrote his own words, attributing the lyrics to "Charlotte G. Homer," the most frequent of his numerous pen names. His most popular hymns were "Higher Ground," "The Glory Song," "His Eye Is on the Sparrow," and "Will the Circle Be Unbroken?"

Inevitably, Fanny was requested to supply Gabriel with hymns, which she did increasingly as the years went by. Among those for which Gabriel supplied the tunes were "Hold Fast," "Lead Me, My Saviour," and "Sunshine on the Hill." The last was by far the most successful of their joint efforts—the hymn had come to Fanny by "divine inspiration" during a ride in Sankey's carriage while the singer was describing the effects of dusk on the surrounding countryside—but even so, Fanny was not able to achieve hits with the thin, bespectacled composer with the enormous walrus mustache. Like most of her hymns of this period, the lyrics Fanny provided for Gabriel were more or less repeats of her previous hymns, paraphrased for the fifteenth or twentieth time, often sterile imitations of their precursors.

Besides Gabriel, there were several other younger musicians with whom Fanny worked. Some of them wrote music that was more complicated and sophisticated than that of their predecessors. One of the younger composers was Adam Geibel, who became a close friend of Fanny's. Born in Baden, Germany, in 1855 and brought to America as a child, he was, like Fanny, blinded at an early age by inept treatment of an eye infection. Like her also, he had gone on to get an excellent education and become a skilled musician, well known both as an organist and as a composer of secular music. Among his most famous compositions was "Sleep, Sleep, Sleep," a song which became the theme of Fred Waring's popular radio program in the 1930s and 1940s. Geibel set many of Fanny's poems to music, the most successful of which being "Beautiful Waters of Eden."

Another new musician was Mary Upham, a distant cousin of Fanny's who had been a well-known concert singer before she decided, for religious reasons, to give up singing all secular music. She married a lumber dealer, Reuben Currier, and lived in Springfield, Massachusetts, and as time went on Fanny was a frequent visitor in their home. Fanny wrote a number of hymns for Mrs. Currier, many of which were published in a hymnal called O Sing Unto the Lord. The best known of these was "Press Towards the Mark."

Victor Benke was another composer of the new school. Born in Germany in 1872, Benke was the organist at the Bowery Mission when Fanny first met him. He specialized in martial hymns, which he wrote in a style reminiscent of John Philip Sousa. Among his hymns using Fanny's lyrics were "Girded for Battle" and "Soldiers of the King." Perhaps the most successful hymn for which Fanny supplied Benke the words was "Child, I Loved Thee Long Ago," which sounds something like a typical love song of the time. But even her most successful hymns of this period never approached the popularity of her previous hits.

The most accomplished and successful of Fanny's younger collaborators was Ira Allan Sankey, third and youngest son of her great friend. Born during his father's first overseas campaign, in Edinburgh, Scotland, on August 30, 1874, from early childhood young Sankey manifested "an intense love for the arts, especially music."[3] But at Princeton University he studied to be an architect and civil engineer. However, after his graduation in 1897, he could no longer resist the lure of the field that was his first love and went to work with Biglow and Main. His superior talent was at once recognized by his father and his colleagues, and Allan was soon composing a large number of the tunes for that firm.

Fanny had known young Sankey from the time he was a baby and watched with great interest his progress as a composer. He was big, tall and heavy, with a drooping mustache and dark hair parted in the middle. An amiable young man, he had a "sunny disposition."[4] He was also an excellent musician whose music was the most harmonically sophisticated of any that used Fanny Crosby's poems. It was mellifluous, whereas the tunes of most gospel-hymn writers had a tendency to be choppy. Moreover, young Sankey's melodies were much more complicated than those of his father and their generation. He often adapted themes from classical compositions, but he did so more skillfully than Bradbury or Root. Of all the men for whom she ever wrote, Allan Sankey was the only one whose musicianship she praised without reservation. She often praised one tune or another by Doane or Stebbins or the elder Sankey, but she studiously avoided comments on their musicianship. However, she wrote that young Sankey's music was "unusually sweet and beautiful"[5] and had to admit that as much as she loved Ira Sankey as a person, "the son surpassed the father in sweetness of tone and harmony of expression."[6] Often, when she was with Allan, trying to compose words to one of his melodies, she was so carried away with the ineffable beauty of his composition that she was virtually entranced and temporarily unable to write a line!

Fanny began to collaborate with Allan Sankey in 1899, and their work together continued until both their deaths sixteen years later. Allan was capable, more than any other gospel-hymn tune writer, of expressing the emotional power of Fanny's poems, and he set to music some of her more complicated hymns, such as "God's Peace I'll Know." Although these may have been superior hymns musically speaking, they tended to be too rich and difficult for popular taste. They may have been more beautiful to listen to than the tunes of Doane and Lowry, but they were more difficult to sing and to play on the piano or organ. The most popular of their hymns was "Never Give Up"; for which Allan wrote a simple, straightforward tune in the old style.

> Never be sad or desponding,
> If thou hath faith to believe,

Grace, for the duties before thee
Ask of thy God and receive.

Never give up, never give up,
Never give up to thy sorrows,
Jesus will bid them depart,
Trust in the Lord, trust in the Lord,
Sing when your trials are greatest,
Trust in the Lord and take heart![7]

This Fanny considered one of her most effective poems.

There is a great and wonderful truth embodied in these words. The whole victory of life is in them—"Trust in the Lord and take heart." That means the exercise of courage, the consciousness of being linked to one mightier than ourselves, and it helps one to keep smiling, to keep sunshiny, and to have not only a song on the lip, but one in the heart.[8]

It became popular in the early 1900s, when it was a favorite with the British evangelist Rodney "Gipsy" Smith (1860–1947), who used it continually in his meetings.

Allan Sankey was also vice-president of the Leeds and Catlin Phonograph Company, and through his efforts some of the leading lights of the Moody-Sankey years were persuaded to record their voices for posterity. The elder Sankey preserved on wax the pathetic remains of his once-glorious voice, making several cylinders in which he sang his famous "The Ninety and Nine," as well as "God Be with You," "The City of God," "The Mistakes of My Life," and the old German hymn, "My Jesu, As Thou Wilt." Moody was induced to make at least one recording, reciting the Beatitudes, and Stebbins, Sam Hadley, and others were recorded singing hymns, but there is no evidence that Fanny Crosby ever had her voice recorded.

After the hectic annual trip to Tully Lake in the late summer of 1899, Fanny went to Oneonta, New York, where she conducted a long series of evangelical meetings that eclipsed the Bible Conference at Northfield. Since she was unable to be with Moody and Sankey, she was anxious to convey greetings to them, especially so in the case of Moody, with whom she had had no personal contact for a year. She bade a friend who was en route to the conference to greet her two great friends. "Now, when you come back," she said to the man, "be sure and bring me a message from Mr. Moody and one from Mr. Sankey. Don't forget it."

The gentleman had no trouble speaking to Sankey and relaying Fanny's greeting to him, but he had a hard time getting to see Moody alone. Finally, he came upon Moody as he was seeing J. P. Morgan off to New York in his carriage. As the vehicle rumbled away, Fanny's messenger cornered the white-bearded evangelist and greeted him for the poet. The aged man looked at him for a minute in silence, then said quietly, "Give her my love." Fanny always cherished those few words of greeting, for this was to be the last communication from her beloved old friend.

Fanny returned to Brooklyn, and in November Moody traveled west to conduct a campaign in Kansas City, Missouri. He had maintained a grueling routine for nearly forty years, and as a result he was prematurely old. He had been suffering from a heart condition for several years, and now he was in constant pain. Flushed in the face, he breathed with difficulty, and his frame, already enormous with corpulence, was swollen with dropsy to immense proportions. Indeed, scarcely able to walk, with the slightest exertion leaving him exhausted, he still insisted on conducting the meetings. Even so, the effort was too much for him, and he found that he just could not continue. "I'm afraid I shall have to give up these meetings," he sadly admitted. "It's too bad. It's the first time in nearly forty years of preaching that I have had to give up my meetings. It is more painful to me to give up those audiences than it is for me to suffer from my ailments."[9]

Moody's health had always been excellent, but now, "worn out in the service of the Lord," his body was disintegrating. He was taken back to Northfield by rail, and there he spent a month dying. Delirious with pain, he at times was heard to repeat, partly in quotation of Psalm 30, "I have heard it in the Land of Light from whence I came: weeping may endure for a night, but joy cometh in the morning." On the morning of December 22, joy came. His wife and sons heard him cry joyfully, "Earth is receding. Heaven is opening before me. Is this dying? If this is death, it's sweet. There's no valley . . . this is bliss." He seemed to be suspended between two worlds. After a while, he said to his family, "I have been within the gates. God is calling. I must go." Then once again he seemed to enter the heavenly world. "Dwight! Irene!" he called, naming two of his grandchildren, who had died tragically the year before. "I see the children's faces!" Their father, his son Will, suggested that he must be dreaming. "No, this is no dream, Will." He bade farewell to his wife of nearly forty years, saying, "Mama, you have been a good, dear wife to me," and then fell insensible again, only to be revived by the doctors by means of heart stimulants. Irked by the physicians' "heroic efforts" to prolong his life, he said disappointedly, "What are you doing here? I have been beyond the gates of heaven, and now I am here again!" When, after a short time, he began to sink once more and the doctors tried to give him another injection, Moody refused to have his life prolonged. "It is only keeping the family in anxiety,"[10] he said. A few minutes later, he drifted off to sleep, returning forever to the "Land of Light" whence he had come sixty-two years earlier.

As thirty-two pallbearers carried the bier with his casket on it to its final resting-place on Round Top hill, near his home, Fanny, back in Brooklyn, pondered what manner of man her revered Moody had been. "He was a wonderful man," she said of him. As she thought of his long and useful life, the words from the Apocalypse of John came to her: "Blessed are the dead which die in the Lord from henceforth: Yea, saith the Spirit, that they may rest from their labours; and their works do follow them."[11] Now Moody rested forever from his prodigious labors. To a reporter some years later, Fanny said of her friend, "I have never known a kinder, bigger-hearted man than Dwight L. Moody. His work was a miracle, and a constant inspiration through all my work. His influence was like light—sanative and bracing."[12]

Although the man who had to such an extent inspired her work now lay in dust, Fanny's labors continued. She continued to write hymns, travel, preach, and work in the night missions until spring, when shortly after her eightieth birthday the inevitable collapse came. She fell ill with bronchial pneumonia. "Many thought I was not goir.g to get well," she later said, because, for the second time in four years, she was "almost in sight of the harbor." But, by virtue of her remarkable constitution, and not withstanding her heart condition, Fanny pulled through.

Carrie and Jule had hurried down from Bridgeport to Fanny's room on Lafayette Avenue when they were first informed by neighbors of their sister's illness. This time they insisted that Fanny leave Brooklyn and come with them. It was just not right for an eighty-year-old woman to be living alone. Fanny at first objected, but when Hugh Main and the Sankeys seconded Carrie and Jule and when she came to the understanding with her sisters that she would be returning to the Empire City for frequent visits, she relented. So, in June 1900 Fanny left New York, after a residence there of sixty-five years.

For the first time since she was fifteen, Fanny was making her home with relatives. "My living home wasn't till the later years,"[13] she remarked afterward. She first moved into the two-family house at 251 Fairfield Avenue which Jule owned and where Carrie had been boarding since the death of their mother. As soon as possible, Carrie and Fanny rented a room in the home of Mr. and Mrs. Wilbur Wilson on 2526 North Avenue, across the street from the cemetery where "Mother Dear" and practically all their other relatives were buried. Soon, however, they moved into an apartment in a fine brick house owned by William and Sarah Becker on 756 State Street. There the two would live for the next six years. Their rent was paid by Ira Sankey, who, in addition, sent Carrie a sum of money each month with which to provide for the needs of the poet. (He knew better than to send it to Fanny, who would always find someone worse off than she and give it away!) This dwelling, in a good section of the city, was by far the most congenial residence that Fanny had ever known. The apartment consisted of five large rooms, into which Carrie moved her furniture. It was a pleasant, cozy place and the living room had a bay window, in which Fanny loved to sit and rock. The parlor was dominated by an enormous portrait of Mercy, whose memory both sisters fervently venerated.

Carolyn Rider was a short, heavy-set woman with a long, homely face, but the unimpressiveness of her physical appearance was offset by a lovely smile and twinkling eyes. She has been described as a pleasant, jolly lady, of an exceedingly sweet disposition, who was especially fond of children. Like her famous sister, she was disarmingly frank, open, sincere, and confiding, and hated pretense and deceit. But she was quiet and extremely shy, and public appearances were a kind of purgatory for her. For the sake of her sister, she put up with the hurly-burly of public life, devoting the remaining years of her life to being her sister's eyes. "She has sacrificed her life for me,"[14] Fanny later said of her.

For the rest of her life, Carrie would serve as Fanny's secretary and amanuensis. She read to her all the mail that came to Fanny's "Box 840" in the Bridgeport Post Office and wrote her dictated replies. Every morning she would take down anything in the way of a hymn or poem that "Sister Fan" had composed during the night. Later on, she was able to secure the services of a professional secretary, a young woman named Eva G. Cleaveland, who would relieve her of much of the work; but for the time being, Carrie certainly had her hands full, handling what had been the responsibility of two or three professional secretaries in the offices of Biglow and Main in New York.

Carrie had joined the First Baptist Church in Bridgeport at the age of sixteen, upon marriage to Lee Barnum, and she was a devout member. Fanny occasionally went there with her, but being a Methodist, she went more frequently with Jule to First Methodist Church. Although it was four years before she officially transferred her membership, from the start Fanny took an active part in its life. She became active in the King's Daughters, a charitable organization connected with that church which provided food, clothes, and coal for the poor and ran a hospital. The guiding light of this group seems to have been Alice Young Rector (1861–1941), who, with her physician husband, Orville, ran the hospital, known redundantly as "Rector's Hospital for the Sick." "Rector," as Fanny called Alice, was very pious and somewhat sanctimonious, and claimed that Jesus walked with her every day; like Phoebe Knapp, she could be strong-willed and difficult at times. Nevertheless, she and Fanny got along well, and Rector became one of her most devoted friends in Bridgeport.

Fanny at once became active in Bridgeport's Christian Union, an institution that served the same purpose as New York's rescue missions. The Union, of which the Rev. Charles W. Simpson was superintendent, was on South Main Street in downtown Bridgeport. Every night there was a service and, assisted by converted bums who were now full or part-time Christian workers, Simpson would round up as many derelicts and drunkards as he could for an audience. Several nights a week, Fanny would be the main speaker, if she was in town. Mrs. Clarice Bray Griffins, who as a young girl played the piano in many of these services, vividly recalled to the author "Aunt Fanny's" talks. "You're my girl if you play at my mission," she would tell her schoolgirl pianist. Invariably clad in black, with a bonnet tied under her chin, Fanny would be led to the lectern. In a voice that was young and steady, she would greet "her men," exclaiming, "Dear friends, I'm so happy to see you!" Her manner took away all self-consciousness on the part of those men sober enough to know what was going on. First, she usually recited, flawlessly, a passage of scripture. Then she would preach. She radiated as always a great sweetness and good cheer, speaking on "The Joy of Being a Christian" and testifying to her own experiences and offering to the men the reasons why they should be Christians too. She told them what the Lord could and would do for them, often quoting from her own hymns or those of other authors. In a calm and conversational way, she would lay the "plan of salvation" before them. When she finished and Simpson gave the altar call, Mrs. Griffins recalls that there were *always* one or two men who came forward, "converted."

Fanny was by no means confining herself to Bridgeport. In August, less than two months after she arrived, she went to Northfield, a sadder and quieter place now that Moody was gone. As usual, she stayed with Ira and Fanny Sankey. During this visit, she visited Moody's widow, Emma, and also paid a final call on Daniel Whittle, who was dying. That unfortunate man had been ravaged by an excruciatingly painful disease of the bones ever since his work with the soldiers in Tampa two years before.

"Oh, Major," she said, "I wish I could give you a part of my good health this morning."

The Major, who was in an agony of pain, murmured, "It's all right. . . . The Lord knows best, and all will result in my good." During the visit, the dying evangelist, despite his sufferings, spoke "pleasantly" of some of his favorite hymns. He was not at all bitter or questioning about his illness, but cheerfully resigned to impending death. "All sorrow will fade away," he said, "and all pain depart as dew before the morning sun."[15] Poor Whittle had seven more months of pain to endure, but "that dear, patient man," as Fanny characterized him, bore his torments faithfully until he was released on the day of the Second Inauguration of William McKinley the following year.

It was during this conference that for the second time Fanny spoke to the Northfield audiences. Sankey opened the Sunday meeting by singing "Saved by Grace." Afterward, commenting about how much Moody had loved that hymn, he bade the audience join with him in singing it once more. Then he led Fanny to the lectern, where she made a disappointingly short address and concluded by telling of the joy she experienced when Moody sent his last message to her. Of this modest message, Fanny said, "Oh, praise the Lord! I am so glad that I got that message. I have hidden it in the very depths of my soul as a precious treasure, and by and by, when he and I meet in yon blessed realm, he will remember it and so will I." She closed by reciting the words of a hymn she had written for Sankey, "The Everlasting Hills":

Oh, the music rolling onward,
Through the boundless regions bright,
Where the King in all His beauty
Is the glory and the light!
Where the sunshine of His presence
Ev'ry wave of sorrow stills,
And the bells of joy are ringing
On the everlasting hills.[16]

When the convention was over, Fanny went to Tully Lake and Sankey set sail for Britain, for another campaign. He was in high spirits as he arrived in Ireland, writing Fanny that he had crossed the Atlantic with "no sickness, no sorrow, no sighing" and protesting his love for her "although 3,000 long miles separate us for a 'letter while.'" In Belfast he talked about Fanny so much that a wealthy businessman gave him a present of five pounds in gold for her. When Ira returned in January, however, he was completely exhausted and went with his wife to the Kellogg Sanitarium at Battle Creek, Michigan, for a rest. There Fanny wrote him a letter in verse in which she exclaimed:

But, oh, a sanitarium fare—
No coffee? Well, I do declare
'Tis rather hard, it seems to me;
But doctors say—and they agree—
The sacrifice is right to make
When ordered for the stomach's sake.[17]

The Sankeys soon returned from Michigan. But the career of the "Sweet Singer of Israel" was just about at its close. He was no longer in the limelight of American religious life. Since his voice had lost the brilliance that had so electrified audiences of twenty and thirty years before, his star had been on the wane. And since the death of his "David," "Jonathan" had been in almost total eclipse. He was remembered, but only as a figure out of the past. It was as if he were already dead. In fact, one day Sankey was on a train, sitting beside a total stranger who spoke of the great Ira D. Sankey but did not recognize him. Indeed, his appearance was sadly altered from the days when he moved Moody's audiences to tears by the beloved hymns. Once nearly as fat as Moody, through ill health he had lost a great deal of weight; what little hair he had left was white; and in place of the famous mutton-chop whiskers, he now wore simply a drooping white mustache. The stranger began to speak fondly of the days when Moody and Sankey were winning thousands of people to Christ, not knowing to whom he was speaking. He reminisced about Sankey's once-glorious voice, and added something to the effect that "too bad he died too."

Sankey said nothing about his identity until it was his time to alight. "Before I go, I must tell you—that I am Sankey."

His traveling companion was incredulous. "Don't kid with me," he said impatiently. "Everybody knows that Sankey is dead!" To be dead while blood still courses through one's veins ... to be as a ghost visiting familiar scenes incorporeal and unrecognized ... such was the fate of Ira Sankey, his voice gone, his audiences gone, his fame a thing of the past. Yet he accepted this and continued the one ministry of which he was still capable: writing hymns. Fanny supplied him with many poems which he set to music. Among the most lovely of their hymns of this period is "He Who Safely Keepeth":

He who safely keepeth,
Slumbers not nor sleepeth;
Though by all the world despised,
Wherefore shall I fear?
That which He hath spoken
Never can be broken—
Who can harm the trusting heart
When He is near?[18]

Fanny also still wrote for Phoebe Knapp. The rich widow, resplendent in silk and satin gowns and diamond tiaras, nearing seventy but with the face and figure of a woman of forty,[19] had decided that she and Fanny should publish their future compositions as sheet music. In that way Fanny would be able to profit financially from her efforts more than she did when her poems were bought and published by a music company. Owning the copyright to the sheet music, she could more adequately benefit from whatever popularity the hymns should attain. Fanny insisted that the copyright be Phoebe's property, but the widow made sure that the profits came in full to her blind friend. Among the hymns written in these years were "Thou in Whom Alone I Live," a poem very much reminiscent of "Every Day and Hour"; "At Evening Time It Shall Be Light," an anthem with characteristically pedestrian verse; and

"Open the Gates of the Temple," an Easter anthem. This last proved to be very popular and is still sung occasionally today. A few years later it was recorded by the operatic tenor Evan Williams on an RCA Victor Red Label, thus becoming the first Fanny Crosby hymn to be accorded the distinction of being recorded by a leading classical soloist.

Fanny continued to supply Allan Sankey and Hugh Main with hymns, which they now published not in large hymnals of more than a hundred pieces but in collections of six, seven, and eight hymns. Howard Doane, however, was preparing a new full-length hymnal, which he was going to entitle *Songs of Devotion,* and in order to assist him Fanny went to his summer home at Watch Hill, Rhode Island, to spend the first part of July.

It was at Doane's home that Fanny received a telegram announcing Van's death. Her more-and-less husband, whom she continued to visit and with whom she still maintained amicable relations, had been ill with cancer for over a year and in the last month had suffered a paralytic shock. Harriss and Caroline Underhill had faithfully nursed him in this last sickness. When Fanny heard of the death of the man with whom she had shared more than two decades of happy married life and whom she still considered a very dear friend,[20] she was heartbroken. Her thoughts went back to that June day nearly a half century before when the "voice of love" first spoke within their breast and "all the world was changed," when they "were no longer blind, for the light of love showed us where the lilies bloomed, and where the crystal waters find the moss-mantled spring." Poor Van! It had not been easy to marry a woman already famous. Nor had it been easy to live with a wife so seldom at home. Although they had not been together for years, in a way they continued to love each other to the end.

Three days after Van's death, which occurred on July 18, Howard Doane wrote Adelbert White, now a student at Wesleyan College, who was like a son to the two childless old women on State Street in Bridgeport, and who periodically helped Carrie with the voluminous correspondence that was her responsibility:

> Yours of 19th reached me to-day. Sunday we have no mail. I am also in receipt Telegram from Biglow and Main advising Van's death. I was sorry and grieved to hear it. I thought I would not mention it to Fanny, but finally I felt it was the thing to do. I have done so. I think as you do that it would be unwise for her to try to go now. The excitement and fatigue would surely make her sick and would not do any good. She does not yet know where to have him buried. Will need a little time to quietly think it over. She feels ought to be where she can be buried beside him. Biglow and Main say body will be placed in a vault this afternoon. Fanny will start for Bridgeport Thursday afternoon about 5:30 or 6:00, I think. She is bearing up bravely

under the sad news and knows in whom she has believed and trusts His promise of the Comforter to come in times like these. She sends her love to you, Carrie and all. Sincerely yours,

W. H. Doane[21]

Apparently, Fanny at first thought she might bury Van in Mountain Grove Cemetery, where she planned to be buried. But she decided that it was somehow inappropriate and made arrangements to have the body interred in Olivet Cemetery in Maspeth, Queens, near where the two had first made their home forty-four years before. He rests there to this day—alone—in a single, unmarked grave, quite forgotten. The next spring, the Underhills took Fanny to the spot where Van was buried and she fell upon the grave and wept, placing her hands on the turf and talking to his spirit, trying to assure him that she was "constantly lamenting his temporary loss."[22] Indeed, Fanny had hopes that their separation, begun long before Van's death, was only temporary, and that one day they would meet again where all the tears of earth would be dried and all its wrongs made right.

After the death of her erstwhile husband, Fanny decided that "under the circumstances it would be well to occupy my mind by writing as many hymns as I could. I accordingly secluded myself where I could hear the music of Old Ocean."[23] There, in Van's memory, she wrote, "I Am Satisfied":

If He, my Lord, is with me still,
And in Him I abide,
If He but whisper to my heart,
Then I am satisfied.

• • •

And though at times the things I ask
In love are oft denied,
I know He gives me what is best
And I am satisfied.

From Him my soul, in life or death,
No power shall e'er divide;
I read the promise in His word
And I am satisfied.[24]

Soon afterward, in gratitude for their loving care of Van, Fanny wrote for the Underhills a tribute to their seventeenth-century ancestor, "An Ode to the Memory of Captain John Underhill." Soon after that, she wrote a final tribute to the man she had loved to the end:

The winds a carol murmur, soft and low,
While silver stars, that gem the arch of night
In answering tones, repeat the choral strain:
Sleep on, O Minstrel, calm be thy repose;
Pure as thy spirit, guileless as thy heart,
May golden dreams of past and future years,
Of deeds accomplished, laurels nobly won,
Beguile thy slumber with their magic power,
And bear thee onward to the classic vales,
Where thou in thought hast wandered o'er and o'er,
Hast laved thy brow in sweet Arcadian springs,
And caught the music of Apollo's lyre:
Sleep on, O Minstrel, angels guard thy rest,
Till in her chariot drawn by flaming steeds
Comes the fair goddess of the blushing morn,
And in her beauty smiling bids thee wake.[25]

CHAPTER 20
LIFE BEGINS AT EIGHTY

Fanny was away as much as she was home. Whenever she was in Bridgeport, she held open house on Thursdays, which meant that anyone who cared to could come and talk with the celebrated hymn writer. The rest of her time was spent working with the King's Daughters and at the Christian Union. Even in her eighties, Fanny found little time to rest; resting was for old people, and she was young—she said.

During the fall of 1903, she appeared at the East Baptist Church in Kensington, Long Island, sharing the platform with her great friend, Eliza Hewitt, before the audience of six hundred. A local newspaper reported that

> save for the heavy green glasses she wore and the peculiar manner in which she thumbed a little book which contained her notes in the raised letters of the blind, no one would have imagined that she was sightless. She seemed to be glancing here and there over the lecture room, and frequently referred to sight in a way which would lead one to infer that she possessed it physically as well as mentally.[1]

Of course, Fanny had the reporters fooled, for as we have seen she almost never used braille, and her thumbing through her "little book" was simply a nervous habit. At any rate, Fanny spoke of her blindness: "A great many people sympathize with me," she said, "smiling sweetly," but "although I am grateful to them, I really don't need their sympathy. What would I do with it? You see, I was blind from the time I was six weeks old, and I never knew what it was to see with my eyes. Yet, when I was six years old, I could climb a tree like a squirrel, and ride a horse bareback. I wrote my first piece when I was eight years old." She went on to speak of hymn writing. It was "my life's work and I cannot tell you what pleasure I derive from it. I believe I would not live a year if my work were to be taken away from me."[2]

Fanny had one of the most gratifying experiences of her life in November of the same year. She was in Lynn, Massachusetts, speaking at the YMCA, and as usual she recounted the story of how she came to write some of her hymns. On this occasion, she told how "Rescue the Perishing" was inspired by the conversion of a young workingman who rejoiced, "Now I can meet my mother in heaven, for now I have found her God!"

After the meeting, several people came to shake hands with her, and among them was a man whose voice did more shaking than his hand. Fanny was dumbfounded when he proclaimed, "Miss Crosby, I was that boy who told you more than thirty-five years ago that I had wandered from my mother's God. That evening you spoke, I sought and found peace, and I have tried to live a consistent Christian life ever since. If we never meet again on earth, we will meet up yonder." Without another word, he left without giving his name, but Fanny was deeply moved by this "nameless friend who touched a deep chord of sympathy in my heart."[3]

In January Fanny, accompanied by her niece Ida Leschon, set out on a grueling speaking tour by train. They journeyed first to Philadelphia, where Fanny held a series of evangelical meetings. Traveling north, they went to Albany, New York, and then to Rochester, where Fanny honored various speaking engagements. She was now a national celebrity and at the very pinnacle of her fame, and a newspaper in Rochester observed that there was scarcely a religious service in the United States where at least one of her hymns was not sung. One thing that struck those who saw and heard the blind speaker was her youthful manner. Her face and form did indeed betray her age, though not to the extent as had been the case in the few years before she left New York. But her voice, her mind, and her movements were all those of a woman in her prime, and on the basis of this, reporters observed that "Madame Crosby" could have passed for twenty years less than her actual age.

Fanny and Ida were back in Bridgeport for only a matter of days before it was time to go to New York. February 2, the fortieth anniversary of Fanny's association with Biglow and Main, was to be the occasion of a special celebration in the firm. Many of her old friends and colleagues were present at the banquet prepared by Louise Main and Fanny Sankey. There was Doane, whom Fanny cited as the one who did "much to bring my songs to the front"[4] in the early days. The jolly old "professor," Kirkpatrick, was there too, as was George Stebbins. These and many others assembled to honor the poet who had more than any other person helped to make Biglow and Main one of the leading publishers of church music in the English-speaking world. At the ceremonies Fanny was presented with a golden brooch studded with pearls. Although many were complaining that the firm had overworked Fanny, she herself had been glad to do the work, even if for little pay and at the expense of her talent for writing truly good poetry. It was a work she did for the Lord, and she thanked her friends for "forty years of blessings, peace, and tranquility, like the dew of Hermon and the dew on the mountains of Zion."[5]

Two of Fanny's good friends were absent from the festivities, and one was her hostess in New York. During trips to the Empire City, Fanny apparently was always put up at the Hotel Savoy by Phoebe Knapp. Phoebe was most definitely on the outs with Hugh Main ever since Carleton's publications in the late nineties. Now she had made herself all the more persona non grata by continually claiming that Fanny was underpaid and by enlisting friends in the higher echelons of the Methodist Church to appeal for money for the hymn writer, implying publicly that Fanny was destitute and poorly housed. But inasmuch as Ira Sankey paid for Fanny and Carrie's accommodations in Bridgeport and Hugh Main had arranged for her to receive all the royalties from *Bells at Evening* (which was still in print), Fanny's friends at Biglow and Main had grown exceedingly vexed at the conduct of the rich widow. Fanny nevertheless appreciated Phoebe's devotion and honored her invitations to stay with her, and on this occasion she remained there several days while Ida returned to Bridgeport. During the time she was there, she returned thanks to her friends at Biglow and Main, honoring them with a reception at a Fifth Avenue hotel which was undoubtedly financed by Phoebe herself.

While at Phoebe's, Fanny worked with her on several new hymns which were to be published as sheet music. It was then that Phoebe wrote to Carrie, who had inquired when Fanny could be expected back in Bridgeport. This letter gives a clear picture of the gushing, possessive, dominating, and somewhat eccentric personality of the diamond-spangled dowager:

Dear Mrs. Ryder:

I am taking the best care of our dear Fanny—whom we both love. Each time that she comes to me I am so satisfied (and as never before)—that someone in Bridgeport cares for the personal interests of the dear one—and I am happy indeed!

Is this "as never before" a reference to the will business of fourteen years previous? Phoebe continues, saying that

I cannot possibly let her go home until Friday next in the afternoon—just now I need her and she is having a good time. Sincerely hoping that you are well,

Then Phoebe inserts an inexplicable paragraph:

Fanny sends lots of love and says that for just once she is going to *try* and commence to be good. That is going to be hard work as we all know. For she has been keeping bad company of late and I hear nothing but Mr. Dooly and upon mention of his name she begins a wild dance—and I, awe-stricken, say "shades of night envelope us" and withdraw.

Your friend,

Mrs. J. F. Knapp[6]

203

To what Phoebe is referring is unknown. Who was Mr. Dooly? What does Phoebe mean when she speaks of Fanny beginning a "wild dance" at the mere mention of his name? Can she have been literally dancing at the age of eighty-four? The situation and context of this rather weird paragraph lie hidden amid the obscuring mists of the past. No letter or document that has come down to us can shed light upon Fanny and this mysterious Mr. Dooly.

Before she left New York, Fanny called upon her second old friend who was not present at the banquet, Ira Sankey. For a year now he had been stone blind, sitting quietly in deep depression at his house in Brooklyn, living with his memories and awaiting death. He had not been well after returning from Europe in 1901, and the rest at Battle Creek had helped only temporarily. Moreover, things were not improved when the manuscript of an autobiography on which he was working was lost in a fire that destroyed the sanitarium while he was there. Starting over from scratch, he had not yet finished when in January 1903 his sight began rapidly to fail. It was discovered that he was suffering from glaucoma, and in February surgery was performed, but with no success, for the disease was too far advanced. Rumors began to spread that Sankey had gone blind, but Ira instructed his family to deny them, since he hoped to recover and did not want to alarm his friends unnecessarily. However, as the rumors grew more persistent, his sons, Allan and Edward, called a press conference the first week in March in which they confirmed that their father had indeed lost his sight.

Fanny had been devastated upon learning that her "neverfailing friend" was, like her, bereft of sight, and she made regular trips from Bridgeport to see him in Brooklyn. She tried her best to help and encourage the singer, whom she usually found in tears. She would sit with him, "read" scripture to him, pray with him, and encourage him to sing with her some of the hymns they had written together. She succeeded in improving his spirits somewhat, for whenever she left, Ira told his wife that he felt as if an "angel-hand of strength" had been held out to him. "Her presence has been to my heart as a healing balm."[7] Indeed, Sankey's family and friends were sure that the "chalice full of consolation" which Fanny brought "wonderfully helped" Ira in the physical and spiritual trial through which he was passing.[8] Unlike Fanny, who never knew any condition but blindness, Sankey lost his sight when he was too old— or thought he was—to begin life over again. He managed to finish the autobiography in truncated fashion, but after that he simply gave up. He no longer tried to compose tunes and appeared no more in public. Life was over and death was the only thing left to hope for, so Sankey spent the rest of his days sitting in his bedroom, lost in memories, or sitting at his harmonium, playing over and over again the songs of happier days.

After her return from New York, Fanny was but a few days in Bridgeport. On February 19, 1904, she and Carrie took a train to Boston, where they were met by Dr. A. C. Dixon of the Ruggles Street Baptist Church. There, two days later, she spoke on the subject of George Washington. Throughout the spring she traveled about, preaching, lecturing, recounting the story of her life. Whenever she was in Bridgeport, she busied herself with speaking at the Christian Union, working with Alice Rector and the King's Daughters, and receiving the seemingly endless streams of "pilgrims" who descended whenever she was in town. And although Thursday was her official open house day, she never refused a visitor.

In early July, Fanny, along with Carrie, journeyed west to Buffalo, where she was the major speaker at a Christian Endeavor convention. Despite her advanced years, she spoke three times a day, often to crowds of more than three thousand, and not only gave sermons but also lectured on mission work and the methods of hymn writing. On one Sunday in Buffalo, she preached twice, at ten thirty at the Delaware Avenue Methodist Church and at noon at the Central Presbyterian Church. In all her appearances in Buffalo, Fanny deeply moved her hearers, but never as many as on the night when, carried away by an impulse, she rose and joined the soloist.

On that night a baritone was singing "Saved by Grace," which was still immensely popular. Fanny, who was scheduled to speak later, sat behind him on the platform. Suddenly, when the soloist, Jacobs, came to the third stanza, Fanny spontaneously leaped to her feet and began to sing, "Some day, when fades the golden sun. Beneath the rosy-tinted west. . . . " The notes at first seemed "quavering and faltering," as one might expect of an eighty-year-old woman, and Jacobs lowered his powerful voice so that hers might be heard by the audience. But as the chorus "And I shall see Him face to face . . . " progressed, her voice became higher and stronger, until it filled the entire hall and held the audience spellbound with its beauty and pathos. There was much weeping when she and Jacobs finished their impromptu duet.[9] It was spontaneous acts like this one, as much as her prepared talks and sermons, that tended to make hearts captive to the little old lady in ancient garb and to the gospel which she proclaimed.

From Buffalo, stopping to lecture at various places on the way, Fanny, still in the company of her sister, made her way to Binghamton. People marveled at her almost miraculous vitality. It amazed even Carrie, who although more than twenty years her sister's junior, nevertheless remarked, "She can tire out everyone present, then go home fresh!"

Someone asked Fanny in Binghamton how long she was going to continue her vigorous activity. "How long," she replied, "am I going to travel and lecture? Always! There is nothing that could induce me to abandon my work. It means nothing to be eighty-four years of age because I am still young! What is the use in growing old? People grow old because they are not cheerful, and cheerfulness is one of the greatest accomplishments in the world!"[10] Fanny

205

felt that as long as she kept busy, she would always be "young." She often reiterated that she doubted whether she would live a year if she were somehow forced to abandon her work. It was this that kept her going.

Fanny apparently did not go to Ocean Grove or Northfield that year. Emma Moody was now dead, and with Whittle gone and Sankey confined to his home in Brooklyn, the Bible conferences had lost their appeal for her. She did go to Tully Lake, however, where she participated in Round Table. Fanny also made her annual visit to the Indian reservation, and this year she and Eliza Hewitt were accorded the great honor of being adopted into the Eel Clan of the Onondaga tribe. Albert Cusick, the tribal chief, performed the traditional rite that made the two women official members of his tribe. Fanny had always been "deeply interested" in the welfare of American Indians, and the adoption into the Onondagas delighted her. Now that she was a "genuine Indian," she began to collect Onondaga folk tales, which she often related in her lectures and sermons.

Fanny also journeyed to East Orange, New Jersey, where she and Carrie visited with friends for a week. From there she went to visit Ira, addressed "her men" at the Naval YMCA in Brooklyn, and conducted an evangelical meeting for the Y's Railroad Branch, right in the roundhouse of the Lackawanna Railroad in Hoboken, New Jersey. Returning to Bridgeport "brown and merry," she was there only long enough to prepare for her autumn travels. Then she was off to New England and lectures at the First Baptist Church in Taunton, Massachusetts, where newspapers urged their readers to take advantage of what would probably be their last chance to see and hear the celebrated old woman. But at eighty-four, Fanny seemed to have as much energy as Carrie, who was sixty, and Ida, who was forty-five, and the two younger women had to alternate as her traveling companions.

Fanny always made an effort to be at home for two occasions: her mother's birthday and Christmas. She and Carrie and Jule and Ida still celebrated Mercy's birthday as if she were alive. The sisters and Ida would put a fresh vase of flowers beneath Mercy's huge photograph and set a place at table for the deceased matriarch. Fanny would recite a poem she wrote each year in honor of "Mother Dear," just as she had when her mother was alive.

Christmas was a happy occasion. Fanny and her sisters usually celebrated the feast day at the home of niece Laura Tait. There the whole Morris clan would assemble: Henry and Florence Booth and their children, Florence and Ralph; Albert and Clara Morris and their children, Albert and Marjorie; and, of course, the three aged sisters and the host family, William and Laura Tait and their daughters, Mary and Natalie. Albert Morris, Jr., later recalled that his grandaunt, though "slight and spent," displayed "a ready wit."[11] There was a family dinner, in which Aunt Fanny would enliven the lulls in conversation with humorous poems composed on the spot, and then in the afternoon, while the children rested, Fanny made little gifts to be put into the "grab-bag" which provided the evening's entertainment. She also made up humorous little poems which were copied and distributed to every member of the family. She loved to play with the children, and on one occasion, her grandnephew, Ralph Booth, begged her to go for a ride on his sled. To the absolute horror of the parents, Aunt Fanny gladly consented and seated herself on the conveyance while he pulled her around the backyard in the snow.

In early March 1905, Fanny, in the company of Carrie, left for a lecture tour of more than two weeks. On the fifth, she spoke at the YMCA at Fitchburg, Massachusetts, to 750 people packed into a hall built for only 650. The audience sang several of her hymns before a clergyman from the area read a passage of scripture and Fanny stepped forth, holding a little book tight in her hands. She gave no sermon or lecture as such but, as she did so often, told about her life, about how God had enabled her to overcome her handicap and how he had inspired her hymns. She then discussed and interpreted nine of her most popular hymns. After Father Martini had delivered the benediction, Fanny proceeded to greet and shake hands with the audience. It was estimated that she shook at least 350 hands that night.

Next she traveled to western New York, where she spoke to a mass meeting of the Railroad YMCA. In Rochester she also spoke to the members of the YMCA's Women's Auxiliary and was given a tribute by Mrs. Caroline Atwater Mason (1853–1939), a well-known author of religious novels. After giving an evangelical sermon in a rescue mission, Fanny and Carrie left Rochester to journey farther west, stopping at the School for the Blind in Batavia. Then she started east again, addressing the Railroad YMCA in Albany on March 18. There, as always, she had great success, and those who heard her marveled at her vitality and "sonorous and musical" voice.[12]

On March 24, Aunt Fanny would be eighty-five. To honor her, a group of New York clergymen, with the encouragement of Hugh Main and Allan Sankey, decided to hold a Fanny Crosby Sunday in churches on March 26. Adelbert White served as secretary of the Fanny Crosby Day Committee, and Mrs. Ann Cobham, whom Fanny frequently visited in Warren, Pennsylvania, served as assistant. Together, they saw to it that the celebration was publicized nationwide. Dr. Louis Klopsch, editor of the widely circulated *Christian Herald,* advocated that all Christian churches honor the aged hymn writer on the designated Sunday. On Fanny Crosby Day, her hymns would be used exclusively, and ministers and priests of all denominations would preach on her life as an example of Christian witness. Fanny would, in effect, while still alive, be the subject of a "saint's day" of the type that the Roman Catholic Church normally observes for heroes of the faith long since deceased. Moreover, a "love offering" would be taken for her in all the churches where her "day" was observed.

Fanny was nonplussed when she learned of the honor, but she made no attempt to stop the plans. "Am I pleased?" she asked rhetorically, in response to a question. "Certainly. Who would not be? Just so long as the celebration in honor of my work is by those who have loved my songs, both the celebration and the contemplated offering will be like the crowning blessing at the close of a long and busy life!"[13] She wanted to make certain that it was God, and not she, who received the glory.

And so the celebration was held. Fanny Crosby Day was observed not only in America but in England and in such unlikely countries as India and Tasmania. She received many tributes, including letters of congratulation from common folk and places she had never visited. A lady from Mississippi sent some flowers she had gathered. A tribute also came from Grover Cleveland in Princeton. Fanny had frequently visited him ever since he moved there after the end of his second term and had given him much comfort when he had recently lost his eldest daughter, Ruth, who had been her special pet. He commended her for her "continuous and disinterested labor in uplifting humanity and pointing out the way to an appreciation of God's goodness and mercy."[14]

Fanny attended a reception given by Hugh Main a few days early. On her birthday, she appeared at a reception at the First Methodist Church in Bridgeport. Looking like a "fragile flower," the poet appeared with Reuben and Mary Currier and was led to a special pew, draped with an American flag. Suffering from a bad headache, Fanny was led to the rostrum by her physician, and in a voice that was not that of an emaciated old woman but, rather, was "strong and filled the edifice," she publicly thanked the doctor, saying, "I prize your friendship, and I suspect that I shall send for you early unless my headache should soon fly away." She spoke briefly of her God, "the sunshine of my soul," and warmly thanked her audience for their love, blessing them as she turned to sit down. The choir sang a hymn she had written for the occasion, "O Land of Joy Unseen," set to music by a parishioner, Fred King. Sunday she gave the evening message at the First Baptist Church, Carrie's congregation. The crowd was so huge that it filled not only the large sanctuary but also the Sunday school rooms. In that address, Fanny thanked God for all the "kindness and affection" shown her in the last few days and throughout her long life, "as I realize the source from which they have come."[15]

At birthday services in Bridgeport, and wherever throughout the nation Fanny Crosby Day was observed, love offerings were taken for the blind hymnist. At First Baptist she was given a dollar for every year of her age. All in all, when the festivities were over, she was the recipient of several thousand dollars, which this time she did not refuse. She was overwhelmed by the display of a nation's love and her heart was "full" as she rejoiced that "yea, I have a goodly heritage!"[16]

CHAPTER 21
"MRS. CROSBY'S MATTER"

Fanny was on the road again in the autumn of 1905, lecturing in Massachusetts and New Jersey. During the time she found herself at home she was busily engaged in putting the finishing touches to her autobiography, *Memories of Eighty Years*. This seemingly innocuous project had a stormy career that had begun three years before. In order to understand it, we need to go back to the spring of 1903.

Because Fanny Crosby was an internationally known figure who had lived a long and interesting life, it is understandable that many people had pressed her to write an autobiography. Partial accounts of her life and career had appeared over the years in various magazines and journals. Lowry had written a brief sketch of her life as an introduction to *Bells at Evening*, and, two or three years after that, Will Carleton's articles had appeared in his *Every Where* magazine. Fanny was so very modest she could not understand why anyone would be interested in her poor life, but Adelbert White convinced her of a genuine public interest in it. He offered to help compile the volume, and Carrie also volunteered to help. Accordingly, in April 1903 Fanny dispatched White to the New York Institution for the Blind, to ascertain from the present superintendent, William Wait, "any information from the Institution records, or anything you may have, concerning the years I was there."

Before anything else was done, complications rapidly developed. Carleton, knowing the interest of the public in a Fanny Crosby autobiography, told Fanny of his intention to organize the articles he had written about her into book form. He offered her the same royalty (25 percent) that he received from Harper's for his own books of poetry, but Fanny told him that she was not at all concerned about the royalties and gave him permission to organize the autobiography from the articles. Although she would have preferred to have written her own autobiography, she conceded that the articles were Carleton's property and was reluctant to deny him permission to do with them as he wished. This did not please White and the personnel of Biglow and Main. Not only did her friends feel that Fanny should write her own autobiography, they remembered the hard feelings associated with the Carleton articles when they were published, and how they had interfered with the sale of *Bells at Evening*.

They suspected that *Fanny Crosby's Life-Story, by Herself* was simply a moneymaking scheme that Carleton was undertaking for his personal profit. Not unexpectedly, Phoebe Knapp became involved in the matter. Still looking out "for the personal interests of the dear one," this elderly do-gooder was convinced that Fanny deserved more worldly substance and was not satisfied with anything anyone connected with Biglow and Main had done for her. That Ira Sankey paid for Fanny and Carrie's rent and gave Carrie a monthly sum to provide for most of Fanny's expenses did not satisfy Mrs. Knapp. She thought that Fanny ought to have a house of her own. She enlisted the services of Bishop Charles Caldwell McCabe (1836–1906), a Methodist prelate who was a mutual friend of both Phoebe and Fanny and had been a guest many times at the Knapp residence. Phoebe apparently told him that Fanny was destitute, and he began to make it known publicly that Fanny was in severe financial straits and was "willing to accept financial assistance." McCabe did consult Fanny, but only to ask her if she would be willing to accept "a testimonial of [the] love and admiration" of the people of America. She could not very well refuse that, but she was never told that this "testimonial" would be drawn from the purses of her admirers on the basis of a "plea of poverty."[1]

McCabe and Mrs. Knapp then convinced Carleton to circulate a "publisher's advertisement" along with *Fanny Crosby's Life-Story*. This advertisement, which came with the book, contained an extract from a letter by Fanny, together with her signature, with the statement that she hoped, by means of the book, "to become a welcome guest in many homes." But, while Carleton had obtained her permission to reproduce the articles in book form, he did not consult her about adding this statement, as well as the statement that the book was being sold so that Fanny might be "enabled to have a house of her own, in which to pass the remainder of her days." This, of course, tended to give people the impression that poor Aunt Fanny had no place to live. Combined with the statements of McCabe and Mrs. Knapp, it caused great concern in many circles for the welfare of the "queen of hymn writers." Mary Root, the aged widow of the man who had first set Fanny's words to music, was one of several old acquaintances who wrote to Fanny. Mrs. Root had been alarmed not only by the Carleton book but also by an article about Fanny by Marion Harland, a female journalist who apparently had written quite a sob story. The venerable Mrs. Root, in a tremulous hand, wrote, urgently inquiring about Fanny's circumstances and Fanny immediately replied, saying that she was not in "straitened circumstances" but, on the contrary, was well accommodated in a spacious apartment rented for her by Ira Sankey. White tried in vain to trace the other article as rumors continued to spread that Fanny Crosby, underpaid and neglected by her "callous and rapacious publishers," was living in direst poverty and squalor.

210

Fanny Crosby's Life-Story, by Herself, compiled by Will Carleton, went over like a lead balloon with Fanny's publishers. While the text said nothing unfavorable about them, it neglected to say anything positive about the firm and its members, except that Fanny had cordial, "even affectionate," relations with them. It should be pointed out that this was because the book dealt primarily with Fanny's early life, before she had become associated with Biglow and Main. Carleton always said he did not intend to slight or offend Fanny's mentors, but Main, Doane, and others indignantly complained that they did not receive as much recognition as they deserved for the part they had played in Fanny's career. Hugh Main raved in a letter to White that "Carleton's book is a *biased* affair and does not do Fanny justice to say nothing of those who had the *most* to do with her popularity."[2] In addition to jealousy, Fanny's friends had other, more serious reasons for disapproving of Carleton's book. Initially, Carleton had promised Fanny 25 percent of the profits, but for various reasons he retracted the offer and cut the percentage to 10. Most of Fanny's friends felt that if anyone was taking advantage of Fanny, it was not Biglow and Main, who arranged for the poet to reap all the profits of *Bells at Evening,* but rather Carleton. They argued that if he really wanted to help Fanny, he would have given her a much larger percent of the profits. They were incensed that after nearly a year of publication, *Life-Story* had brought Fanny exactly $285 in royalties, while Carleton was claiming that he was selling the book to save the hymn writer from poverty and buy her a home. As Fanny's lawyer put it, "I think Mr. Carleton drew plans for this home when he wrote 'Over the Hills to the Poorhouse'!"[3]

White and Carrie, in particular, were concerned about the future of Fanny's own autobiography, which the poet still planned to compile. If she ever got around to writing it, they were going to work out an arrangement similar to that of *Bells at Evening,* in which all the proceeds from the book's sale would go to her. Publication of Carleton's supposed autobiography would doubtless seriously hurt the market for the genuine account of Fanny's life, for most people would be unwilling or unable to buy a *second* autobiography, even if they had good reason to believe that it was the complete and authentic one.

Fanny tried to stay out of the imbroglio, which certainly embarrassed her. She was not concerned whether she received 10 percent, 25 percent, or nothing at all, and according to Carleton's biographer, "with that perfect candor and generosity characteristic of her," she had told Carleton "that the articles were his property, as he had written them."[4] Nevertheless she was concerned because the "autobiography" did not present a complete picture of her life. Put together from sketches dealing chiefly with her early years, it told little of her life after she became a hymn writer. To give a more accurate and complete picture was something that she felt she owed the public, now that the Carleton autobiography was published. Moreover, she resented the fact that Carleton had published excerpts from her letter and added to it his own statement that the book was being sold to buy her a house. She was quite happy where she was and had no desire to be a homeowner. Fanny also did not like the implication that she was kept in poverty by the stinginess of Biglow and Main. If she had ever been in poverty, it was by choice. Now, in Bridgeport, she felt that, far from being in want, she was in almost embarrassing luxury, due to the beneficence of Ira Sankey. Accordingly, Fanny wrote to Carleton asking him to withdraw the advertisement and telling him that she had never given permission to reproduce part of her letter. Carleton, thinking she had been pressured, ignored her, and Fanny, not wanting a legal fight, took no further action.

Bert White, however, wrote to Carleton, urging him in strong language to withdraw the advertisement. After Carleton replied rather evasively, White wrote to Doane, who responded that he was in "entire sympathy." He had told Fanny the summer before that Carleton's book "looked like a scheme to gather in a few shekels for himself with a little notoriety." He went on to say that the book wronged the publishers of Bells at Evening and Fanny. "And the way the book is being sold on the sympathies of the public is not right. I sincerely hope you will open up the matter and let the public know the facts." He urged White to use legal means to stop the sale of Carleton's "fraudulent" book. "I know Mrs. Crosby," he wrote. "She is sweet-spirited, tender-hearted, and would suffer wrong before she would do wrong to anyone." Nevertheless, he urged White to consult attorneys to stop Carleton's "nefarious work."[5] White, however, apparently found no legal means of stopping Carleton.

In December White and Doane convinced Fanny to make a public statement in the Watchman, a widely circulated religious magazine:

Of late many inquiries have come to me in regard to my health* and home, and once and for all I would say that I am in my usual health and have a comfortable home. Concerning a book that is being sold ostensibly to buy me a home, I wish to say that it was mainly not written by me, but was compiled from incidents of my life first for a magazine five years ago: and finally was issued in a book with my toleration rather than my consent. Before the book was published, I asked that the "Publisher's Announcement" in the book be withdrawn. It is not an adequate biography, especially of the last forty years of my life, when I have been writing hymns. I have never authorized anyone to advertise that the book is being sold to raise

---

*There were rumors circulating at this time, possibly fostered by the Knapp-Carleton-McCabe faction, that Fanny was in poor health, even in a dying condition.

212

money to buy me a house, and personally, and through legal counsel, I have requested that it be not so advertised. My royalty on the book has been less than 10% and has amounted to less than $325.

My requests have been disregarded . . . when these facts are fully known to all, the publishers can sell the book as they desire; only I have no wish to increase its sale for my own benefit, which, of course, is very small.[6]

She also sent a letter to the editor of another religious magazine, dealing with the fact that Bishop McCabe had been raising funds for her. While she permitted him to allow for her friends "making her a testimonial of their love," she never understood that this appeal would be made on "the plea of [her] poverty."[7] Even Ira Sankey was unable to remain silent. When he learned of "Mrs. Crosby's matter," as Doane had called it, he was so enraged that he made his last public statement in a brief article published in a magazine named *The Christian*. In it he implied that the Carleton business had been of Satanic origin and commented, echoing the wheat and tares passage in scripture, "An enemy hath done this."[8]

"Mrs. Crosby's matter" came to an end shortly before Fanny Crosby Day in 1905, when Will Carleton, who previously assumed that the commotion raised against him was simply the work of "interested friends," realized that Fanny herself was offended and stopped lecturing and advertising for the book. In the midst of the controversy, his wife had died suddenly, and now it was just as well with him that the matter be dropped. Despite their use of questionable methods, neither Carleton nor the Bishop nor Mrs. Knapp had any fraudulent intent but were sincerely motivated to help Fanny. Unlike some of her friends, Fanny realized this and remained on good terms with all three until their deaths.

It was during the winter of 1904–5 that Fanny did most of the work on her autobiography, *Memories of Eighty Years*. She was assisted by Carrie and Eva Cleaveland, the stenographer, who took down what she dictated, and by Adelbert White, who organized her rambling recollections into a coherent narrative. He read to Fanny what he had written and obtained her approval for its final form. In the autobiography she placed the major emphasis on her hymns and the stories behind them. Accordingly, she wrote to Doane and others for various incidents associated with the hymns, which had come to their notice but escaped hers. She was very concerned about recounting cases in which the hymns had helped someone as well as the incidents that inspired their writing. Fanny would rather have praised her friends than to have called attention to herself, and men like Stebbins and Kirkpatrick had to chide her and urge her to write about herself and not so much about them. She tried to get Kirkpatrick to send clippings and documents relative to his life, but he refused. When Fanny wrote again, insistent, Kirkie took a firmer stance. The "Quakerdelphian," as he liked to style himself, flatly stated, "I really have no . . . clippings that would be of use to you concerning myself, Sweney, or anyone else that I would care to let be reproduced."[9]

Not all Fanny's friends were that modest. Hugh Main, who had been most upset about the Carleton book because it did not say enough of "those who had the most to do with her popularity," wrote White to make sure that Fanny accorded sufficient mention to a long catalogue of names that included those of Root, Bradbury, Doane, Lowry, Sherwin, Philip Phillips, Danks, Sweney, Kirkpatrick, Moody, Sankey, and, of course, himself. He concluded, "I suppose, if she believes in the Golden Rule—that she should have to mention Mrs. Knapp and Carleton, but under the circumstances, I would be short of ink just after the mention."[10] Main's view, which was apparently adopted by White, prevailed, and in many places the autobiography becomes a long catalogue of names of various people whom she honors simply by mentioning. She never mentions Carleton, and mentions Phoebe only in connection with "Blessed Assurance." *Memories of Eighty Years*, like so much Fanny did, was written in haste and suffers accordingly. When it went to press in 1906, it was still in many ways rough and disconnected. It accorded accolades of praise to those who "had the most to do with her popularity," and it described some of her hymn-writing and home-mission activities of the preceding forty years, but it is less interesting, less readable, and less finished than Carleton's "nefarious" production. The articles from which he drew in compiling it had been prepared by Fanny in more relaxed circumstances and under less pressure, so the earlier account is in many ways more lively, more witty, and slightly more coherent than *Memories*.

The book was published by the James H. Earle Company of Boston, and, as with *Bells at Evening*, all the proceeds from its sale went to Fanny. Grover Cleveland helped promote it by contributing a written endorsement included in the publisher's announcement. To further encourage sales, the aging Doane, blue-lipped, watery-eyed, and trembling, gave a series of lectures on Fanny, just as Carleton had done to promote *Life-Story*. The next month James Earle wrote to White that *Memories* "is starting off better than I was anticipating. Had not the field been raked with that most unfortunate Carleton book, we could have been quite sure of some handsome returns to the saintly author."[11] As most books were at the time, *Memories* was sold mostly by subscription and was advertised not only by statements by Cleveland or speeches by Doane but by schoolchildren who went from door to door. Even though the overall sales were disappointing to White, they netted Fanny about a thousand dollars. What with the autobiographies, the donations resulting from lectures by both Carleton and Doane, and the love offerings of Fanny Crosby Day, Aunt Fanny was catapulted, albeit reluctantly, from poverty into something resembling affluence. She never changed her life-style, and the increased income simply meant that she had more to give away. She did save some money, but only so that she might provide something for relatives when she died.

Fanny was particularly grateful for the devotion of Bert White "in the work of compiling, copying, and arranging" her book. In an "introductory statement" she cites him, stating that "he has sacrificed every other consideration and patiently devoted himself to my interest."[12] Although she saw him less after the publication of the book, Fanny maintained ties with the young scholar, who was now living in New Haven, doing graduate work at Yale. White occasionally visited Fanny in Bridgeport and kept up a regular correspondence, in which the hymnist playfully signed her letters "Zenobia" and called White "Deacon" and "Hezekiah."

Aunt Fanny, as she was now almost universally called, was writing fewer hymns; she had cut back writing from about two hundred hymns a year to about fifty, a quota she was to maintain for the rest of her life. The reason was not Fanny but her publishers: Biglow and Main were turning out fewer new hymnals. Since Lowry's death, Doane's *Songs of Devotion,* to which she had contributed more than forty poems, was one of the few they published. Most of their hymnals now reproduced hymns published in earlier collections which had been popular over the years. In 1903, Fanny had written more than seventy hymns for a collection published by Funk and Wagnall's, *Gloria Deo,* but that was the only additional book to which she was asked to contribute.

After publication of *Memories of Eighty Years,* the declining demand for hymns was by no means in the forefront of Fanny's mind. Her days were filled with concern for "Sister Carrie." In her autobiography she expressed gratitude to God for sparing both her sisters, but this was not to be for long, for in the summer of 1906 Carrie had developed intestinal cancer. She failed gradually to the point where she could no longer care for herself, nor Fanny for her, with the result that both women were forced to leave the Becker house and stay with their niece, Florence Morris Booth. Florence and Henry Booth and their two nearly grown children lived in a fine house on 226 Wells Street, some blocks north of the former residence.

Fanny was visiting Reuben and Mary Currier in Springfield, Massachusetts, when the first copies of *Memories* reached Carrie. No longer able to write, she had Florence communicate the news to Bert White. At that time, in mid-November, Florence described Carrie as doing "very poorly" and being very uncomfortable.[13] She lingered through the winter and spring into early summer, when her condition became so bad that she had to enter Bridgeport Hospital. After an unsuccessful operation she lived another thirty-six hours but never regained consciousness, dying just after midnight on June 25, at age sixty-three. The newspapers in Bridgeport praised the "sterling character," "sweet and loveable disposition" and "blameless life" of "the woman who had been a friend to all."[14]

Many of her friends feared for Fanny's well-being, knowing her close she had been to her younger sister, and many thought that she could not survive the blow. Indeed, Fanny was all but crushed by Carrie's death, but no sooner had she buried Carrie than she was knocked reeling by another blow. Jule's daughter, Ida, soon fell ill with intestinal problems and was operated upon in August. The surgeons, as in Carrie's case, found they could do nothing, and three weeks later, on September 6, Ida died at forty-eight. Although Fanny felt profoundly the loss of the sister and the niece who had provided her with so much companionship in late years, she resigned herself, saying, "Well, it is God's will, and they are much happier."[15] Her attitude to the loss is expressed in the annual poem written on her mother's birthday, which she dictated almost faster than her remaining sister could write it down:

How we loved our dear departed
Only you and I can tell,
But we know, amid our sorrow,
Jesus doeth all things well.

●　　●　　●

Let us then in calm submission
Meet our trials, one by one,
With a prayer to our Father
That His will, not ours, be done.[16]

216

CHAPTER 22
THE PROTESTANT SAINT

Fanny was to spend the rest of her life with the Booths on Wells Street. Here her niece Florence tried to be the same kind of companion Carrie had been. She has been described as a "tall, slim, pretty woman" with a pleasant disposition.[1] She left business matters entirely to Eva Cleaveland, who came every day and handled all the correspondence and took down all the hymns and poems that Fanny composed. In her late years, Fanny traveled less than she had in the past, but at home she did not get much rest, for she was constantly besieged by many visitors, including journalists who made her the subject of numerous articles in newspapers and magazines. It is from these years that we get the most comprehensive picture of her thought, personality, and appearance.

In her later years, Fanny Crosby was physically little more than a skeleton. Her desiccated body seemed to be more animated by her spirit than by its wasted muscles and sinews, and although her physical form was "homely,"[2] to say the least, there was a spirit that shone through the decaying shell that made her beautiful. Her smile was said to have been lovely, and all reports speak of the great sweetness and beauty of her voice. She spoke with the rural New England accent that omits r and pronounces the final o as er, as in "Longfeller," one of her favorite poets.

For someone so tiny, Aunt Fanny was a remarkably heavy eater. After downing a bowl of hot coffee after she arose at 11 A.M. she would eat a large dinner and, later, an equally heavy supper. She was very careful, however, about what she ate. She ate little meat but, instead, large quantities of eggs, fruit, and vegetables. She drank coffee and tea in large volumes. "There are things I'd love to eat," she said, "but my Angel-Guardian says 'You'd better not!'" Extremely fastidious in dress and housekeeping, Fanny was especially fussy about her wig, which had to be "just so" (according to Florence Paine, her grandniece) before she would come downstairs. Every morning she had someone read one of the New York papers to her.

During her free moments at home, Fanny spent a great deal of time at the piano in the Booth parlor. According to Mrs. Paine, she "could go from one extreme to another,"[3] beginning with a classical composition, proceeding to her own hymns, finishing with ragtime. She delighted in "pepping things up"—playing old hymns in a jazzed-up style. She also improvised and invented compositions of her own but would not permit anyone to write them down. J. L. Cummings, a friend of hers from Springfield, Massachusetts, described her as "always ready to sing." Whenever she went to the homes of friends, she found the fellowship lacking something unless there was a songfest. The daughter of one of her New York friends recalls how, when she was a guest at their home, the family would gather around the piano and sing and often Fanny would cry out, "Open the window and let this music rise to heaven!"[4]

Nearly every day when she was at home, Fanny was met by a solid stream of visitors on pilgrimage, as it were, to see the saint of Wells Street. So many wanted to meet her that they had to call Eva Cleaveland for appointments. People came from all walks of life and for all sorts of reasons. Many asked her advice in educating or rehabilitating a blind child, and this was especially hard for her. "It is an awful ordeal—simply awful!" she remarked.[5] People came for help with other problems, and it is said that no one who ever came to Aunt Fanny went away dissatisfied. Samuel Trevena Jackson, a young New Jersey pastor, was one of Fanny's coterie of younger friends. He wrote, "I must confess that I have not found a person with so many cupfuls of comfort for burdened and distressed souls."[6] She was perhaps even more effective in personal contact than through her hymns. Jackson observed that she "scattered the spirit of joy everywhere she went. Nobody could feel glum or depressed after being with her. Her joy was infectious. People caught in its spirit and gathered it into their own hearts."[7]

People came to Aunt Fanny for help in writing poetry, and in these instances she never withheld assistance. Some came who had no talent at all. She once remarked to her grandniece Florence, or Flossie, that a woman had come with "enough poems to fill a book" but "there was not one line of poetry there."[8] Fanny, however, never liked to tell people to their faces that their work was trash. Once a man read her some horrific "poetry" and informed her of his intention to publish it. "That would be splendid," was all she said.

At the same time, Fanny did get the opportunity to coach some people with real talent. One of them was a young neighbor girl, Blanche Simpson, who came once a week. Escorted to the main parlor by Mrs. Booth, young Blanche found Aunt Fanny seated on a davenport, looking "just like a little Dresden china doll." Fanny made Blanche kiss her before she recited. The poet was highly impressed with the girl's verse and did all she could to assist in developing her talents. After each session, she assigned Blanche a poem to write in a particular meter or style. By the time Fanny died, she was enthusiastic about the progress of this youthful protégée and was convinced that God wanted the young girl to become a hymn writer. She also counseled Blanche about business matters, telling her that there were publishing companies (not necessarily Biglow and Main, however) which did take advantage of those who provided them with hymns. She confided to Blanche that at times she had been taken advantage of by certain persons, and cautioned her to beware of similarly unscrupulous business people.[9]

Many came to Fanny for her autograph. To accommodate them she learned to write her name in her eighties. Before coming to Bridgeport, she had tried to write on only one occasion, and, in Hugh Main's words, "you would not know the result from a pile of spider's legs. She has an idea of how capital letters look, and also such letters as are in the Bibles for the blind, but nothing else." However, she learned to write with a fairly graceful hand.[10]

Many unscrupulous and underhanded people also called on Aunt Fanny. Some seized articles of her clothing or jewelry and kept them to venerate as relics. For instance, one day a woman asked her, "Can I have that cross?" Fanny always wore around her neck a gold crucifix, and although she was very fond of that particular crucifix, she said that her visitor could have it. Immediately the woman reached out and snatched the cross from Fanny's neck and vanished without so much as a thank you. After that, Florence felt that they had constantly to watch and screen the visitors.

People appealed to Fanny by mail too. Each day Eva Cleaveland read her many letters like the one from the invalid woman in Canton, Missouri, who wrote for money to buy medicine. Others wrote for assistance in publishing poetry. Fanny spent many hours listening to people's poems and advising correspondents on how to improve their verse.

Fanny's day usually ended at midnight. During the evenings, she dictated replies to correspondence and then retired to her room, where she prayed and wrote hymns for several hours. In later years, she slept poorly and always spent hours awake in prayer for the intentions of those who had besought her by day. She also prayed for churches and other Christian institutions. By dawn, she was usually asleep.

The one fact most people knew about Fanny Crosby was that she was blind, and she was often referred to as "the blind poetess" or "the blind hymn writer." But she did not like this and hated to be called "the blind woman." One day a man came to her and said, "The minister preached about afflictions to-day, and then I thought of you."

"Thank you," said Fanny, "but I think you should know that I do not consider myself afflicted!"[11]

"A great many people sympathize with me," she said on another occasion, "but, although I am grateful to them, I really don't need their sympathy. What would I do with it?"[12]

Far from feeling self-pity, Fanny felt that on the whole it was a special gift of God that she was blind. She often said, "It was the best thing that could have happened to me," and, "How in the world could I have lived such a helpful life as I have lived had I not been blind?"[13] She felt that she would never have had the opportunity for an education had she not been blind, and had she not gone to the Institution in New York she would not have had the contacts to enable her to write hymns for a nationally known publishing firm. Moreover, she felt that sight must be a distraction, and she attributed her great powers of concentration to blindness. She also felt that lack of sight enabled her to develop a wonderful memory and enhanced her appeal as a speaker. It created a bond of sympathy between her and her audiences that made them more receptive to the gospel message. She always said that the blind could function much better in the world than most sighted people imagined. At least, *she* could. Seeing her at home or in familiar surroundings, people often remarked that only her dark glasses gave the slightest hint that she was blind. In fact, Fanny claimed that she could "see," or, more properly, *perceive*, with her other senses what most people normally perceive with sight. She had very acute hearing and was so sensitive to any discordance or disharmony that a strain of music sung or performed off-key could wake her from a sound sleep. For example, once a man who had been denied access on the grounds that she was asleep got her to wake and come out of her hotel room by simply walking down the hall and whistling off-key.

Many wondered whether she harbored some bitterness toward the mountebank who prescribed the poultices that burned out her eyes. She would always say, very tenderly, "*Don't* blame the doctor. He is probably dead before this time. But if I could meet him, I would tell him that he unwittingly did me the greatest favor in the world."[14] Besides, she often expressed doubt whether even the best of medical treatment could have really helped her already defective eyes.

Fanny felt that her lack of sight was more than compensated for by a "soul-vision" that she felt was made all the keener by physical darkness. She believed she could see into the spiritual world. We know that she was subject to visions in which she said she clearly saw objects and persons, and apparently she was often aware of the state of the souls of those persons with whom she dealt. She could tell who was sincere, who was phony, who was malevolent, and who was good-hearted. Physical lack of sight, she said, contributed to her abundance of spiritual insight. In one of her poems she wrote, "Sightless, I see, and, seeing, find soul-vision, though my eyes are blind." Her attitude toward blindness was inseparably connected with her religion and faith, a faith in which she saw that "all things work for good for them that love the Lord."

Fanny's spiritual counsel was so helpful and uplifting that many people asked her to write about her theology, but "I have never thought much about theology," she said. Indeed she had no interest in theology in the sense of an academic discipline in which religious beliefs are systematized or put on a philosophic basis. Fanny Crosby's faith was not something she had derived from reason, and she saw spiritual wisdom proceeding not so much from the mind as from the heart and soul and from fellowship with Christ. She never asked herself "Is this rational?" or "Is this logical?" but, rather, "Is this from God?" She did not care so much in *what* she believed, but in *whom* she believed. She also believed that so long as one believed scripture and held fast to Christ, purity of life and deed was sufficient. More important than theology, she said, were character and kindness.[15] Holiness of life was the true touchstone of faith in Christ.

These convictions enabled her to transcend the bounds of denominationalism. To her, people were "brothers" or "sisters" no matter what church they belonged to, if they believed in Jesus Christ as revealed by scripture. As we have seen, although she was for many years a member of the Methodist Church, she never had qualms about attending and even preaching and speaking in churches of other denominations. Distinctions of academic theology and church polity were superfluous and irrelevant, so long as Christ and his word were central to the believer.

The ultimate authority in Fanny Crosby's life of faith was the Bible. She lived into the time when scholars known as biblical critics were, in many ways, taking scripture to pieces and seemingly reassembling it according to the inclinations of human reason. Fanny was disturbed by this phenomenon, believing that the Bible should be the "absolute authority" for the Christian life. Reason should be employed to help to understand scripture, but scripture should not be subordinated to what its interpreters feel is "rational." For Fanny, scripture was the absolute "norm of faith," and her numerous religious experiences, her visions and voices, her incisive thoughts and penetrating insights—all these had to be examined in light of scripture. "This Book is to me God's treasure house," she said. "It is my bread of life, the anchor of my home, my pillar of fire by night, my pillar of cloud by day. It is the lantern that lights my pathway to my paradise Home."

In her later years, where the terms "fundamentalism," "liberalism," and "modernism" came into being, Fanny was often asked where she stood regarding the Bible, and such questions vexed her sorely. "I have no time to cavil over the Sacred Volume or raise questions of no value about the Word," she said. In keeping with her lack of interest in "theology," she refused to pigeonhole beliefs about scripture, but she believed that God spoke through scripture, and through every part of it. She also believed that it was important for each individual Christian to hear the voice of God from each passage and believe that its message was absolutely binding for their life. She felt that a sermon should be preached and received as an oracle from heaven and that clergymen in their messages should be absolutely faithful to sacred scripture. For a pastor to preach on politics or poetry was a heresy which has "done

221

more real harm to the growth of the kingdom of God among men than anything else."[16]

Fanny wrote and said little that has been preserved about the Lord's Supper, although certain people who knew her said that she had a great love for the Sacrament. In fact, in later years when she studied Roman Catholicism, she found nothing objectionable in the doctrine of Transubstantiation, which asserts that the bread and wine are literally changed into the body and blood of Christ. No doubt she regarded Communion as a private matter.

For Fanny, the true essence of Christianity was something to which the scriptures and the sacraments merely pointed: a real and personal relationship with God. And it is probably accurate to say that she had a greater sense of the realness and personal-ness of relationship with God than most people. Everyone ought to strive to attain a closer relationship with God; to her this was the glory of being a Christian.

Fanny went to God with all her needs, great and small, firmly believing that God answered prayers—if the request was in the best interest of the one who prayed. Like other faithful Christians, she knew that God often did not grant what was asked, but she was convinced that, if God refused her, he had something better in mind. "All must have their sorrows and disappointments," she said, "but we must never forget that Jesus will answer our prayers if for our good, and answer them so much more fully and completely than we have dared to dream."[17] At the same time, Fanny was not of the school that thinks there is no evil in life. She believed in a real Satan and believed that the evil in the world was real and not apparent. And although he does not "order" it, yet God "permits" evil, at times, in order to bring some good from it. As an example of this, Fanny sometimes cited the case of her own blindness. "Now God did not order that," she said, for the doctor who mistreated her eyes "broke a law of nature." Nevertheless, she felt her handicap "carried out God's plan."[18]

She could be incredibly cheerful, even in suffering, and while sometimes the reason for her difficulties would not be readily apparent, she knew that there *was* a good reason and that God was permitting this affliction for some good. "Our Lord afflicts His children only to bring them closer to Him. I walk by faith, not by sight. I am ready to suffer if only for His glory. When we reach those heavenly shores, we shall know why these earthly ties were broken,"[19] she said, in reference to the bereavements of her later years. She would often quote Hebrews 12:6, saying, "Whom the Lord loveth, he chasteneth," and commenting, "If I had no troubles, I'd think the Lord didn't love me!"[20] In addition, she felt that, whatever happened, "everything will come out right in the end," for "I have heard my heavenly Father say, 'What I do, thou knowest not now, but thou shalt know hereafter.'"

Many supposed that the cheerful disposition that manifested itself in Fanny

Crosby's later years was the result of a naturally happy disposition, but this was not necessarily so. We have seen how she was much beset by depression and discouragement early in life, and even in old age she admitted that her "life has been short of many things that some people would probably rather die than be without."[21] She had had "many a hard struggle, with bread and rent to pay," but she "never lost faith in the promise, 'Thy bread shall be given and thy water sure.'"[22] She had suffered, but she could in later years look back and see how God had brought her through troubles. "I am happy as a lark, for He who takes care of the sparrow will never forget Aunt Fanny," she once said, adding that "many a storm has beaten on this old bark of mine, but I always enter the harbor" and "many sorrows which have been heartrending have crossed my path, but out of Gethsemane I have reached Olivet, where angel-voices have beckoned me to the lands of eternal sunshine."[23]

Often asked why some of her happiest hymns were death hymns, Fanny replied, "Since my childhood, death has simply seemed to me a stepping-stone to something better. Why should I feel sad about that? I have had moments when it almost seemed I had reached heaven. Could I possibly be less happy when I reach home for good?"[24] If her life on earth could be so joyful, then what must the glories of paradise be like? At times she, like her beloved Moody, became "homesick for heaven." Often, in beautiful visions, she was seized by a desire to throw off all earthly encumbrances and depart, only to be told by her Guardian Angel that she still had work to do on earth.

In one such vision, toward the end of her life, Fanny found herself, walking "beside a clear river" with her Guardian Angel. "On the other side of the river were beautiful trees—perfect trees, with no sign of age or decay; and under the trees people were walking, and they were perfect too, and it looked so peaceful and lovely that I said to my Guide, 'Let me cross over the River,'"[25] but she was forbidden, for the time being, to do so.

Of her dead relatives, she was often heard to say, "Oh, well, they're better off. They've just passed into the glorious land."[26] In that glorious land she expected to see them again. "What a grand treat," she said, "to meet all those we have known and loved here and talk over the events of the past."[27] Of her destination she was so certain that she criticized Lord Tennyson for writing, "I hope to see my Pilot face to face when I have crost the bar," saying, "I *know* I'll meet my Pilot face to face!"[28]

With such a hope set before her, how could she help but be a happy person? Her joy was not merely a calm and "holy" serenity, a dignified and subdued felicity, but often an outright merriness and jollity. She was considered a very funny person, noted for her wit and humor. A great practical jokester as a girl, she was playfully mischievous even in old age. Her sermons and lectures were full of funny stories and whimsical anecdotes, and she felt that the best way to chide or to criticize was through making people laugh at themselves and their own foibles. Indeed, she often showed disapproval through a humorous comment. Once, at Phoebe Knapp's apartments, she met a grave and pompous bishop and was turned off by the prelate's overdone sobriety. So when the churchman had to excuse himself to leave, Fanny called out, loudly, in the presence of numerous guests, "For heaven's sake, Bishop, stay sober!"[29] Fanny disliked talk that made light of sacred things. Once a young man called on her whom she found appallingly irreverent. After he left, she remarked to Florence, "Oh, for a hammer to knock a lump of reverence into that man's head!"[30]

Aunt Fanny had a special love for children, even in her old age. Whenever she spoke in a church, she would usually give a "children's sermon" in addition to the regular talk. As we have seen, she liked, even despite her age, to play with her grandnieces and nephews, and took an interest in the children in her neighborhood. At times, when she was in town, parents would leave their little ones in Aunt Fanny's care, and few things delighted her more than this. Many people who lived into the seventh decade of this century carried fond memories of Aunt Fanny from their earliest childhood in Bridgeport.

By the time she was in her later eighties, Fanny Crosby was indeed known as "the Methodist saint." The social worker Ann Cobham, whom Fanny frequently visited at her estate in Stoneylonesome, near Warren, Pennsylvania, was not alone when she said that the hymnist was "the most wonderful person living." Thousands of people throughout the nation and the English-speaking world agreed with her.

CHAPTER 23
"I DON'T WANT TO DIE YET"

"I am staying indoors until the weather shall moderate," Fanny wrote to White during the winter of 1907-8. She seldom went out now in wintertime, but she was far from idle, what with the constant streams of visitors who came for advice and help. When the weather did improve, away she went. In March she boarded the train at Bridgeport and traveled alone to New York, where she was met by Phoebe, with whom she spent a week. At her annual banquet she was asked about her more than eight thousand hymns. Which did she consider the best? Significantly, she remarked, "I have not yet written my best hymn."[1] Although she felt that many of her hymns had been used by God for great good, she still felt that from an artistic point of view she had not written very many great ones. Her output had been rushed, but perhaps now, since much less was being asked of her, she could get down to writing her greatest.

After her birthday, Fanny spent a week attending a Methodist convention in Brooklyn. One afternoon she called on Ira Sankey in what would prove to be her last visit to this beloved old friend. Ira was now dying. For three years he had been suffering from a sickness that caused him excruciating pain and had reduced him to a near-skeleton. Fanny found his condition "really pathetic." When she told him that "the entire Christian world is praying for your recovery," the sick man shook his head and said to tell his friends that "I hope to meet them all bye and bye in the land where there is no more sorrow or pain and where God shall wipe away all tears from our eyes." Ira bade Fanny to meet him in heaven, "at the pearly gate at the eastern side of the city." There, he said, "I'll take you by the hand and lead you along the golden street, up to the throne of God, and there we'll stand . . . and say to Him: 'And now we see Thee face to face, saved by Thy matchless, boundless grace!'"[2]

After the convention, Fanny set off for Perth Amboy, New Jersey, for two weeks of speaking engagements. Although she must have known that she was meeting with Sankey for the last time, when she bade adieu to Phoebe Knapp at the Hotel Savoy she had no way of knowing that for her, too, it was to be the last good-bye. At Perth Amboy she stayed with her old friend William Rock, the Surface Car executive, where, she wrote to White, "I am recovering from my birthday week's dissipations."[3] From there she proceeded to

Princeton, where, staying at the home of friends, she spoke at a "sacred concert" on Good Friday at the Presbyterian church. On Sunday, she preached the Easter sermon.

Before leaving Princeton, she paid one last visit to her old friend, Grover Cleveland, who was in an enfeebled and emaciated condition. She was deeply concerned about him as she rode to New Haven, where she visited Bert White at Yale. Then, on the morning of June 25, she learned that Grove was dead. A reporter called on her that day, asking her if she knew of the ex-President's passing. "Oh, yes," she said sadly, "they told me today he was dead. I could not think it was possible. It almost broke my heart. It seems to me that I cannot give him up." She paused. "Yes ... I can give him up, for I have learned to know, 'Thy will be done.'" She hailed Cleveland as a "lovely, noble character" and a "noble, faithful Christian gentleman." And she consoled herself that they had a "deep, warm friendship that death cannot break, for the cords will be united and we shall see and know each other in the land of the blest." She was especially shaken because the news came on the first anniversary of Carrie's death, but, as in the case of Van's demise, she immersed herself in work. She had been commissioned to write a magazine article on her friendship with Cleveland and was determined to "keep my thoughts to the work." In this case, she felt, "work is a blessing."[4]

This summer was to be the saddest of Fanny's long life. Not much longer than two weeks after she learned of Cleveland's death, she was stunned by the news that Phoebe Knapp was dead. Still vigorous and youthful-looking in her early seventies, Phoebe had gone to Poland Spring, Maine, for a vacation and there, on July 10, she suffered a stroke and died. Then, a month later, Sankey's soul was freed. On the morning of the thirteenth of August, he drifted off into a coma, singing the opening lines of Fanny's "Saved by Grace":

Some day the silver cord will break
And I no more as now shall sing,
But, oh, the joy when I shall wake
Within the palace of the King!

By nightfall, he was gone.

Fanny must have felt quite lonely now. Not only had she outlived most of her friends of her own age, she had outlived most of those who were a generation younger. She had seen generations come and go, and yet she remained. Unlike many very old persons who wonder why they are left behind, Fanny remained basically "as happy as a chickadee," secure in the confidence that she would eventually be forever united with those she had loved, and secure in the confidence that God still had work for her to do on earth.

She continued to write hymns, mostly for Allan Sankey and Charles Gabriel, a few for Hugh Main. For Main she wrote a successful hymn on the transitory nature of earthly life entitled "We're Traveling On." It was the last of her major hymns. She continued to speak regularly at the Christian Union and maintained her ministry of cheer by private meetings, letters, and lectures. She tried to visit every patient that came to Rector's Hospital for the Sick, praying for them and cheering them.

Fanny's lifetime had spanned many changes in America. She had seen the invention of the telephone, as well as the telegraph, steam engine, phonograph, moving picture, bicycle, typewriter, X-ray, elevator, sewing machine, safety match, anesthetics, reaper and mower, submarine, typesetting machine, automobile, airplane, and radio. Fanny did not "belong to that class of people who, looking back over many years, think the old times better than our own." As she watched with wonder and great interest the developments of her lifetime and even in the fields of music and literature, she had no great criticism for modern inventions. She came to know and somewhat appreciate poetry of the modern idiom—poetry without rhyme and rhythm and so unlike that which she had been nurtured upon and wrote. She enjoyed the popular songs of the day and toyed with the idea of writing secular songs once again, as she had done fifty years before, feeling that her lyrics could "elevate above their present standard" the songs of the day.[5]

Aunt Fanny was profoundly disturbed by other trends she saw developing in American society. The growing tendency toward materialism troubled her, and she saw the beginning of the breakdown of the American home and family structure. At odds with the feminist movement, she complained that modern women seemed eager to do everything but "the work that ought to be done at home," adding, "I may appear a little old-fogeyish, but I have firm convictions on this very vital question."[6] She was convinced that the strength of a nation lay in family and home life, and when that broke down so did the nation. "The people of the United States must know," she said, that "if the home fails, the Church is shorn of its strength, the community crumbles, the State is unstable, the nation is doomed."[7] At the center of the home should be God, and Fanny saw with great concern the increasing lack of interest in Christianity among Americans. "When I was a child," she said, speaking of the Bible, "this book had a practical place both in home and nation." Her mother and grandmother, she recalled, "took pains that I knew the Bible better than any other book." This had been true of most families at that time, but now this had changed and Fanny was alarmed. The growing doubts and disbelief of scripture saddened her. "No Christian nation can be great which ignores the Sacred Book," she lamented. Moreover, she felt that America could not endure "if the heads of the families are prayerless."

The nation too, she felt, must be headed by a man of prayer. With William

H. Taft, a rather nominal Unitarian, in the White House, Fanny commented that she felt that it was impossible for the nation to survive with "prayerless Presidents." Without a return to the faith of her fathers, America had no future at all. She saw all this reflected in the life of the church itself, where attendance was falling off. She was appalled at the few men who took an interest in religion. While the streets were full of men and boys engaged in all kinds of worldly pursuits, yet "Go to the church and see forty bonnets to one bald pate." She feared that from the generation rising about her "there will not be men enough in heaven to sing bass."[8]

Within Protestantism, there were movements that appalled Fanny. Many of the modern theologians had come to question the authority of scripture and had come to see a large part of it as myth and legend. Fanny was deeply troubled about trends she perceived developing among the clergy. She was troubled when told of many young people losing their faith in college and seminary. "First they took Santa Claus away from me. Then they took away my God," lamented a young seminarian she had known.

Fanny seldom went to church services now, and perhaps the trend toward "modernism" was one of the reasons, but no certain case can be made for this. First Methodist Church in Bridgeport, under its pastor, the Rev. Dr. George M. Brown, whom Fanny loved and respected, still preserved the orthodox faith.

The infrequency of her church attendance is a mystery. She was growing quite frail, but this did not stop her from traveling up and down the East Coast, fulfilling various speaking engagements, and she continued to speak at churches when invited to do so. In fact, about the only times that she appeared at First Church now were when she was asked to speak. She told Henry and Florence that, since they were Anglican, it would be "too much trouble" for them to take her to her church and then go to another.[9] This reason is not really satisfactory, since in the past Fanny never had any qualms about attending different churches and going wherever her hosts had chosen to go. Moreover, in Bridgeport there was a cabbie who was totally devoted to her and served as her chauffeur, taking her wherever she wanted to go free of charge, so transportation was really no problem. When asked by friends about the reason for her infrequent attendance, she told them, "I can worship God just as well here, by myself, as I can at church."[10] This is a strange and baffling statement, coming from one who had been a faithful churchgoer most of her life.

Fanny still retained her Methodist membership, however, and continued to work diligently with Alice Rector and the King's Daughters. She became increasingly interested in Roman Catholicism, finding it a "good, strong religion" whose fervent piety she admired.[11] She held highest respect for Pius X, who had opposed the trends toward "modernism" among his own clergy

228

and people and who was noted for the extraordinary holiness of his life. The pastor of St. Patrick's Church on North Avenue in Bridgeport, the Rev. James Nihill, came regularly to see Fanny, and the two would discuss the Roman Catholic faith. Fanny found that Roman Catholicism held but one drawback for her, and it was not a doctrinal one. It was the liturgy. "Why, you're only reading out of a book," she told Nihill. "It's not something you've worked up yourself!" Moreover, she felt that there was too little emphasis on the preached word. "Now, Father," she said, "why don't you stand up and *say* something?"[12]

Not all the developments in American Protestantism filled Fanny with dismay. She followed with interest the career of Dr. W. A. (Billy) Sunday, who in many ways proved himself a successor to her dear Moody. She was also inspired by Dr. J. Wilbur Chapman and his "Chorister," Charles M. (Charlie) Alexander, who in 1909 conducted a successful multinational campaign. She even wrote a poem in their honor.

In March 1910 Fanny celebrated her ninetieth birthday. She was bent nearly double now but continued to travel and lecture, refusing to give in to the ravages of time. She was still busy enough to write to Bert White that "I am so busy I hardly know my name."[13] Her cheerfulness seemed to increase rather than diminish with increasing years. At Samuel Trevena Jackson's church in Hackettstown, New Jersey, she spoke to a packed house of her nine decades "rich with the wealth of good, sparkling with the best spirit of sweetness, and overflowing with the true wine of joy and gladness."[14]

"I come to you," she said, "in the evening of life, with a rod and staff, and I am living in sight of eternity's sunrise." She maintained that "I don't want to die yet, but rather live on for another decade and a half, to the age of a hundred and five." "But," she conceded, "if my heavenly Father wills it otherwise, it is well." She attributed her remarkable longevity to three "angel-guards," which controlled her appetite, temper, and speech.

Fanny traveled to New York—alone—in the spring of 1911, where she appeared as the principal speaker at the "Tent, Open-Air, and Shop Campaign" of the Evangelistic Committee of the Methodist Episcopal Church. There were more than five thousand people at Carnegie Hall that day, and a choir of two thousand voices sang, almost exclusively, her hymns. Fanny arrived in an automobile, and when it pulled up the attendants were so appalled by her feeble and ravaged appearance that one of them cried, "For heaven's sake, get a wheelchair!"

Fanny's strong voice stopped them. "*I* need no rolling chair," she said. "I can stand on my own two feet. My strength is in the Lord." She got out of the car and was led into the hall onto the platform as the choir burst into her hymn "We're Traveling On." She stretched forth her feeble hands and cried (in a "firm, well-pitched voice"), "Men of Empire City, you are dear to my heart!

This scene takes me back to my twenty-five years of mission work! When I came in and you greeted me so warmly, I wanted to weep tears of joy!" And she proceeded to give a long lecture on hymnody. [15]

That October she returned to New York for the last time, to visit with Helen Keller, whom she had first met a decade before. After a day with her gifted friend, whom she considered a modern prophet, she once more visited the Bowery Mission and spoke there. Then in the company of Samuel Trevena Jackson, she went over to Jersey City, where she spoke in the Simpson Memorial Methodist Church and visited with Alice Holmes, who at ninety was somewhat deaf and enfeebled. The two women had not been together for four decades, but Alice recognized Fanny at once by her voice. The two embraced and sat together for hours, holding hands. When Fanny left, Alice said, "Good-bye, Fan. We shall meet again in the better land." [16]

Fanny would never return to the Empire City. For years she had had no trouble getting about by herself; she had been able to count on the help of friendly passersby to cross streets, enter trolleys and subways, and find addresses. But no more. During her stay this time, she boarded a trolley but had to stand for minutes, pushed and jostled and shoved, until the conductor, seeing her dark glasses, called out, "Somebody give her a seat! Can't you see the woman is blind!" [17]

That autumn, everyone felt that the last hour had come for Aunt Fanny when she was stricken with pneumonia, but to everyone's amazement, including her own, she recovered. Fanny looked so frail now that everyone expected her death momentarily. Sometimes the phone would ring, and while Fanny sat talking to callers some excited reporter would inquire of Miss Cleaveland "at what hour Fanny Crosby passed away"!

Fanny still traveled occasionally. In February 1913 she and Florence journeyed to Cambridge, Massachusetts, where she was to speak at the First Baptist Church. The two women were entertained by the pastor, Dr. John Campbell, a Scotsman, and while they were dining the doorbell rang and a delegation from the Salvation Army entered with the request that they be permitted to accompany her to the church with a brass band playing some of her hymns. Fanny was nonplussed and gratefully consented. So the next evening, the band of the Salvation Army's Cambridge Corps appeared at the manse and serenaded Fanny with her own hymns for several minutes. Tears came to her eyes as she thanked the corpsmen for "this unmerited honor to a humble child of God." She and Campbell then took a carriage to the church, with the band preceding them playing such hymns as "Rescue the Perishing" and "Pass Me Not." The next day, she preached to an audience of two thousand. Years later, a man who had been a child at the time could still remember "the little old lady, dressed in black, standing with Dr. Campbell behind the lectern, saying goodbye to the world." [18]

On her return to Bridgeport, Fanny was asked to write a poem to be read at the dedication of Grover Cleveland's birthplace, which was being made a national shrine. Her ninety-third birthday fell on Easter, and she remarked, "If there is anyone in this world happier than I, I want to shake his hand, for I believe myself to be as happy as it is possible for a mortal to be in this world. Life with me glides on like a little boat on a waveless stream, with flowers on each bank."[19] That evening, she appeared at the First Methodist Church for the first time in many months. George Stebbins had come from Brooklyn to be with her, accompanied by Mrs. Jenny Bennett Carpenter, a blind soprano who was a neighbor of Stebbins. Fanny had heard her sing while on a visit to New York several years earlier and had been impressed by her talent. After Fanny spoke and blessed the congregation, Mrs. Carpenter sang "Saved by Grace." Halfway through, Aunt Fanny rose and took her arm and sang with her. The congregation was moved to tears at the sight of the two blind women singing together, arm in arm.[20]

Fanny spent her time, now, as she said in a letter to Bert White, "knitting, always as usual—stopping when callers come in or something more pressing presents itself."[21] She took a few automobile rides and a few trips to see friends, but beyond that she seldom went out any more. As her ninety-fourth birthday approached, Alice Rector and her King's Daughters decided that all Fanny's friends should honor her by wearing her favorite flower, the violet. Hugh Main saw to it that Violet Day came to the attention of the newspapers, and another nationwide birthday celebration was planned. The Sunday before Violet Day, Fanny spoke for what was to be the last time, at First Methodist, and the church was packed with people who had come to hear the ancient poet. A local newspaper reported that she was "feeble in body, yet strong in mind ... buoyant in spirit, with a trust and faith in God as firm as the everlasting hills." The audience sang several of her hymns before she was helped to the lectern by Dr. Brown. She began with a reference to the "sainted" Ira Sankey: "The person who wrote the hymns we have just sung is singing in heaven to-night."

Most of her address was about the efficacy of prayer. Prayer is essential in the life of the believer and a Christian lives by prayer, she said. Some people think that one must kneel or assume a certain physical position to pray, but this is false. "I do not kneel to pray. I no longer have the strength to rise from that position." Likewise, all believers should feel free to pray to God wherever or in whatever position is most convenient.

She gave several examples of God's answering prayers, including her own recovery from pneumonia a year or so before, which she attributed solely to the prayers of her friends. "I want all of you to go to God in prayer in all trials and sorrows. The good will come out of it, and He will answer your prayer better than you think." Of course, one will not always get exactly what he has asked for. "All must have sorrows and disappointments," but one must never forget that, if commended to God, they would issue in good. One must trust God's way as best—his own solution as far better than any we could conceive.

She closed, urging the congregation to "cling to the Saviour" in "this age of change." She deplored the lack of faith and reverence of the day, enjoining the people to pray with her for a nationwide revival. "Let it begin in the hearts of God's children."

"My dear, dear people," she concluded, "I love you dearly, and if I should first cross to the beautiful shore, I know that I shall greet you there!"[22] Nevertheless, she felt that her work was not yet done. "I believe that He still has work for me yet. I don't want to die yet."[23]

But it was now apparent to most, and probably even to her, that she would never approximate her goal of 105 years. She was definitely slowing down and, increasingly, her vivacious soul was prisoner of a decaying body. Florence often had to tell many callers now that her aunt just did not have the strength to meet with them.

CHAPTER 24
NEVER MORE TO SAY FAREWELL

The last day of May, Fanny and Jule celebrated their mother's birthday once more at Jule's home. Approaching death was very much in the minds of the two old women, and Fanny repeatedly said of Carrie, "I know that she is very near me." She also claimed "communion of the spirit" with Ira Sankey and said that it would be a grand day when she went to heaven to once more "behold the sweet faces" of those she had loved. Alice Holmes died that year, and when Fanny learned of her death, she simply said, without a sigh or tear, "She is waiting for me." To Julia she dictated:

Once again, oh, sister mine,
Hearts and hands around us twine,
While together you and I
Look on yonder radiant sky,
Where our friends and kindred dwell,
Never more to say farewell.

•   •   •

They have passed the vale of tears,
Far beyond its toils and years;
In the morning land above,
In a paradise of love,
Of eternal joys they tell,
Never more to say farewell.

•   •   •

Sister, when our work is done,
When the victory we have won,
In the presence of the King,
Of His Glory we shall sing,
And with friends and kindred dwell,
Never more to say farewell.[1]

In the summer of 1914, Fanny went on her last major trip, journeying north with Florence to the home of the Curriers at Longmeadow, Massachusetts. Fanny was now so feeble that she had to be carried to and from trains and automobiles, but she took this debilitation in good humor, quipping, "I'm safe in the arms of the chauffeur!"[2]

Instead of going to a public place to speak, which would have been quite beyond her strength, the nonagenarian was induced to give a talk in the Curriers' backyard. "Let the public come to her this time," said Mary. Many people packed onto the Curriers' spacious lawn, which was festively hung with Japanese lanterns. There Fanny talked, recited, and sang until Florence and Mary feared she would overtax herself and made her stop.

On her return to Bridgeport in August, however, Aunt Fanny paid the price of overexertion and had a mild heart attack. This time death seemed imminent, and Fanny again believed that her time had come. During this illness she had ecstatic visions, and when she was better she reported that these were the most remarkable of her life. She said very little about their nature or contents, except that in one an angel came to her and said, "Be thou faithful and I will give thee the crown of life," an almost word-for-word quotation from the Apocalypse of John. The angel also said, "Be calm and get your strength back as soon as you can, and then go to work for the Master once more."[3] Fanny partially recovered but she knew that it would not be for long, and the doctors warned Florence that her aunt could not live for many more months. Fanny welcomed her approaching end with joy. She was going to "just pass on to the glorious land," and she told her friends, "When I have arrived at my eternal home, they will say, 'Come in, Fanny! Come in!' Then will be the victory through Christ!"[4]

Nevertheless, as her angel had bidden, while life lasted she still had "work for the Master." The circle of the King's Daughters, now known as the Fanny Crosby Circle, took up Travelers' Aid work that year, and, although too frail and sick to participate actively, Fanny enthusiastically gave the organizing women all she could in the way of encouragement, advice, and prayer. Alice Rector later recalled her enthusiasm, how "we had to tell her about all the cases taken care of at the Railroad Station."[5] She could no longer go to the Christian Union to speak, but she continued to pray for it. First and foremost, however, Aunt Fanny felt that the angel wanted her to give the world a few more hymns before she departed. Indeed, Allan Sankey and Hugh Main were planning their first major hymnal in a decade and asked Fanny to make contributions to it, and in the next few months she wrote about a dozen hymns. Among these were "Stand at Your Post," set to music by Victor Benke, "His Fold of Rest," "God's Peace I'll Know," "Joy Beyond the Sea," "O, for a Faith," "How I Thank Thee," "Why Not Believe?" and "O, Saviour, Hear." Among the best was "Keep Thou Me." Her last series of hymns was nearly completed by Christmas, and she was working on what she called a "war hymn," which was in reality a peace hymn. Once fascinated by the "red deeds of war," in the last few years she had moved progressively in the direction of pacifism. The outbreak of the Great War in Europe the previous summer, "a strife whose like has ne'er been told," had filled her with dismay and she wanted peace. "The price of peace must be paid," she said, "in order that any semblance of civilization is to remain on the face of the earth." The hymn, which she dictated to Miss Cleaveland in December 1914, was a plea for peace. It concluded:

> Warriors, sheathe the flaming sword,
> The right shall rule through Christ the Lord,
> Twill not be long, 'twill not be long,
> O, praise His Name, 'twill not be long!
>
> Thou great supreme and judge of all,
> While at Thy feet we humbly fall,
> O, grant our prayer, our earnest plea,
> That all the world at peace may be.[6]

In January, the aged Doane, suffering from "creeping paralysis" and bedridden, able to sit up for only a few minutes each day, decided to write one last song. He sent word to his old colleague that he would like her to write one last piece and accordingly, in early February, she wrote what was to prove her hymnic swan song:

> At evening time it shall be light,
> When fades the day of toil away,
> No shadows deep, no weary night,
> At evening time, it shall be light.
>
> At evening time it shall be light,
> Immortal love from realms above
> Is breathing now the promise bright,
> At evening time it shall be light.[7]

Fanny now began to make preparations for her death and burial. She made Florence and Jule promise that any memorial in her memory would not be a marble or granite monument, such as Barnum had erected to himself close to her plot, but something that could benefit people. She had several suggestions. The Christian Union had been a concern ever since she had come to Bridgeport, and it needed an infirmary. If her friends felt that they had to memorialize her, let them set up a fund in her name to raise money for this

235

infirmary. Or perhaps her friends could set up a home for elderly people. Although her own life had been made cheerful by a young family and by young friends, she was concerned with the loneliness and emptiness in the lives of so many older people in a society in which the increasing tendency was for children to live apart from their aging parents and grandparents. One elderly widow told her that the only time she ever heard a human voice now was when the woman she hired to keep house called her to tell her that a meal was ready. Fanny thought that it might be a good thing if elderly people who had no families could live together in a community; this might be a suitable memorial for her. Or perhaps it could take the form of a fund to help elderly ministers, for whom there was no real pension system in those days. By no means, however, was any money to be spent on a tombstone or a dead monument of marble.

Fanny called in a lawyer to draw up a will in which she left one half of her estate to Florence, in gratitude for accommodating her for so many years. The other half was to be held in trust by Florence for Jule, an arrangement Fanny decided upon because of her sister's advancing years. When Jule should die, her share would go to Florence.

On February 8, Fanny was visited by a group of mission workers and she spoke of her life, telling them that she was especially concerned with four categories of people: railroad men, policemen, prisoners, and the poor. To the mission workers, Fanny reiterated what she had said all her life long about her blindness:

I believe that the greatest blessing the Creator ever bestowed on me was when he permitted my external vision to be closed. He consecrated me for the work which He created me. I have never known what it was to see, and therefore I cannot realize my personal loss. But I have had the most remarkable dreams, I have seen the prettiest eyes, the most beautiful faces, the most remarkable landscapes. The loss of sight has been no loss to me.[8]

During her last weeks, Fanny manifested a peculiar phenomenon. Numerous visitors remarked with wonder that her countenance seemed visibly to shine "full of radiant light."[9] This visible glowing was first observed on isolated occasions as early as 1907, but apparently it became constant in her last days. This was remarked upon by the mission workers as well as by the Rev. H. A. Davenport of the People's Presbyterian Church, who called on her February 9. "I hope to reach heaven sometime," he told her, and bade her pray for him in the other world. She promised to remember him in heaven. On the tenth, Adam Geibel came, and the two blind musicians played a duet at the piano. Father Nihill came later in the day, and Fanny and the priest had their last conversation.

236

On the eleventh, Fanny, who had hithertofore been ambulant, said that she did not feel well and would stay in bed. Her appetite, always so good, at last failed. "Tomorrow I shall be well," she said, and she seemed radiant with joy. All through the day she smiled and kept saying, "I'm so comfortable. I'm so comfortable." At nine at night, she sent for Eva Cleaveland and asked her to take down a letter to a neighbor family which had just lost a young child, assuring them that "your precious Ruth is 'Safe in the Arms of Jesus.'" After completing the letter, she dictated her final testimony to the world:

In the morn of Zion's glory,
When the clouds have rolled away,
And my hope has dropped its anchor
In the vale of perfect day,
When with all the pure and holy
I shall strike my harp anew,
With a power no arm can sever,
Love will hold me fast and true.[10]

Henry Booth was the last one in the household to retire that night. When he came upstairs at two thirty in the morning, he looked in, as he always did, to see how Aunt Fanny was. She was awake, heard him, smiled, and said gently, "All right, Governor."[11] At three thirty, Florence heard her aunt up and walking down the hall, presumably to the toilet. Getting up to assist her, she met Fanny at the doorway to her room and there, to her horror, Fanny fainted in her arms. Florence carried the pathetically meager figure back to bed, awoke her husband and son, and called two doctors, Reich and Godfrey. Fanny was oblivious of those around the bedside. Earth seemed to be receding now. "The morn of Zion's glory" seemed to be breaking upon her. Florence and Henry were struck by the expression of peace and serenity on her face. Then Fanny smiled and "turned towards the eternal fountain," seemingly only to go to sleep. The first of two doctors arrived about four thirty and pronounced her dead of a massive cerebral hemorrhage. Florence screamed and burst into tears, sobbing, "It cannot be! It cannot be!" Eva Cleaveland, however, confided in a letter to Bert White, "We have had reason to fear that she might have a long unconscious illness or suffer or something that way, so that it is a comfort to have her go like this."[12]

According to many witnesses, Fanny Crosby's was the largest funeral ever seen in Bridgeport, surpassing even that of P. T. Barnum. People stood for blocks to file by the bier. In her right hand was the little silk flag she had always carried, and on the casket, at the request of Jule, were engraved the words, My Sister. George Stebbins, Allan Sankey, and Hugh Main were there. Stebbins remarked, to Samuel Trevena Jackson just before the services began, "Fanny wrote for the hearts of the people, and she wrote even better than she knew. She imbued all she ever did with a befitting spirit—the spirit of sweetness."

There were delegations from the King's Daughters, the Grand Army of the Republic, and from the Bridgeport and Hartford chapters of the Daughters of the American Revolution (of which Fanny was a member). The church was full of the flowers which Fanny had loved. The choir sang her favorite hymn, Heber's "Faith of Our Fathers," and Pastor Davenport prayed—at very great length. Then the choir sang "Safe in the Arms. of Jesus" and "Saved by Grace," as many wept openly. Dr. Brown gave the eulogy, in which he said, "You have come to pay tribute and to crown a friend. There must have been a royal welcome when this queen of sacred song burst the bonds of death and passed into the glories of heaven." Poetic tributes were read. As the congregation filed out, everyone was given a violet, and passing before the bier they dropped the flowers in until it seemed that she was sleeping in a bed of violets. As Blanche Simpson put it:

Face to face with Him in glory,
Safe in Jesus' tender care,
Earthly pains and cares forgotten,
Lips, now still, once spoke in prayer,

Thoughts so filled with loving kindness,
Heart seemed bursting, full of love,
Eyes that saw not worldly beauty,
Glory in the light above.

●　　●　　●

Like a sweet and lovely violet,
Now asleep on Jesus' breast,
Never wilt thou be forgotten,
Sweetly there, thy soul's at rest.[13]

That afternoon, Jule wrote White, who could not attend:

I have come home from the cemetery and dear Aunt Fanny is gone from the earth. I am sending you the clippings from the paper which explain the service. How I shall miss her! Mr. Main and Mr. Sankey were both at the funeral. It was cloudy all day and raining hard now. The enclosed flowers were in Fanny's hand. I know *you* will *prize* them.[14]

But Fanny was not so dear to Jule after she read the will. Notwithstanding her own capers with her mother's estate two decades before, Jule was beside

238

herself with rage that her share of Fanny's estate of $2,000 was to be held in trust for her by Florence. She was in high dudgeon and hired a lawyer in a futile attempt to challenge the will, claiming that Fanny was senile when she made it. In April, when the mess hit the papers, a dismayed Florence wrote to Bert White:

You can't imagine how sorry I am that those said clippings ever came out. I am not here to defend myself, if I wish, but poor Aunt Fanny who wanted peace. I can say from first to last, it was *false*. And she was perfectly right in changing the will. While, it is quoted, silence is golden. I have followed that saying. Well, it is better not to dwell on such things.[15]

The rest of Fanny's associates also began to die. On Christmas Eve, Doane succumbed to pneumonia at age eighty-four. Three days later, Allan Sankey had a heart attack. On the twentieth, he had married Anna Underhill Neighams, whose first husband had jumped out of a window a few days after their wedding. She and Allan were planning to take a cruise to the Caribbean, and despite his illness, Allan insisted on going, because the *S. S. Korona* was scheduled to leave the next day. His doctors said he ought to remain hospitalized and warned that if he went on the trip he would certainly die. Sankey was adamant. The cruise was delayed two days, and on December 29, ashen-faced, he boarded the ship with his wife. At 1 P.M. it left New York harbor; at 3 he was dead. Eliza Hewitt, after major surgery, died on April 24, 1920. The next year, Kirkpatrick, who at age eighty had, after the death of his wife, married Sweney's widow, died of a heart attack while writing a hymn. Hugh Main retired, and his firm was bought out or merged with the Hope Publishing Company of Chicago. He donated all his music books to the Newberry Library in Chicago before dying in Newark at eighty-six on October 7, 1925. George Stebbins lived on in Catskill, New York. He lost his wife and son and went to live with a sister, who, in turn, died a few years later. Nevertheless, he continued to write music, giving a setting to at least one previously unused poem of Fanny's, and lived until October 1945, just four months short of his hundredth birthday.

Of Fanny's family, Jule died of cancer of the breast at eighty on January 16, 1921; she was Fanny's last close blood relation. Florence Booth lived until October 1935, and her husband Henry until 1946. Laura Tait died in 1935, and her brother, Albert Morris, died in 1930. Adelbert White, after a distinguished career at the University of Nebraska, died in 1951, and Eva Cleaveland, the faithful secretary, lived in Bridgeport until 1956.

In 1920, on the hundredth anniversary of Fanny's birth, an infirmary was opened by the Christian Union in memory of its benefactress, Fanny J. Crosby. A chapel in it was also named for her. Two years later, as a result of a campaign to raise funds for a suitable memorial, a large mansion of twenty-eight rooms was endowed in Bridgeport as the Fanny Crosby Memorial Home for aged men and women.

Until 1955, there was nothing to mark Fanny Crosby's grave except a tiny marble stone with the words *Aunt Fanny* and the inscription, "She hath done what she could." Even that was more than she had asked. But on May 1 of that year, a large marble slab was erected on her grave, because citizens of Bridgeport decided that the "relatively inconspicuous marker with only vague identification" was "unworthy of the fame of Fanny Crosby Van Alstyne." [16] It reads:

In grateful and loving memory of
Fanny J. Crosby

Who inspired and edified Christians
all over the world
by the writing of more than 3000 hymns and poems [17]

Born in Southeast, N.Y. March 24, 1820
Married March 5, 1855 [sic], to Alexander Van Alstyne
Died in Bridgeport, Connecticut, February 12, 1915

Blessed assurance, Jesus is mine!
Oh, what a foretaste of glory divine!
Heir of salvation, purchase of God,
Born of His spirit, washed in His blood.

NOTES

INTRODUCTION
1. Samuel Trevena Jackson, *Fanny Crosby's Story of Ninety-Four Years* (New York: Revell, 1915), p. 119; hereafter referred to as *Fanny Crosby's Story*.
2. Fanny Crosby Papers.
3. Jackson, *Fanny Crosby's Story*, flyleaf.
4. Charles H. Gabriel, *The Singers and Their Songs: Sketches of Living Gospel Hymn Writers* (Chicago: Rodeheaver Co., 1916), p. 3.
5. Fanny Crosby Papers.
6. Ibid.
7. George C. Stebbins, *Reminiscences and Gospel Hymn Stories* (New York: Doran, 1924), p. 278.
8. Fanny Crosby Papers.
9. William J. Reynolds, *A Survey of Christian Hymnody* (New York: Holt, Rinehart & Winston, 1963), p. 107.
10. Fanny Crosby Papers.

CHAPTER 1: THE BLIND GIRL
1. Mrs. Theodosia Gay Swenson, conversation, July 1971.
2. Frances J. Crosby, *Memories of Eighty Years* (Boston: James H. Earle, 1906), p. 9; hereafter referred to as *Memories*.
3. Ibid.
4. Mrs. Swenson and consultation of Census of 1850.
5. Crosby, *Memories*, p. 9.
6. Jackson, *Fanny Crosby's Story*, pp. 30–31.
7. Ibid., p. 33.
8. Ibid.
9. Crosby, *Memories*, p. 12.
10. Mrs. Swenson.
11. Frances J. Crosby, *Fanny Crosby's Life-Story, by Herself* (New York: Everywhere Publishing Co., 1903), p. 16; hereafter referred to as *Life-Story*.
12. Crosby, *Memories*, pp. 22–23.

CHAPTER 2: "OH, WHAT A HAPPY CHILD AM I"

1. Crosby, *Memories*, pp. 20–21.
2. Fanny Crosby Papers.
3. Crosby, *Memories*, pp. 24–25.
4. Ibid., p. 14.
5. Mrs. Paine.
6. Crosby, *Life-Story*, p. 18.
7. Ibid., p. 25.
8. Ibid., p. 26.
9. Ibid.
10. Jackson, *Fanny Crosby's Story*, p. 35.
11. Fanny Crosby Papers.
12. Crosby, *Memories*, p. 28.
13. Ibid., p. 35.
14. Ibid., p. 27.
15. Mrs. Paine.
16. Crosby, *Memories*, pp. 30–31.
17. Ibid.
18. Frances J. Crosby, *Bells at Evening* (New York: Biglow and Main, 1903), pp. 144–45; hereafter referred to as *Bells*.
19. Crosby, *Memories*, p. 36.
20. Ibid., pp. 32–33.
21. Crosby, *Life-Story*, p. 28.

CHAPTER 3: "MY HAPPY HOME"

1. Crosby, *Memories*, p. 38.
2. Ibid., p. 39.
3. Ibid.
4. Ibid., p. 40.
5. Ibid.
6. George Frederick Root, *The Story of a Musical Life: An Autobiography* (Cincinnati: John Church, 1891), p. 39.
7. Crosby, *Memories*, p. 41.
8. Frances J. Crosby, *The Blind Girl and Other Poems* (New York: Wiley and Putnam, 1844), p. 21.
9. Crosby, *Life-Story*, p. 34.
10. Crosby, *Memories*, p. 44.
11. Crosby, *Life-Story*, p. 37.
12. Crosby, *Memories*, p. 194.
13. Ibid., p. 49.
14. Crosby, *Life-Story*, p. 54.

CHAPTER 4: "THE BLIND POETESS"

1. Diary of Thomas Morris, courtesy of Miss Marjorie C. Morris, Bridgeport, Connecticut.
2. Crosby, *Memories*, pp. 72–73.
3. Crosby, *Bells*, p. 89.
4. Crosby, *Memories*, p. 60.
5. Ibid., p. 62.
6. Crosby, *Life-Story*, p. 56.
7. Crosby, *The Blind Girl and Other Poems* (New York: Wiley and Putnam, 1844), pp. 66–67.
8. Crosby, *Life-Story*, p. 66.
9. Fanny Crosby Papers.
10. *Washington Daily Globe*, January 24, 1844.
11. Ibid.
12. Crosby, *Memories*, p. 70.
13. Jackson, *Fanny Crosby's Story*, p. 57.
14. George Henry Sandison, "Fannie Crosby: Writer of Hymns," *National Magazine*, vol. IX (1898), pp. 549–50.

CHAPTER 5: PRESIDENTS, GENERALS, AND BRATS

1. Crosby, *Memories*, pp. 63–64.
2. Crosby, *Life-Story*, p. 58.
3. Jackson, *Fanny Crosby's Story*, p. 44.
4. Crosby, *Memories*, p. 80.
5. Ibid., p. 79.
6. *Congressional Globe, New Series, Containing Sketches of the Debates and Proceedings of the First Session of the Twenty-Ninth U.S. Congress* (Washington: Blairs and Rives, 1846), May 8, 1846.
7. Ibid., May 13, 1846.
8. *New York Tribune*, March 8, 1848.
9. Crosby, *Memories*, p. 84.
10. Ibid.
11. *New York Tribune*, May 25, 1848.
12. Crosby, *Life-Story*, p. 100.
13. Crosby, *Memories*, p. 86.
14. Ibid.

CHAPTER 6: AT THE CROSS

1. *New York Tribune*, July 29, 1849.
2. Crosby, *Life-Story*, p. 90.
3. Ibid., p. 91.

4. Ibid.
5. Ibid., p. 93.
6. Crosby, *Memories*, p. 92.
7. Fanny Crosby, *Monterey and Other Poems* (New York: R. Craighead, 1851), p. 6.
8. Crosby, *Life-Story*, p. 78.
9. Crosby, *Memories*, p. 96.
10. Ibid., p. 95.
11. Ibid.
12. Ibid., pp. 95–96.
13. Ibid., p. 95.
14. Ibid., p. 96.
15. Fanny Crosby Papers.

CHAPTER 7: THE VOICE OF LOVE
1. Martin F. Tupper, *My Life as an Author* (London: Sampson, Low, Marston, Searle, and Rivington, 1886), p. 266.
2. Crosby, *Memories*, p. 99.
3. Jackson, *Fanny Crosby's Story*, p. 33.
4. Alice Young Rector, *Fanny Crosby: The Blind Hymnist* (Bridgeport: n.p., 1921), p. 4.
5. Crosby, *Life-Story*, p. 109.
6. Jackson, *Fanny Crosby's Story*, pp. 54–55.
7. Crosby, *Life-Story*, pp. 43–44.
8. Fanny J. Crosby, "Cleveland as a Teacher in the Institution for the Blind," *McClure's Magazine*, vol. 32 (April 1909), p. 582.
9. Allan Nevins, ed., *The Letters of Grover Cleveland, 1850–1908* (Boston: Houghton Mifflin, 1933), p. 4.
10. Crosby, *Life-Story*, p. 119.
11. Crosby, *Memories*, p. 105.
12. Crosby, "Cleveland as a Teacher . . . ," p. 581.
13. Crosby, *Memories*, p. 105.
14. Crosby, *Life-Story*, p. 121.
15. Crosby, "Cleveland as a Teacher . . . ," p. 582.
16. Ibid.
17. Rexford A. Tugwell, *Grover Cleveland* (New York: Macmillan, 1968), p. 17.
18. Sheet music, New York Public Library.
19. Crosby, *Bells*, p. 130.
20. Crosby, *Memories*, p. 112.
21. Jackson, *Fanny Crosby's Story*, p. 54.
22. Crosby, *Life-Story*, p. 81.

23. Ibid.
24. Anna Russell Vance, *Records of the Griswold, Crane, Paddock, Howes, Smith, and Russell Families* (Milwaukee: Smith and Tate, 1898), appendix.
25. Crosby, *Life-Story*, p. 82.
26. Crosby, *Memories*, p. 117.
27. Jackson, *Fanny Crosby's Story*, p. 55.
28. Ibid.
29. Letter, Ralph Howes Paine to C. Bernard Ruffin, May 1971.
30. Jackson, *Fanny Crosby's Story*, p. 55.

CHAPTER 8: A PURPOSE FOR LIVING
1. C. Edward Hopkins, *History of the YMCA in North America* (New York: Association Press, 1951), p. 25.
2. Ibid.
3. Paulus Scharpff, *History of Evangelism*, tr. by Helga B. Henry (Grand Rapids: Eerdmans, 1964), p. 171.
4. Scrapbook, Bridgeport Public Library.
5. Ibid.
6. Fanny Crosby Papers.
7. Lowell Mason and David Greene, *Church Psalmody: A Collection of Psalms and Hymns, Adapted to Public Worship* (Boston: Perkins and Marvin, 1831), p. 1.
8. Ira D. Sankey, *My Life and the Story of the Gospel Hymns* (Philadelphia: P. W. Ziegler, 1906), p. 133; hereafter referred to as *My Life.*
9. Jacob H. Hall, *Biography of Gospel Song and Hymn Writers* (New York: Revell, 1914), p. 27.
10. Jackson, *Fanny Crosby's Story*, p. 118.
11. Crosby, *Memories*, p. 114.
12. Crosby, *Life-Story*, p. 114.
13. Crosby, *Bells*, p. 149.
14. Sheet music, Library of Congress, Washington, D.C.
15. Crosby, *Memories*, p. 116.
16. Ibid.

CHAPTER 9: W. B. BRADBURY & CO.
1. Robert Lowry, ed., *Bright Jewels for the Sunday School* (New York: Biglow and Main, 1869), #47.
2. Fanny Crosby Papers.
3. Crosby, *Memories*, p. 119.
4. Robert Lowry et al., eds., *Pure Gold for the Sunday School* (New York: Biglow and Main, 1871), #22.
5. Alfred B. Smith, *To God Be the Glory: The Inspiring Life Story of*

William Howard Doane, One of America's Pioneer Gospel Song Composers (Grand Rapids: Singspiration, 1955), p. 29.
6. Crosby, *Bells*, p. 154.
7. Crosby, *Memories*, p. 125.
8. Ibid., p. 118.

CHAPTER 10: "MUSIC FOR THE MASSES"
1. Jacob H. Hall, *Biography of Gospel Song and Hymn Writers* (New York: Revell, 1914), p. 79.
2. Crosby, *Bells*, p. 158.
3. Material provided by Hymn Society of America.
4. Jackson, *Fanny Crosby's Story*, pp. 76–77.
5. Crosby, *Bells*, p. 160.
6. Although Fanny Crosby frequently claimed in later years that "Rescue the Perishing" was written in New York, Doane, after reading Fanny's autobiography of 1906, wrote to H. P. Main to remind Fanny that it was written in Cincinnati. This would tend to be borne out by the fact that Fanny always stated that her work with the night missions began in the late seventies.
7. Fanny Crosby Papers.
8. Ibid.
9. Hall, *Biography*, p. 79.
10. Ibid., p. 73.
11. Crosby, *Bells*, p. 21.
12. Crosby, *Memories*, p. 122.
13. Jackson, *Fanny Crosby's Story*, p. 66.
14. Crosby, *Memories*, p. 183.
15. Scrapbook on George C. Stebbins, Moody Bible Institute, Chicago, Illinois.
16. Crosby, *Memories*, p. 120.
17. Crosby, *Bells*, p. 180.
18. Jackson, *Fanny Crosby's Story*, p. 118.

CHAPTER 11: DAVID AND JONATHAN
1. *New York Times*, October 25, 1875.
2. Ibid.
3. *New York Times*, October 24, 1875.
4. Ibid.
5. Ibid.
6. Ibid.
7. Ibid.

8. Paul Dwight Moody, Letter to the Editor, "Moody Becoming a Veiled Figure," *Christian Century*, August 2, 1923, p. 979.
9. D. L. Moody Centenary Committee, *Moody's Illustrations* (East Northfield, Mass.: Northfield Schools, 1937), p. 6.
10. Ibid.
11. Crosby, *Memories*, p. 126.
12. Charles Ludwig, *Sankey Still Sings* (Anderson, Ind.: Warner Press, 1947), p. 91.
13. Paul Dwight Moody, *My Father: An Intimate Portrait of Dwight Moody* (Boston: Little, Brown & Co., 1938), p. 124.
14. *New York Times*, October 24, 1875.
15. *New York Times*, May 10, 1876.
16. Ibid.
17. Earl W. Fornell, *The Unhappy Medium: Spiritualism and the Life of Margaret Fox* (Austin: University of Texas Press, 1964), pp. 118-23.
18. *New York Times*, June 29, 1879.

CHAPTER 12: THE QUEEN OF GOSPEL SONG

1. *New York Times*, January 2, 1877.
2. Sheet music, Library of Congress, Washington, D.C.
3. *Bridgeport Morning Telegram and Union*, March 25, 1905.
4. Morris S. Daniels, *The Story of Ocean Grove* (New York: Methodist Book Concern, 1919), p. 25.
5. Ibid., p. 158.
6. Crosby, *Bells*, pp. 112-13.
7. Ibid., p. 113.
8. A. J. Showalter, *The Best Gospel Songs and Their Composers* (Dalton, Ga.: A. J. Showalter Co., 1904), unpaged.
9. Crosby, *Bells*, p. 183.

CHAPTER 13: RESCUING THE PERISHING

1. S. Hopkins Hadley, *Down in Water Street* (New York: Revell, 1902), p. 28.
2. Alvin Harlow, *Old Bowery Days* (New York: D. Appleton and Co., 1931), p. 401.
3. Hadley, *Water Street*, p. 28.
4. R. M. Offord, ed., *Jerry McAuley: Apostle to the Lost* (New York: American Tract Society, 1885), p. 69.
5. *New York Times*, February 13, 1906.
6. "Jeremiah McAuley," article in *The National Cyclopedia of American Biography* (New York: James T. White & Co., 1909), p. 523.

7. Crosby, *Memories*, p. 148.
8. Hadley, *Water Street*, p. 44.
9. Fanny Crosby Papers.
10. Ibid.
11. Crosby, *Memories*, p. 144.
12. *New Haven Register*, March 24, 1908.
13. Ibid.
14. Fanny Crosby Papers.
15. Crosby, *Memories*, pp. 146–47.
16. Ibid.
17. Ibid.
18. Ibid.
19. Jackson, *Fanny Crosby's Story*, p. 97.

CHAPTER 14: "THE VALLEY OF SILENCE"
1. Fanny Crosby Papers.
2. Crosby, *Memories*, p. 167.
3. Fanny Crosby Papers.
4. Crosby, *Memories*, p. 181.
5. Ibid., p. 172.
6. Ibid., p. 178.
7. Ibid., p. 183.
8. Crosby, *Bells*, p. 197.
9. Crosby, *Memories*, p. 179.
10. Ibid., p. 187.
11. Crosby, *Bells*, p. 174.
12. Mrs. Paine.
13. Crosby, *Life-Story*, p. 124.
14. Ibid., pp. 124–25.
15. Ibid., p. 125.
16. Crosby, *Memories*, p. 167.
17. Crosby, *Life-Story*, p. 125.
18. Ibid.
19. Crosby, *Memories*, p. 166.
20. Crosby, *Life-Story*, p. 126.
21. Ibid., p. 127.
22. Letter, H. P. Main to E. F. Belden, June 26, 1894, in Newberry Library, Chicago, Illinois.
23. Crosby, *Life-Story*, p. 180.

CHAPTER 15: TO WIN A MILLION MEN
1. I. D. Sankey, *My Life*, p. 136.

2. Ibid., p. 252.
3. *Brooklyn Daily Eagle,* March 23, 1925.
4. Jackson, *Fanny Crosby's Story,* p. 98.
5. Fanny Crosby Papers: Letter, Ira D. Sankey to Frances J. Crosby, March 23, 1890.
6. Jackson, *Fanny Crosby's Story,* p. 66.
7. Fanny Crosby Papers.
8. Ibid.
9. I. D. Sankey, *My Life,* p. 268.
10. Crosby, *Memories,* p. 182.
11. I. D. Sankey, *My Life,* pp. 257-58.
12. Ibid., p. 252.
13. Ibid.
14. Robert Lowry et al., eds., *The Royal Diadem* (New York: Biglow and Main, 1873), #49.
15. Fanny Crosby Papers: Letter, W. Howard Doane to Frances J. Crosby, December 30, 1905.
16. I. D. Sankey, *My Life,* p. 242.
17. Ibid., pp. 273-74.
18. Charles Merrill Smith, *How to Become a Bishop Without Being Religious* Garden City, N.Y.: Waymark Books, 1967), p. 82.
19. Robert Reyburn, *Clinical History of the Case of President James Garfield* (Washington, D.C.: 1893), p. 8.
20. C. M. Smith, *How to Become a Bishop,* p. 81.
21. Henry Harrison Hadley, *The Blue Badge of Courage* (New York: Saalfield Publishing Co., 1902), p. 288.

CHAPTER 16: DRUNKS, OPERETTAS, AND CONVENTIONS

1. Jackson, *Fanny Crosby's Story,* p. 68.
2. Ibid.
3. Ibid.
4. John R. Sweney et al., eds., *Songs of Redeeming Love* (Philadelphia: Walden and Stowe, 1882), #48.
5. S. Hopkins Hadley, *Down in Water Street* (New York: Revell, 1902), p. 46.
6. Henry Harrison Hadley, *The Blue Badge of Courage* (New York: Saalfield Publishing Co., 1902), p. 157.
7. Crosby, *Memories,* p. 152.
8. H. H. Hadley, *Blue Badge,* pp. 181-85.
9. Crosby, *Memories,* p. 152.
10. William R. Moody, *The Life of Dwight L. Moody* (New York: Revell, 1900), p. 362.

11. Ibid., p. 364.
12. Ibid., p. 367.
13. I. D. Sankey, *My Life*, pp. 377-78.
14. Ibid., p. 378.
15. Ibid.
16. Crosby, *Memories*, pp. 240-41.
17. Scrapbook, Bridgeport Public Library.
18. Crosby, "Cleveland as a Teacher in the Institution for the Blind," *McClure's Magazine*, vol. 32 (April 1909), p. 583.
19. Scrapbook, Bridgeport Public Library.
20. Crosby, *Memories*, p. 169.

CHAPTER 17: THE "HEART'S SONG"

1. John C. Pollock, *Moody: A Biographical Portrait* (New York: Macmillan, 1963), pp. 277-78.
2. Paul Dwight Moody, *My Father: An Intimate Portrait of Dwight Moody* (Boston: Little, Brown & Co., 1938), pp. 31-32.
3. *New York Times*, March 5, 1890.
4. Ibid.
5. Ibid.
6. Katherine Moody Spalding, *An Afternoon with Fanny Crosby* (Bridgeport: n.p., 1911), p. 3.
7. Fanny Crosby Papers.
8. Crosby, *Memories*, p. 156.
9. Ibid.
10. Ibid., p. 186.
11. Crosby, *Bells*, p. 202.
12. Crosby, *Memories*, p. 186.
13. Crosby, *Bells*, p. 202.
14. Crosby, *Memories*, pp. 184-85.
15. Fanny Crosby Papers.
16. Letter, Dr. Sarah S. Schooten to C. Bernard Ruffin, July 15, 1971.
17. George C. Stebbins, *Reminiscences and Gospel Hymn Stories* (New York: Doran, 1924), pp. 276-78.
18. Crosby, *Memories*, pp. 129-30.

CHAPTER 18: "WHO THE HELL IS MOODY?"

1. George Henry Sandison, "Fannie Crosby: Writer of Hymns," *National Magazine*, vol. IX (1898), p. 548.
2. Crosby, *Memories*, p. 141.
3. *New York Times*, September 28, 1896.
4. Ibid., November 9, 1896.

5. Ibid., November 10, 1896.
6. Ibid.
7. Ibid., November 11, 1896.
8. Charles Stelze, *A Son of the Bowery: The Autobiography of an East-Side American* (New York: Doran, 1926), pp. 118–19.
9. Ibid.
10. A. Elwood Corning, *Will Carleton: A Biographical Study* (New York: Lanmere Publishing Co., 1917), p. 74.
11. Ibid.
12. Jackson, *Fanny Crosby's Story*, p. 173.
13. Ibid.
14. *Brooklyn Daily Eagle*, February 12, 1915.
15. Fanny Crosby Papers.
16. Crosby, *Memories*, pp. 159–60.
17. Basil Miller, *Fanny Crosby: Singing I Go* (Grand Rapids: Zondervan, 1950), p. 92.
18. Ibid.

CHAPTER 19: "NEVER GIVE UP"
1. Crosby, *Memories*, pp. 122–23.
2. Jacob H. Hall, *Biography of Gospel Song and Hymn Writers* (New York: Revell, 1914), p. 351.
3. Crosby, *Memories*, p. 184.
4. Ibid.
5. Ibid.
6. Jackson, *Fanny Crosby's Story*, p. 70.
7. Ibid., p. 71.
8. Ibid.
9. J. Wilbur Chapman, *The Life and Work of Dwight L. Moody* (New York: W. E. Scull, 1900), p. 267.
10. William R. Moody, *The Life of Dwight L. Moody* (New York: Revell, 1900), p. 554.
11. Crosby, *Memories*, p. 111.
12. Scrapbook, Bridgeport Public Library.
13. Mrs. Paine.
14. Fanny Crosby Papers.
15. Crosby, *Memories*, p. 137.
16. Ira D. Sankey, ed., *Sacred Songs and Solos* (London: Morgan & Scott, n.d.), #979.
17. Fanny Crosby Papers: unidentified newspaper clipping, March 1901.
18. Ira Allen Sankey, *Hallowed Hymns, New and Old* (New York: Biglow and Main, 1907), #100.

19. *Brooklyn Daily Eagle,* July 11, 1908.
20. Crosby, *Memories,* p. 179.
21. Fanny Crosby Papers: Letter, W. H. Doane to H. A. White, July 21, 1902.
22. Crosby, *Life-Story,* p. 82.
23. Crosby, *Memories,* p. 179.
24. W. Howard Doane, ed., *Songs of Devotion* (New York: Biglow and Main, 1903), #195.
25. Crosby, *Memories,* pp. 246–47.

CHAPTER 20: LIFE BEGINS AT EIGHTY
1. Fanny Crosby Papers.
2. Ibid.
3. Crosby, *Memories,* p. 146.
4. Jackson, *Fanny Crosby's Story,* p. 65.
5. Fanny Crosby Papers: Letter, F. J. Crosby to H. P. Main and associates.
6. Fanny Crosby Papers: Letter, Phoebe Knapp to C. W. Rider, February 1904.
7. Jackson, *Fanny Crosby's Story,* p. 18.
8. Ibid., p. 17.
9. Fanny Crosby Papers.
10. Ibid.
11. *Bridgeport Post,* April 24, 1955.
12. Fanny Crosby Papers.
13. Ibid.
14. Crosby, *Memories,* pp. 109–10.
15. *Bridgeport Morning Telegram and Union,* March 25, 1905.
16. Ibid., March 27, 1905.

CHAPTER 21: "MRS. CROSBY'S MATTER"
1. Fanny Crosby Papers.
2. Ibid.: Letter, H. P. Main to H. A. White, December 7, 1904.
3. Ibid.: Letter, Charles Clowe to H. A. White, September 21, 1904.
4. A. Elwood Corning, *Will Carleton: A Biographical Study* (New York: Lanmere Publishing Co., 1917), p. 75.
5. Fanny Crosby Papers: Letters from W. H. Doane to H. A. White, January 28, 1904 and February 11, 1904.
6. Ibid.: Letter, F. J. Crosby to editor of the *Watchman,* December 15, 1904.
7. Fanny Crosby Papers.
8. Ibid.
9. Ibid.
10. Ibid.: Letter, H. P. Main to H. A. White, December 7, 1904.
11. Ibid.: Letter, J. H. Earle to H. A. White, December 6, 1906.

12. Crosby, *Memories*, p. 6.
13. Fanny Crosby Papers.
14. *Bridgeport Morning Telegram and Union*, June 26, 1907.
15. Mrs. Paine.
16. Fanny Crosby Papers.

CHAPTER 22: THE PROTESTANT SAINT
1. Mrs. Blanche Simpson Main, interview, July 1972.
2. Fanny Crosby Papers.
3. Mrs. Paine.
4. Anonymous lady, interview in New Haven, Connecticut, spring 1970.
5. Mrs. Paine.
6. Jackson, *Fanny Crosby's Story*, p. 14.
7. Ibid.
8. Mrs. Paine.
9. Mrs. Main.
10. Newberry Library, Chicago: Letter, H. P. Main to E. F. Belden, June 26, 1894.
11. Fanny Crosby Papers.
12. Ibid.
13. Mrs. Paine.
14. Crosby, *Life-Story*, p. 25.
15. Scrapbook, Bridgeport Public Library.
16. Jackson, *Fanny Crosby's Story*, p. 121.
17. Fanny Crosby Papers.
18. *Springfield Daily Republican*, February 13, 1915.
19. Fanny Crosby Papers.
20. *Springfield Daily Republican*, February 13, 1915.
21. Jackson, *Fanny Crosby's Story*, p. 131.
22. Ibid., p. 128.
23. Ibid., p. 172.
24. Scrapbook, Bridgeport Public Library.
25. Fanny Crosby Papers.
26. Mrs. Paine.
27. Crosby, *Life-Story*, p. 56.
28. Jackson, *Fanny Crosby's Story*, p. 176.
29. Katherine M. Spalding, *An Afternoon with Fanny Crosby* (Bridgeport: n.p., 1911), p. 4.
30. *Springfield Daily Republican*, February 13, 1915.

CHAPTER 23: "I DON'T WANT TO DIE YET"
1. Fanny Crosby Papers.

2. Crosby, *Memories,* p. 133.
3. Fanny Crosby Papers.
4. Scrapbook, Bridgeport Public Library.
5. Fanny Crosby Papers.
6. Jackson, *Fanny Crosby's Story,* p. 145.
7. Ibid., p. 149.
8. Ibid., p. 121.
9. Mrs. Paine.
10. Ibid.
11. Ibid.
12. Ibid.
13. Fanny Crosby Papers.
14. Jackson, *Fanny Crosby's Story,* p. 169.
15. Scrapbook, Bridgeport Public Library.
16. Jackson, *Fanny Crosby's Story,* p. 16.
17. Mrs. Paine.
18. Letter, Edward Carey to C. Bernard Ruffin, June 23, 1971.
19. Scrapbook, Bridgeport Public Library.
20. Fanny Crosby Papers.
21. Ibid.: Letter, F. J. Crosby to H. A. White, October 4, 1913.
22. Fanny Crosby Papers.
23. Ibid.

CHAPTER 24: NEVER MORE TO SAY FAREWELL
1. Fanny Crosby Papers.
2. Ibid.
3. *Brooklyn Daily Eagle,* February 12, 1915.
4. *New York Times,* May 3, 1911.
5. Ibid.
6. Alice Young Rector, *Fanny Crosby: The Blind Hymnist* (Bridgeport: n.p., 1921), p. 5.
7. Allan Sankey, *An Evening of Song and Story with Fanny Crosby* (New York: Biglow and Main, 1915), p. 27.
8. Fanny Crosby Papers.
9. *Brooklyn Daily Eagle,* February 12, 1915.
10. Fanny Crosby Papers.
11. Rector, *Fanny Crosby,* p. 2.
12. Fanny Crosby Papers: Letter, E. G. Cleaveland to H. A. White, February 12, 1915.
13. Courtesy of Mrs. Blanche Simpson Main.
14. Fanny Crosby Papers: Letter, J. M. Athington to H. A. White, February 15, 1915.

15. Ibid.: Letter, F. M. Paine to H. A. White, April 15, 1915.
16. *Bridgeport Post*, April 24, 1955.
17. This is probably the approximate number of hymns which were published. Altogether, Fanny wrote about 9,000 hymns.

Heroes of the Faith

Now available...

Classic biographies of outstanding men and women of the faith, in special deluxe gift editions.

Heroes of the Faith is designed for library or personal use, in matching hardcover bindings that will stand up to years of use.

Start building your *Heroes of the Faith* library today, for only $5.99 a volume. You would ordinarily expect to pay twice as much for books of this quality!

Titles Available:

Fanny Crosby

Dwight L. Moody

George Muller

John Wesley

$5.99 each*

(*price may change without notice)

At Your Bookstore

Be sure to ask for *Heroes of the Faith* editions, and begin to build your library today.

If not available at your local bookstore, you may write to the address below. Include $5.99 for each book you want to order, plus $2.00 for postage. Please allow two weeks for delivery.

Barbour and Company, Inc.
164 Mill Street
Westwood, New Jersey 07675